Future of Business and Finance

The Future of Business and Finance book series features professional works aimed at defining, describing and charting the future trends in these fields. The focus is mainly on strategic directions, technological advances, challenges and solutions which may affect the way we do business tomorrow, including the future of sustainability and governance practices. Mainly written by practitioners, consultants and academic thinkers, the books are intended to spark and inform further discussions and developments.

More information about this series at http://www.springer.com/series/16360

Melissa Lukings • Arash Habibi Lashkari

Understanding Cybersecurity Law and Digital Privacy

A Common Law Perspective

Springer

Melissa Lukings
Faculty of Law
University of New Brunswick
Fredericton, NB, Canada

Arash Habibi Lashkari
Canadian Institute for Cybersecurity
University of New Brunswick
Fredericton, NB, Canada

ISSN 2662-2467 ISSN 2662-2475 (electronic)
Future of Business and Finance
ISBN 978-3-030-88703-2 ISBN 978-3-030-88704-9 (eBook)
https://doi.org/10.1007/978-3-030-88704-9

This Springer imprint is published by the registered company Springer Nature Switzerland AG.
The registered company address is: Gewerbestrasse 11, 6330 Cham, Switzerland

Melissa Lukings

For my family and friends, whether biological or chosen; near or far:
AA, AHL, AMR, BCW, BEJ, CJD, CRT, DLL, JHMD, HAGL, HES, HJ, KNH, MAL, MKLL, MKNL, NCO, PAL, RLG, SSD, and everyone who fits under the "extended family and friends" designation.
You know who you are.
And for my feline companions; my furbaby beneficiaries; my treasured cat children: Miss Kitty S. Bird; Sir Thomas K. Brodie; Lady LaLuna de Fats Purrtato; Mister George J. Flanders; and the late Oliver "Olliebug" von Trashnugget.

Arash Habibi Lashkari

For
My wife Farnaz and children, Kourosh and Kianna,
And my father Bahman, mother Zeynab, and sister Ziba,
And my teachers and lecturers, for all the lessons you've taught me.

Preface

The internet, digital media, and online communication have become an integral part of our modern world. Over the past few decades, we have seen the internet evolve, becoming anchored within our households, and a near requirement for accessing education. Our previous hardwired telephone systems were replaced first by mobile phones and then by smartphones. Our cars, our watches, our appliances, all are connected and help to keep us connected to each other. Economically, our commercial endeavors have shifted to increase their reach to a wider range of potential customers, no longer limited by distance creating the online economy.

While we are more connected than ever before, our connectedness has become necessarily dependent on our having sustainable and reliable access to digital technology and online networks. As our society has shifted away from the paper filing methods of the past and onto digital platforms, we have begun storing greater amounts of data, records, media, creative content, and other valuable information online. More still, to improve access to banking and financial services, many of these corporations have launched digital platforms, apps, and other networked methods to the delight of many consumers. Even more recently, we have seen health care service provision move from an in-person clinical model to a model based on online remote consultation, even from the comfort of our own homes. The access and freedom we have with our ability to share information is unprecedented in our history.

This interconnectedness, however, comes with its own novel set of risks and necessary risk assessments. Rather than protecting our stored records in locked filing cabinets, in offices and storage rooms—carbon copied, printed, or written on paper—we are increasingly moving toward full digital integration with online cloud-based platforms for data storage. While we no longer have to safeguard our documents and data with security guards, locking systems, alarms, and other physical protective mechanisms, we have also removed the barrier of distance from accessing our stored records. Rather than safeguarding our data from localized tangible physical intrusion, we must now work to create and maintain safeguards and protective standards that will prevent remote intangible digital intrusion; cybersecurity—a whole new world.

In the not-so-recent past, we relied on physical safeguards to prevent data theft and unauthorized access. When those safeguards failed, we would turn to the legal system—criminal or civil depending on the severity of the theft or breach—to penalize or provide a remedy in law for the act. It should not come as a surprise that our shift onto online platforms has created an obstacle in our ability to apply the law as it was previously written and applied. In this way, our law has had to evolve from our former concept of privacy law and security in law to our newer fields of data privacy law and cybersecurity in law for our online medium.

"Understanding Cybersecurity and Digital Privacy—A Common Law Perspective" is the second book in the *Understanding Cybersecurity Series (UCS)*, following the precursory publication, "Understanding Cybersecurity Management in FinTech" mid-way through 2021. In this installment of the series, we discuss the theory and principles of legal application in (data) privacy and (cyber) security which underpin our digital relationships; personal, professional, commercial, and organizational.

This book provides insight into the pre-digital concept of property ownership, possession, interest, and privacy which form the basis of our tort and property laws. We examine the roots of systems of law and legal governance, building up to an analysis of cybercriminal activities and the issues which arise in dealing with these new areas under the old law. We discuss the methods used by a selection of common law countries in addressing privacy and online interpersonal matters, providing a comparison between these models. Finally, we take a look at the upcoming trends in data privacy and cybersecurity law.

Fredericton, Canada

Melissa Lukings
Arash Habibi Lashkari

Introduction

The field of cybersecurity is dynamic and rapidly changing; new technologies are created and quickly evolve and expand into newer areas and applications. While the speed of new technological evolution is necessary to maintain competition in the industry, it has also allowed our digital world to surge ahead in development much more quickly than our laws and legal systems are able to evolve to accommodate these changes.

When we look to apply our legal structures to this dynamic field, it is unsurprising that we seem to keep coming up short. The field of law and legal education is rooted in traditional, long-standing principles. The common law is shaped through years of nuanced legal evolution, reflecting the social changes of the time, but this is nowhere near the dynamic speed of change that we see in cybersecurity. While this is both necessary for the fundamental purposes of the law, it is also an impediment, reflecting the need for greater flexibility in the application for our legal systems. Herein lies the issue.

Merging these two distinct worlds: one dynamic and one static, we are first faced with the task of filling in the knowledge gaps which unintentionally serve to keep these areas apart. We can see this in the metaphor of the "ivory tower" of academia; where those who specialize in one area may know the intricacies of that area but not how to relate the area of specialization to others. In aiming to address the inherent challenge of connecting the cybersecurity tower and the legal tower, we have created this book.

Our first chapter starts out by describing the foundations of law, including the purpose and principles of law. We discuss the concept of jurisprudence and some of the major theories of legal jurisprudence which have been influential in the development and evolution of the law over time. From there, we extend our discussion to the sources of law and legal influence, the various systems and categories of law, and some of the forms of legal governance. Finally, we round off chapter one with a look into the concept of constitutionalism and the interplay between constitutionalism and the division of jurisdictional power and authority.

Chapter two discusses the legal concept of property and the nature of privacy in a legal context; outlining some of the historical perceptions of property before moving on to distinguish between the interwoven concepts of ownership, possession, and interest. We examine the relationship between property and privacy, as well as the intersection of property, privacy, and cybersecurity within the law and legal system.

Chapter three, on cybersecurity and cybercrime, starts off by categorizing cybercriminal activities into cyber-enabled, cyber-dependent, and cyber-supported offences, and describing the nature of these types of offences. We discuss the growing prevalence of cybercrime, including digital privacy infringement, data theft, and other online-based offences. We finish off the third chapter by neatly sorting the specific subsets of criminal offences, respectively, within each of the three branches of cybercriminal activity categorization.

The fourth chapter looks at the global relevance of cybersecurity law, using four common law nations as comparators: Canada, Australia, the United Kingdom, and the United States. Using tables, we compare and contrast the methods of regulating cyber offences between these four example nations. After establishing an understanding of some of the different strategies employed by individual nations to apply existing law to the online world, we will follow by outlining some of the national and international considerations which influence individual national or state policies pertaining to cybersecurity, data privacy, regulation, and online criminal activity.

In our fifth and final chapter, we discuss some of the emerging issues in cybersecurity and data privacy law. We outline the issues which arise with globalization and the difficulty of navigating jurisdictionally on an international stage. That is followed by an examination of the relationship between digital marketplaces and the online consumer. We then venture onto the DarkNet, giving an overview of anonymized dark marketplaces as well as the rise of digital transactions and online exchanges made using cryptocurrencies. We then branch into a discussion on some of the existing challenges to law enforcement, as well as the complexity of digital sovereignty and data governance in law. Finally, we finish off this fifth and final chapter by discussing some of the potential future directions for further research and exploration into the field of cybersecurity law.

By reading this book, readers will become familiar with two different perspectives: that of the law and that of cybersecurity. Included in this book are some of the most current topics and emerging issues in cybersecurity, including: cryptocurrency, online anonymization, DDOS attacks, and digital content regulation.

Contents

1 Legal Foundations 1
1.1 Purpose and Principles of Law 1
1.1.1 Salmond on the Classifications of Law 2
1.1.2 The Rule of Law 2
1.2 Jurisprudence 4
1.2.1 Natural Law Jurisprudence: Observation and Realization 5
1.2.2 Analytical Jurisprudence: Definition and Clarification 6
1.2.3 Normative Jurisprudence: Evaluation and Reformation 9
1.3 Sources of Law 10
1.3.1 Legislation/Statutory Law 10
1.3.2 Legal Precedent/ Case Law/Common Law 11
1.3.3 Sources of Legal Influence 12
1.4 Systems of Law 13
1.4.1 Common Law 14
1.4.2 Civil Law 14
1.4.3 Religious Law 15
1.4.4 Customary Law 16
1.4.5 Legal Pluralism 16
1.4.6 Case Hypothetical: Systems of Law 16
1.5 Categories of Law 17
1.5.1 International Law vs Domestic Law 17
1.5.2 Recognition of Sovereignty 18
1.5.3 Public Law versus Private Law 19
1.5.4 Case Hypothetical: Categories of Law 19
1.6 Legal Governance 20
1.6.1 Authoritarianism 21
1.6.2 Monarchism 24
1.6.3 Elitism 24
1.6.4 Socialism 25
1.6.5 Democracy 26
1.6.6 Case Hypothetical: Legal Governance 27

1.7 Constitutionalism 27
1.7.1 Division of Jurisdictional Powers 29
1.7.2 Branches of Legal Governance 30
1.8 Summary 31
References 32

2 Property and Privacy in Context 37
2.1 Perceptions of Property 37
2.2 Ownership, Possession, and Interest 38
2.2.1 Distinguishing Ownership from Possession 38
2.2.2 Ownership 39
2.2.3 Possession 39
2.2.4 Interest 41
2.2.5 Case Hypothetical: Ownership, Possession, and Interest . . . 43
2.3 Property and Privacy 44
2.3.1 Classifications of Property 45
2.3.2 Private Property Versus Public Property 47
2.3.3 Privacy 47
2.3.4 Differentiating Personal from Private 47
2.3.5 Legislative Example: Canadian Consumer Privacy Protection 49
2.3.6 Case Hypothetical: Consumer Privacy Protection 50
2.4 The Intersection of Property, Privacy, and Cybersecurity Law 51
2.4.1 Criminal Law/Statutory Law 52
2.4.2 Tort Law/Common Law 53
2.4.3 Case Hypothetical: Intersection of Criminal and Tort Law 53
2.5 Summary 55
References 56

3 Cybersecurity and Cybercrimes 59
3.1 Categorizing Cybercrimes 59
3.1.1 Cyber-Enabled Offences (On/Offline) 60
3.1.2 Cyber-Dependent Offences (Online) 65
3.1.3 Computer/Cyber-Supported Offences 80
3.1.4 National (Cyber)Security Offences 85
3.2 Growing Prevalence of Cybercrime 91
3.3 Categorizing Cybercrimes in the Law 91
3.4 Summary 93
References 95

4 Global Relevance 97
4.1 Review of Canadian Cybersecurity Laws 98
4.1.1 Regulating Governmental Relationships 98

4.1.2 Regulating Businesses, Organizations, and Commercial Enterprises . . . 99
4.1.3 Regulating Interpersonal Relationships and Criminal Activities . . . 100
4.2 Review of Australian Cybersecurity Laws . . . 102
4.2.1 Regulating Governmental, Business, and Organizational Relationships . . . 102
4.2.2 Regulating Interpersonal Relationships and Criminal Activities . . . 105
4.3 Review of United Kingdom Cybersecurity Laws . . . 108
4.3.1 Regulating Government, Businesses, and Organizations . . . 108
4.3.2 Regulating Interpersonal Relationships and Criminal Activities . . . 109
4.4 Review of United States Cybersecurity Laws . . . 110
4.4.1 Regulating the Federal Government and Governmental Agencies . . . 111
4.4.2 Regulating Sector-Specific Industries: Healthcare . . . 111
4.4.3 Regulating Sector-Specific Industries: Banks/Financial Institutions . . . 112
4.4.4 Regulating Interpersonal Relationships and Criminal Activities . . . 113
4.5 Common Law Countries, in Brief . . . 114
4.6 National Considerations . . . 115
4.6.1 Identity and Diversity . . . 115
4.6.2 Identity in Politics . . . 118
4.6.3 Constitutional Values . . . 121
4.7 International Considerations . . . 121
4.7.1 Treaties and International Agreements . . . 123
4.7.2 The *Tallinn Manual* and Cyber Warfare . . . 125
4.7.3 International Legal Principles in Cyberspace . . . 133
4.7.4 International Dispute Resolution . . . 133
4.8 Summary . . . 135
References . . . 135

5 Emerging Issues . . . 137
5.1 Globalization and Jurisdictionally . . . 137
5.1.1 Determining Jurisdiction . . . 138
5.1.2 Online Jurisdiction . . . 139
5.1.3 Case Hypothetical: Jurisdiction . . . 139
5.2 Digital Marketplaces and the Consumer . . . 142
5.2.1 Rights of the Consumer in the Global Marketplace . . . 142
5.2.2 Commercial Electronic Messages . . . 144
5.2.3 International Commercial Application . . . 146
5.3 Anonymized DarkNet Markets and Cryptocurrencies . . . 148
5.3.1 Illegal Content and Dark Web Marketplaces . . . 150

5.3.2 Differentiating the Dark from the Deep 153
5.3.3 Cryptocurrencies 159
5.3.4 Corporate Considerations 160
5.4 Challenges to Law Enforcement 165
5.4.1 Decentralization 166
5.4.2 Detection, Tracing and Localization 166
5.4.3 Jurisdiction and Enforcement 168
5.4.4 Digital Evidence Collection 168
5.4.5 Example in Law: Canada's Evidence Act 169
5.4.6 Case Hypothetical: Challenges to Law Enforcement 170
5.5 Digital Sovereignty and Data Governance 171
5.5.1 Challenges to Digital Sovereignty in International Cyber Law 171
5.5.2 Online Content Regulation 172
5.5.3 Digital Content Creation and the Gig Economy 172
5.6 Future Directions 175
5.7 Summary 175
References 176

Conclusion 179

Author Biographies

Melissa Lukings Melissa Lukings is a Juris Doctor (JD) candidate at the Faculty of Law, University of New Brunswick (UNB), a former graduate of Memorial University of Newfoundland (MUN) holding a Bachelor of Arts degree in Linguistics, and an intersectional research assistant with a background in social justice, grassroots organization, data privacy, and cybersecurity law. Lukings is currently working on a handful of research projects covering a wide variety of topics, ranging from cybersecurity and privacy law to legal reform and access to justice within the Canadian judicial system.

During 2020 and 2021, Lukings co-authored a ten-part article series, entitled "Understanding Canadian Cybersecurity Laws," which was published by IT World Canada. The article series was recognized with a Gold Medal for the Best Blog Column in the Business Division of the 2020 Canadian Online Publishing Awards, which was remotely held in February 2021.

In April 2021, following the publication of the final article in the Understanding Canadian Cybersecurity Laws series, Ms. Lukings was invited to appear, on two occasions, as an expert witness and individual advocate for the purpose of providing testimonial evidence in a hearing before the House of Commons of Canada's Ethics Committee—formally known as the Standing Committee on Access to Information, Privacy and Ethics (ETHI)—which studies matters related to the Offices of: the Information Commissioner of Canada; the Privacy Commissioner of Canada; the Commissioner of Lobbying of Canada, and certain issues related to the Office of the Conflict of Interest and Ethics Commissioner.

Following her appearances before the Ethics Committee, Ms. Lukings was cited in the final publicized report from the Ethics Committee, which was formally presented to the Members of Parliament in the House of Commons of Canada and made freely available to the public on June 17, 2021.

Over the years and into the present, Ms. Lukings has been a notable activist, with an extensive background of involvement within non-profit organizations, particularly those with a primary mandate founded on principles of: harm reduction; mental health advocacy, education, and awareness; crisis and suicide intervention; violence prevention; sexual health and reproductive justice; human rights; and access to justice within gender-based marginalized community networks. Outside of professional and academic work, Ms. Lukings enjoys spending quality time experiencing the joys of life with her small following of cats.

Arash Habibi Lashkari Dr. Arash Habibi Lashkari is the founder of the Understanding Cybersecurity Series (UCS). This is an ongoing and extendable research and development project, which will culminate with a varied collection of online articles and blogs, books and papers, open-source codes, and datasets tailored for researchers and readers at all levels. Dr. Lashkari is a senior member of the Institute of Electrical and Electronics Engineers (IEEE), an Associate Professor in the Faculty of Computer Science at the University of New Brunswick (UNB), and the Research Coordinator at the Canadian Institute for Cybersecurity (CIC).

Dr. Lashkari has over 20 years of teaching experience, spanning several international universities, and was responsible for designing the first cybersecurity Capture the Flag (CTF) competition for post-secondary students in Canada. He is the author of ten published books and more than 90 academic articles on a variety of cybersecurity-related topics. He has been the recipient of 15 awards at international computer security competitions—including three gold awards—and was recognized in 2017 as one of Canada's Top 150 Researchers.

In 2020, Dr. Lashkari was recognized with the prestigious Teaching Innovation Award from the University of New Brunswick (UNB) for his intuitive teaching methodology, the Think-Que-Cussion Method. Also, his teaching technique has been nominated for the Reimagine Education, world level teaching and education award for 2021.

Over the last six years, Dr. Lashkari has done extensive work on cybersecurity repository dataset generation; producing a total of twelve novel cybersecurity datasets during that time. Building on over two decades of concurrent industrial and development experience in network, software, and computer security, Dr. Lashkari's current work involves the development of vulnerability detection technology to provide protection to network systems against cyberattacks. He simultaneously supervises multiple research and development teams working on several projects related to network traffic analysis, malware analysis, Honeynet, and threat hunting. His other research interests focus on cyber threat detection, big data security, and darknet traffic analysis.

Dr. Lashkari's newest research and development project, the Understanding Cybersecurity Series (UCS), is a project that will feature a mixed collection of online articles, published books, datasets, and open-source codes. The online articles—published as blogs—will target a readership audience including computer and software engineers, researchers and developers, IT professionals and administrators, youth, students, seniors, and other interested readers. Some of the existing online articles in the project so far include: the ten-part Understanding Canadian Cybersecurity Laws (UCCL) series and the six-part Understanding Android Malware Families (UAMF) series. The first part of the UCS entitled Understanding Canadian Cybersecurity Laws (UCCL), was recognized with a

Gold Medal at the 2020 Canadian Online Publishing Awards. The third part of the UCS entitled Understanding Cybersecurity Management in Fintech (UCMF) is also under process and will be released from August for 6 months.

The published books and papers in the Understanding Cybersecurity Series (UCS) will target a readership primarily consisting of academic scholars and advanced educators, post-secondary students, researchers and developers, corporate decision-makers, industry professionals, government legislators, and legal practitioners. The first book, which has been published by Springer and entitled Understanding Cybersecurity Management in Fintech (UCMF), provides infrastructure security solutions for a target audience of financial experts, software developers, financial technology innovators, and cybersecurity researchers.

Legal Foundations 1

In this chapter, we will create the necessary context for future chapters, by starting with the foundations of the law and the legal system. This chapter will be the base for everything that follows. To begin, we will discuss the origins and purpose of law, including the jurisprudential theories of law. We will outline the sources and systems which shape our application of legal theory, and the intersectionality of the areas of legal practice. Finally, we will wrap up this chapter by exploring the concepts of legal governance, democracy, and constitutionalism.

1.1 Purpose and Principles of Law

In its most basic form, law is any rule of action and includes any standards or pattern to which actions are or ought to be confirmed. The law serves many purposes including: establishing standards; maintaining order; resolving disputes; and protecting liberties and rights.

Sir John William Salmond KC (1862–1924) [1] was a highly regarded legal scholar, practitioner, public servant, university lecturer, knight, and judge of the Supreme Court of New Zealand [2]. Salmond was appointed as Counsel to the Law Drafting Office of New Zealand in 1907 and stayed there until he was appointed as Solicitor-General in 1911 [3]. Salmond received the designation of King's Counsel in 1912, was knighted in 1918, and appointed a judge of the Supreme Court of New Zealand (now known as the High Court) in 1920.[1] Salmond also authored several legal texts over his lifetime. Two of his texts, in particular, *Salmond on*

[1]This is now known as the High Court.

M. Lukings, A. Habibi Lashkari, *Understanding Cybersecurity Law and Digital Privacy*, Future of Business and Finance, https://doi.org/10.1007/978-3-030-88704-9_1

Jurisprudence[2] and *Salmond on Torts*,[3] are both now regarded as legal classics. Salmond provided the following opinion regarding the function of law.

"The term 'Law' denotes different kinds of rules and Principles. Law is an instrument that regulates human conduct/behavior. Law means Justice, Morality, Reason, Order, and Righteous from the perspective of the society. Law means Statutes, Acts, Rules, Regulations, Orders, and Ordinances from the point of view of the legislature. Law means Rules of court, Decrees, Judgment, Orders of courts, and Injunctions from the point of view of Judges. Therefore, Law is a broader term which includes Acts, Statutes, Rules, Regulations, Orders, Ordinances, Justice, Morality, Reason, Righteous, Rules of court, Decrees, Judgment, Orders of courts, Injunctions, Tort, Jurisprudence, Legal theory, etc."

1.1.1 Salmond on the Classifications of Law

In his work, Salmond recognizes eight kinds of laws:

1. *Imperative law*—the command of the sovereign must be general and the observance of law must be enforced by some authority.
2. *Physical or scientific law*—these are laws of science which are the expression of the uniformities of nature.
3. *Natural or moral law*—Natural law is based on the principles of right and wrong whereas Moral laws are laws based on the principles of morality.
4. *Conventional law*—system of rules agreed upon by persons for the regulation of their conduct towards each other.
5. *Customary law*—any system of rules which are observed by men as a custom and has been in practice since time immemorial.
6. *Practical or technical law*—rules meant for a particular sphere by human activity.
7. *International law*—rules which regulate the relations between various nations of the world.
8. *Civil law*—the law enforced by the State [4].

1.1.2 The Rule of Law

The *Rule of Law* is a legal principle which suggests that every person is subject to the law, including people who are lawmakers, law enforcement officials and judges [5]. The principle of the Rule of Law goes back to ancient philosophers, including Plato and Aristotle. While the modern use of the phrase "the rule of law" has been credited to Samuel Rutherford, John Locke, and A. V. Dicey, the development of the fundamental legal concept of the Rule of Law can be traced back through history and

[2]Officially titled *Jurisprudence or The Theory of the Law.*

[3]Officially titled *The Law of Torts.*

linked to many ancient civilizations as far back as ancient Greece, Mesopotamia, India, and Rome [6].

Plato, an Athenian philosopher in the Classical period of ancient Greece, advocated for a benevolent monarchy ruled by an idealized philosopher king. While the philosopher king would be above the law, Plato expressed the ideal that the best men of the benevolent monarchy would be good at respecting existing laws.

> Where the law is subject to some other authority and has none of its own, the collapse of the state, in my view, is not far off; but if law is the master of the government and the government is its slave, then the situation is full of promise and men enjoy all the blessings that the gods shower on a state. [7]

Aristocracy describes a form of government that places power and authority in the hands of a small and privileged ruling class, called the aristocrats [8]. The term is derived from the Greek term *aristokratia,* which describes this idealized beneficial monarchy and can be translated as "rule of the best." In jurisprudence, the "rule of the best" described a system of governance where only the best of the citizens, chosen through a careful process of selection, would become rulers. In this system, hereditary rule would be forbidden, unless the children of the incumbent ruler performed best and were better endowed with the attributes that make a person fit to rule in comparison to every other citizen in the polity.

In comparison to Plato, Aristotle was more strongly opposed to letting the highest officials wield power beyond guarding and serving the laws; what we now recognize as the legal principle of the Rule of Law.[4] Aristotle describes this concept in *Politics* as:

> It is more proper that law should govern than any one of the citizens: upon the same principle, if it is advantageous to place the supreme power in some particular persons, they should be appointed to be only guardians, and the servants of the laws.[5]

In ancient China, during the third century BC, members of the school of legalism argued for using law as a tool of governance, but they promoted the "rule *by* law" as opposed to the "rule *of* law", meaning that they placed the aristocrats and emperor above the law [9]. In contrast, the Huang-Lao school of Daoism rejected the theory of legal positivism in favor of a natural law to which even the ruler would be subject [10].

In the ninth century, Alfred the Great—an Anglo-Saxon king—reformed the law of his kingdom and assembled a law code, which he grounded on biblical commandments [11]. He held that the same law had to be applied to all persons, whether rich or poor, friends or enemies [12].

Stephen Lanton (1150–1228), the Archbishop of Canterbury, was responsible for drafting the first version of the *Magna Carta Liberatum*, more commonly known as

---

[4] Aristotle, *Politics* 3.16.

[5] Aristotle, *Politics* 3.16.

the *Magna Carta*. The *Magna Carta* was a royal charter of English civil liberties which was granted by King John on June 15, 1215, under threat of civil war. By signing this document in agreement of the terms, King John conceded that he, as the King of England, was subject to the laws of the realm like every other citizen. This moved King John and future sovereigns and magistrates back under the rule of law, preserving ancient liberties by *Magna Carta* in return for exacting taxes [13]. The *Magna Carta* was reissued, with further alterations, in 1216, 1217, and 1225.

By declaring the sovereign, himself, to be subject to the Rule of Law and by documenting the liberties held by "free men," the *Magna Carta* provided the foundation for individual rights in Anglo-American jurisprudence. From 1215 onward, no British citizen, no matter their political position, could ever be considered to be above the law. This eventually expanded to include all commonwealth citizens. Clause 29 of the *Magna Carta* is considered by many to be the foundation of the Rule of Law in England as well as the first declaration in Western history to formally impose the Rule of Law [14]. The *Magna Carta* has also been used as a foundational aspect of many later-established constitutions. The Due Process Clause of the United States Constitution was partly based on a combination of common law principles and the *Magna Carta* (1215), which had by then become a foundation of English liberty against arbitrary power wielded by a governing body or ruler [15].

The Rule of Law can be contrasted with the tyrannical or oligarchical system of legal governance, in which the rulers are perceived to be above the power of the law [16]. The Rule of Law can also be absent in democracies and monarchies when there is neglect or substantial ignorance of the law [17]. As well, if a government has insufficient corrective mechanisms for restoring the Rule of Law where it is lacking, then the principle of the Rule of Law within that society become gradually more apt to decay, allowing for corruption to become embedded within the governmental systems of that society, and making it even more difficult to restore the Rule of Law over time.

1.2 Jurisprudence

Jurisprudence, or legal theory, consists of the theoretical study or knowledge of the law and legal systems [18]. The word "jurisprudence" comes from the English derivation of the Latin word *jurisprudentia* which means "astuteness in the law". Scholars of jurisprudence seek to explain the nature of law in its most general form and provide a deeper understanding of legal reasoning, legal systems, legal institutions, and the role of law in society [19]. Over the course of history, there have been many forms of legal theory. We can categorize these theories into three main branches: (1) natural law; (2) analytical jurisprudence; and (3) normative jurisprudence.

1.2.1 Natural Law Jurisprudence: Observation and Realization

In *De Legibus*, Marcus Tulius Cicero (106 BC—43 BC) wrote that both justice and law originate from what nature has given to humanity, from what the human mind embraces, from the function of humanity, and from what serves to unite humanity [20]. For Cicero, natural law provides the obligation to contribute to the general good of the larger society. The purpose of positive laws is to provide for "the safety of citizens, the preservation of states, and the tranquility and happiness of human life" [21]. In this view, "wicked and unjust statutes" are "anything but 'laws,'"because "in the very definition of the term 'law' there inheres the idea and principle of choosing what is just and true" [22]. In *De Re Publica,* Cicero wrote that:

> "There is indeed a law, right reason, which is in accordance with nature; existing in all, unchangeable, eternal. Commanding us to do what is right, forbidding us to do what is wrong. It has dominion over good men, but possesses no influence over bad ones. No other law can be substituted for it, no part of it can be taken away, nor can it be abrogated altogether. Neither the people or the senate can absolve from it. It is not one thing at Rome, and another thing at Athens: one thing to-day, and another thing tomorrow; but it is eternal and immutable for all nations and for all time." [23]

The work and writings of Cicero continued to influence the discussion of natural law for many centuries to come, up through the era of the American Revolution. In his summary of medieval natural law, Thomas Aquinas even quoted Cicero's statement that "nature" and "custom" were the sources of a society's laws. [24]

1.2.1.1 Natural Law

Natural law is a system of law based on a close observation of human nature, and based on values intrinsic to human nature that can be deduced and applied independent of positive law [25]. According to the natural law theory, all people have inherent rights, conferred not by act of legislation but by "God, nature, or reason" [26]. Natural law theory can also refer to "theories of ethics, theories of politics, theories of civil law, and theories of religious morality" [27].

Thomas Aquinas (1225–1274) was an immensely influential scholastic theologian, legal philosopher, highly esteemed jurist, and the foremost classical proponent of natural law. HIs major work of legal philosophy, *Treatise on Law*, forms topics 90 to 108 of the *Prima Secundæ,* of the *Summa Theologiæ*, Aquinas' masterwork of scholastic philosophical theology [28]. In his writing, Aquinas distinguished between four kinds of law: eternal law, divine law, natural law, and human law. These four models of law have formed the basis of evolution for many of our current legal systems and some continue to be a source of legal influence.

1.2.1.2 Eternal and Divine Law

Eternal law refers to divine reason; the plan for the universe which is known only to God. Man needs this plan, for without it he would totally lack direction.

Divine law comprises any body of law that is perceived as having been derived from a transcendent source, such as the will of God or gods—that is, in contrast to human-made or secular laws. Aquinas described divine law as being that which is revealed in the scriptures and is God's positive law for mankind. Similar to natural law, divine law is viewed as existing independent of the will of man, with divine laws being perceived as being superior to—or of having greater authority than—human-made laws.

The natural law-based theories, according to Aquinas, is the "participation" in the eternal law by rational human creatures, and is discovered by reason. Natural law today refers to the body of unchanging moral principles that are regarded as the basis for all human conduct. It is a theoretical perspective, grounded in ethics and philosophy, that posits that all human beings possess intrinsic values that govern our reasoning and behavior, and that these values are not created by society, governments, or court judges.

The paradigmatic view of natural law holds that:

1. The natural law is given by God.
2. It is naturally authoritative over all human beings.
3. It is naturally knowable by all human beings.

1.2.1.3 Human Law

Human law refers to the set of laws which are made by humans, supported by reason, and enacted for the common good. Aquinas considered all human laws to be derived from the natural law, which in turn is a participation in the eternal law of God. To use an example provided by Aquinas himself, "that one must not kill may be derived as a conclusion from the principle that one should do harm to no man."

1.2.2 Analytical Jurisprudence: Definition and Clarification

Analytical jurisprudence is a philosophical approach to law that draws on the resources of modern analytical philosophy to try to understand its nature. The history of analytical jurisprudence can be traced back at least as far as the work of Jeremy Bentham (1748–1832), an English philosopher, jurist, social reformer, legal positivist, and founder of the modern theory of utilitarianism.[6] Theories of analytic jurisprudence include: (1) legal positivism; (2) legal realism (3) sociological jurisprudence; (4) critical legal studies; (5) critical rationalism; (6) legal interpretivism; and (7) therapeutic jurisprudence.

1.2.2.1 Legal Positivism

Legal positivism is a philosophy of law that emphasizes the conventional nature of law—that it is socially constructed. Under legal positivism, law is synonymous with positive norms, that is, norms made by the legislator or considered as common law or

[6]Jeremy Bentham is also known for having described theories of natural law and divine law as being "nonsense on stilts."

case law. In the legal positivist perspective, the source of law is founded in the establishment of that law by some legal authority which is recognized socially.

Legal positivism contends that:

1. Laws are commands of human beings.
2. There is not any necessary relation between law and morality, that is, between law as it is and as it ought to be.
3. Analysis (or study of the meaning) of legal concepts is worthwhile and is to be distinguished from history or sociology of law, as well as from criticism or appraisal of law, for example with regard to its moral value or to its social aims or functions.
4. A legal system is a closed, logical system in which correct decisions can be deduced from predetermined legal rules without reference to social considerations.
5. Moral judgments, unlike statements of fact, cannot be established or defended by rational argument, evidence, or proof [29].

1.2.2.2 Legal Realism

Legal realism is a subset of analytical jurisprudence that perceives creativity in the interpretation of legal texts as being justified and necessary in order to assure that the law serves good public policy and social interests. Legal realism runs contrary to *legal formalism*—the theoretical perspective that legal reasoning is, or can be, modelled as a mechanical, algorithmic process as, in the formalist perspective, giving judges the authority to change the law to serve their own ideas regarding policy would undermine the rule of law [30].

In the formalist perspective, giving judges the authority to change the law to serve their own ideas regarding policy would undermine the rule of law.[7] As a defining feature of the common law system is the ability of judges to incrementally alter the law in accordance with the evolving needs and interests of the society, the tension between legal formalism and legal realism is especially relevant in common law legal systems, which depend on judicial precedent. Unsurprisingly, legal realism has been favored in some common law jurisdictions, where the kind of legal codifications associated with civil law, and more strict legal formalism, are virtually unknown.

1.2.2.3 Sociological Jurisprudence

Sociological jurisprudence is the study of the law in practice, including the actual effects of the law within society, and the influence of social phenomena on both the substantive and procedural aspects of law. In essence, sociological jurisprudence examines the relationship between the law and the society to which that law is applied. This is based on the belief that this law remains unclear unless you analyze it

---

[7] That is, that everyone is subject to the law, including people who are lawmakers, law enforcement officials and judges.

with relation to an actual social phenomenon. With the aim of making the law an effective instrument of social control, sociological jurisprudence emphasizes the working law, actual social conditions and social situations rather than the abstract legal concepts and content. It places the value of individual betterment over the interest of the state or general interest.

Proponents of sociological jurisprudence hold a greater concern for the functioning and workings of the law, rather than the nature of law itself. Sociological jurists focus strongly on the social purposes, goals and expectations of law rather than the sanctions and coercive nature of the law. Jurists who subscribe to the sociological jurisprudence perspective are more likely to consider law as a body of authoritative guides that help to enable decision-making, as opposed to an abstract content of authoritative directives. As this school of thought considers law as a socio-legal institution that can be created and modified consciously, it synthesizes with both the analytical method of legal practice and historical approach to the study of law.

1.2.2.4 Critical Legal Studies

Critical legal studies is a newer theory of jurisprudence, having only been developed since the 1970s. The theory of critical legal studies holds that the law is largely contradictory, and can be best analyzed as an expression of the policy goals of a dominant social group [31].

1.2.2.5 Critical Rationalism

Critical rationalism is a form of rational skeptical philosophy which holds that scientific theories and any other claims to knowledge can and should be rationally criticized, and (if they have empirical content) can and should be subjected to tests which may falsify them. The term was coined by Karl R. Popper as a response to "uncritical or comprehensive rationalism", the justifications perspective that only what can be proved by reason and/or experience should be accepted. In this way, claims to knowledge may be contrastingly and normatively evaluated. Popper argued that comprehensive rationalism cannot explain how proof is possible and that it leads to inconsistencies [32].

1.2.2.6 Legal Interpretivism

Legal interpretivism refers to the philosophical explanation of the impact of institutional practice—the legally significant action and practices of political institutions—on legal rights and obligations. It says that how institutional practice affects the law is determined by certain principles, identified by interpretation, which explain why the practice should have that role [33].

1.2.2.7 Therapeutic Jurisprudence

Therapeutic jurisprudence is the approach to law which looks at the extent to which substantive rules, legal procedures, and legal actors produce therapeutic or anti-therapeutic consequences for individuals involved in the legal process, which can have an impact on the emotional and psychological wellbeing of an individual, either positively or negatively [34]. Supporters of therapeutic jurisprudence seek to ensure that the law is a positive social force, promoting better well-being and overall mental health [35]. By positioning itself as a form of lens, or field of inquiry, therapeutic jurisprudence can be extremely wide-ranging in its ideas and principles. It draws on insights from various disciplines—like psychology, criminology and sociology—as well as often overlapping with other approaches to law—such as restorative justice and mental health law [36]. The flexibility of this approach allows for its practical adaptation for a wide variety of situations.

1.2.3 Normative Jurisprudence: Evaluation and Reformation

Normative jurisprudence involves the examination of normative, evaluative, and otherwise prescriptive issues about the law, such as restrictions on freedom, obligations to obey the law, and the grounds for punishment. As normative jurisprudence is concerned with "evaluative" theories of law, it deals with what the goal or purpose of law is, or what moral or political theories provide a foundation for the law. Prominent normative jurisprudencial perspectives include theories like virtue jurisprudence, deontology, and utilitarianism.

1.2.3.1 Virtue Jurisprudence

Virtue jurisprudence is a normative and explanatory theory of law that utilizes the resources of virtue ethics to answer the central questions of legal theory, including the view that the laws should promote the development of virtuous characters by citizens. Virtue jurisprudence focuses on the importance of character and human excellence—or virtue—to questions about the nature of law, the content of the law, and legal judgments [37].

1.2.3.2 Deontology

Deontology is the view that laws should reflect our obligation to preserve the autonomy and rights of others [38]. Historically, deontological thought regarding law is associated with the work of Enlightenment-era philosopher Immanuel Kant and that of contemporary legal philosopher Ronald Dworkin.

Immanuel Kant argued that in order to act in the morally right way, people must act from duty *and* that it is not the consequences of actions that make them right or wrong, but the motives of the person who carries out the action [39].

Dworkin's theory of "law as integrity," as described in his book *Law's Empire*, has judges interpreting the law in terms of consistent moral principles, especially justice and fairness, and is among the most influential contemporary theories about the nature of law. Dworkin's theory is "interpretive" in that it describes the law as being whatever follows from a constructive interpretation of the institutional history of the legal system. Dworkin argues that in every situation where people's legal rights are controversial, the best interpretation involves the right answer thesis, the thesis that there exists a right answer as a matter of law that the judge must discover.

1.2.3.3 Utilitarianism and Consequentialism

Utilitarianism refers to the family of ethical theories that prescribe actions that maximize happiness and well-being for all affected individuals. Utilitarianism is a version of *consequentialism*, which states that the consequences of any action are the only standard of right and wrong. Unlike other forms of consequentialism, such as egoism and altruism, utilitarianism considers the interests of all humans equally. While there were earlier writers who presented theories that were strikingly similar, utilitarianism as a distinct ethical position only emerged in the eighteenth century, having begun with Jeremy Bentham—an English jurist, philosopher, and social reform advocate—in the Introduction to his *Principles of Morals and Legislation.*

> Nature has placed mankind under the governance of two sovereign masters, pain and pleasure. It is for them alone to point out what we ought to do, as well as to determine what we shall do. [40]

Jeremy Bentham theorized that happiness or pleasure is the only thing that is good for its own sake. He believed that humans, by nature, are motivated exclusively by the desire for pleasure—also known as "psychological hedonism"—and that ethically they should seek to maximize pleasure—otherwise known as "ethical hedonism". In *The Principles of Morals and Legislation*, Bentham attempted to determine what a system of laws would look like if it was constructed on a purely utilitarian basis. According to Bentham, seven factors should be considered in weighing the value of a pleasure or pain: (1) intensity; (2) duration; (3) degree of certainty; (4) propinquity or remoteness; (5) fecundity[8]; (6) purity[9]; and (7) extent or scope of impact.

1.3 Sources of Law

The four primary sources of law are statutes, cases, and regulations. These laws and rules are issued by official bodies within governmental bodies. There are other sources for what constitutes appropriate conduct, such as religion and ethics, which may have an influential impact on law, but are not considered to be primary sources.

1.3.1 Legislation/Statutory Law

Statutory law refers to the laws which are implemented through enacted legislation. Statutes, or Acts, are laws made by the (federal) Parliament or the (provincial/territorial) Legislature. The implementation of a new statute can create a new law,

---

[8]The tendency to produce further pleasure or pain.

[9]Whether it is purely pleasurable or painful, or a mixture of the two.

or modify or nullify a previously existing law. The rules that address the details and practical applications of the law expressed in each Act are known as its Regulations. The authority to make Regulations in relation to an Act is assigned within that Act itself. Put simply, statutory law refers to the entirety of written laws that are passed through the body of the legislature and voted on by the members of the governing body. Keywords to look for when determining whether a law is a statute or legislation can include terms like: Charter, Code, Constitution, Act, etc.

1.3.2 Legal Precedent/ Case Law/Common Law

In some legal systems, the concept of sources of law in jurisprudence can also refer to the body of previous court decisions, known as legal precedent. Other terms for legal precedent include: case law, common law, judge-made law, judicial precedent, and precedential law.

Legal precedent refers to a court decision that is considered as authority for deciding subsequent cases involving identical or similar facts, or similar legal issues. If the facts or issues of a case hugely differ from those in a previous case, then the previous case cannot be used as legal precedent for determining the outcome of the new case. Once a case is decided by a judge by applying the principle, a case on similar facts which may arise in future must also be decided by applying the same principle. The basis for legal precedent is founded in the doctrine of stare decisis. This area of law is also known as case law, common law, judge-made law, etc. The doctrine of judicial precedent is based on two rules:

Rule 1: A court which is lower in a hierarchy is completely bound by the decisions of courts which are above it.

Rule 2: Higher courts are bound by their own decision, in general, in matters related to precedence.

1.3.2.1 Treatment of Legal Precedents

There are a few different subtypes of legal precedents, the main types being: (1) binding precedents; (2) persuasive precedents; (3) original precedents; and (4) declaratory precedents.

A *binding precedent* is a previous legal decision which subsequent courts are required to follow. When a court is required to follow precedents, or previous legal decisions, it means that the previous judicial decision was binding, that is, that all subsequent cases will be bound by the previous decision. When a judicial decision is based on a precedent case, it is being made according to the principle of *stare decisis*, which is to "stand by the decision already made."

A *persuasive precedent* is a previous judicial decision which a subsequent court if not required to follow. When a court is not required to follow a judicial precedent, but the precedential case is strikingly similar to the case in question, then the previous judicial decision is instead referred to as a non-binding or persuasive precedent. While persuasive precedents are not binding on a decision-maker, they can be highly influential in the resulting decision made by a court, especially where there is a high level of similarity in the facts of the two cases.

An *original precedent* is a judicial decision in which a new law is created and applied in a legal matter. This occurs when a judge must come to a decision without the option of following a previous decision, as the specific facts in the case have not previously come before a court. Original precedents are responsible for the creation of new laws, which we may also refer to as judge-made law [41].

A *declaratory precedent* is when there is only one possible application of a previously decided rule in a legal matter, which can be intuitively applied to the case. In this situation, the decision-maker would simply be applying an existing law to a legal matter.

1.3.2.2 Doctrine of Legal Precedent

When the *doctrine of legal precedent* is applied—that is, when a previous judicial decision can be compared and contrasted with the current case—there can be four outcomes. The precedent provided by the previous case can be: (1) applied; (2) adopted; (3) distinguished; or (4) overruled [42].

For a precedent to be *applied* or *adopted* means that it was positively influential in the decision of the case to which the precedent was compared. A previous judicial decision is said to have been *applied* when it is found to be a binding precedent, in that the principles underpinning the previous decision are used to evaluate the issues of the subsequent case. Where a previous judicial decision is not found to be judicially binding, but is persuasive to the eventual outcome of the decision, then we can say that the previous decision was *adopted* by the court.

Alternatively, when a precedent case is not positively influential on the outcome of a decision, then the precedent can be said to have been either *distinguished* or *overruled*. A precedent case is *distinguished* when the principles which underpin the previous decision are found to be specific to—or otherwise heavily premised upon—certain factual scenarios which cannot be applied to the subsequent case because of the absence of, or material difference in, the relevant and material facts of the case. Put simply, if a precedent case is different enough from the case with which it is being compared, then the precedent case can be distinguished from the latter case [43].

Finally, a precedent can be *overruled* either on appeal or through the determination of subsequent cases—by either the same or a higher level of court—if it is found that the principles underpinning the previous decision were made through erroneous interpretation and/or application of the law or if the principles underpinning the previous decisions have been overtaken by new legislation or other relevant developments [44].

1.3.3 Sources of Legal Influence

While not considered to be primary sources of law, there are many additional personal, social, political, financial, or other factors which may have some level of

Fig. 1.1 Sources of Law and Legal Influence

influence on the law and/or judicial decision-making. While this is not ideal, it seems nearly inherent—as humans—to experience preference and opinions based on individual ideologies. Sources of legal influence can include anything which may influence or impact the perspective of a decision-maker or governing body, such as: religious ideologies, personal values, social norms, political influence, internalized bias, and many other influencers. Figure 1.1 shows some of the sources of law and sources of influence on law.

1.4 Systems of Law

Black's Law Dictionary tenth Ed., definition 2, differentiates "common law" jurisdictions and legal systems from civil law jurisdictions, there are five major legal systems used in the world, with each of those systems having their own structural subsets. Those systems are: (1) common law; (2) civil law; (3) religious law; (4) customary law; and (5) legal pluralism.

1.4.1 Common Law

Common law countries are those which adhere to the doctrine of *stare decisis*, which is the principle in common law systems that a precedent—an earlier decision or ruling in a previous legal case—is either binding or persuasive for a court when deciding future cases with similar issues or established facts. Historically, the common law system originated in medieval England from uncodified judge-made case law and gave authority to prior court decisions—which we have discussed as legal precedent [45].

The goal of the common law legal system in deciding cases based on precedent and according to consistent principled rules is that cases that have similar facts will yield similar and predictable outcomes, which will aid in maintaining the fundamental principles of justice. Common law systems place great weight on court decisions, which are considered law with the same force of law as statutes. While they often have statutes as well, common law legal systems rely more heavily on legal precedent. Common law systems are adversarial, rather than investigatory, with the judge moderating between two opposing parties [46].

1.4.2 Civil Law

Civil law is the most widespread system of law in the world, in force in various forms in about 150 countries, historically drawing heavily from Roman law—one of the most intricate known legal systems prior to our modern era. The civil law system took inspiration from the framework of ancient Roman law, was influenced by Canon Law[10] in the Middle Ages, and developed into the current referable system or codified core principles which acts as the primary source of law.[11]

Globally, civil systems vary widely, both in procedure and substantive law, which often varies between nations, however they do have some trademark characteristics. The most pronounced features of civil systems are their legal codes with concise and broadly applicable texts that typically avoid factually specific scenarios. The short articles in a civil law code deal in generalities and stand in contrast with ordinary statutes, which are often very long and very detailed. Nations which use a civil law system have comprehensive and frequently updated legal codes [47]. Most importantly, case law is a secondary source in these jurisdictions. France and Germany are two examples of countries with a civil law system. Table 1.1 distinguishes between the main features of the common and civil legal systems.

[10] A variety of religious law.

[11] Also called a "codex".

Table 1.1 Distinguishing common law and civil law legal systems

	Common Law	**Civil Law**
Synonyms and Subsets	Anglo-American law English law Judge-made law Precedential law	Continental law French law Germanic law Roman law
Primary Source (s) of Law	Case law / Legal precedent	Codified laws / Legislation
Creators of Law	Both the Judiciary and the Legislative bodies	Legislative bodies
Role of Judiciary	Evaluation and creation of law through legal precedent	Interpretation and application of the law as codified
Clarity vs Flexibility	Less clarity; great flexibility	More clarity; less flexibility
Legal Procedure	Adversarial: Trial judge focuses on issues of law and legal procedure; acting as a referee between the prosecution and the defense.	Inquisitorial: Trial judge acts as inquisitor and actively participates in the process; fact-finding, questioning, raising issues, etc.
Example Nations	Australia Bangladesh Canada Hong Kong Pakistan United States	Brazil France Germany Kuwait Lebanon Russia

1.4.3 Religious Law

Religious law includes ethical and moral codes taught by religious traditions and used as a basis for law. Religious legal systems then, are those in which the law is rooted in the religious doctrine, interpretations of those texts, or traditions within a given religion. Different religious systems hold sacred law in a greater or lesser degree of importance to their belief systems [48].

Some countries incorporate some aspects of religious law into civil or common law systems.[12] We can see this in Islamic nations which have legal systems based in whole or in part on religious material, with a portion of those nations opting to mix the traditional religious law with features of the civil or common law legal systems. In other countries, elements of Hindu, Buddhist, Confucian, or Sikh laws can be found incorporated into the legal structure [49].

[12] See: Legal Pluralism.

1.4.4 Customary Law

Customary law legal systems are generally found at the tribal or local level in districts, counties, and villages, and is a vast set of practices that vary from community to community. Countries that do not historically have strong formal justice systems may rely upon customary law, which frequently becomes a function of tribal or village elders in the absence of a functioning formal justice system, as in a conflict or post-conflict country. These traditional rights and obligations are generally unique to a particular society or culture. Customary law is based on longstanding local customs which greatly shape the ideas of justice. The laws of customary legal systems are usually unwritten; orally dispensed by elders and passed down through generations. Oftentimes, customary law practices can be found within pluralistic legal system jurisdictions, in combination with common, civil, or religious systems of law. It generally uses a case-by-case approach to dispute resolution, sometimes involving informal mediation or arbitration, and typically does not include a formal trial. Customary law frequently becomes a function of tribal or village elders in the absence of a functioning formal justice system, as in a conflict or post-conflict country [50].

1.4.5 Legal Pluralism

Legal pluralism, also called a hybrid or mixed law legal system, includes any legal systems where countries have mixed legal systems that draw on common law or civil law traditions and mixed with customary or religious laws [51]. Some examples include:

- Nepal's legal system combines Hindu legal concepts and common law [52].
- Sri Lanka's legal system combines civil law, common law and customary law [53].
- Many Pacific island countries recognize customary law as well as common law [54].
- In some African countries, customary law still has great influence, and local values play a role in informal justice systems and accountability [55].

1.4.6 Case Hypothetical: Systems of Law

Country X is a national federation made up of three united provinces: Province A, Province B, and Province C. Prior to becoming the federation collectively known as Country X, each of these three provinces used their own unique system of law.

Province A has always based their laws, legal enforcement, and judicial decisions on a collection of *legal codes and statutes*. When a case appears before a court in Province A, the judiciary applies the *codified law*, as it is written, to the specific matters in the case. Each case is heard individually and on its own merits. The outcome of a case is neither influenced by previous decisions made in similar cases nor does it serve to influence future judicial decisions. In this way, Province A would be considered to use a *civil law* system of law.

Province B has a system of law which is primarily based on replicating the lines of reasoning and legal application as applied in *preceding cases* and *previous judicial decisions*. In this way, Province B gives *deference to the judgements* made by previous decision-makers. This allows for a more fluid application of law—taking into consideration the developing legal goals, attitudes, social norms, and values of a region—which serves to gradually shape and shift the application of the law over time, as those goals, attitudes, norms, and values evolve. In this case, Province B would fall under the umbrella of the *common law* legal system.

Province C uses a blended system of law which is based on *religious law* with the added influence of *customary law*. Although not written or prescribed through canonical material, the customary law itself was heavily influenced by the dominant religion and the laws prescribed within its associated materials. Province C can either be seen as using a system based on *religious law* or, alternatively, it can be identified as a *pluralistic system* of religious and customary law.

As a nation in its entirety, Country X has come to the agreement that any legal matter which is localized to one of the provinces can be enforced and decided based on the presiding legal system of that province. For matters which occur between or across provinces, Country X has a complex set of rules for determining the system of law to be applied which varies depending on the nature of the legal matter. Based on its jigsawed cocktail of legal systems, Country X can be said to be using a *pluralistic* system of law. *Legal pluralism*, in this context, refers to the blend of *civil law*, *common law*, and *religious/customary legal systems* which apply within each jurisdiction, that being, the province—or provinces—in which the law is being applied.

1.5 Categories of Law

As we can see from the earlier sections of this book, the law can be many things, is formed from many influences, and can be vastly different between individual nations. When we talk about laws, it can be helpful to narrow the scope of the discussion to the specific subcategory or branch of law, as we can use a taxonomical structure to categorize different species of related creatures. In law, we can distinguish (for the most part) between international and domestic law, as well as between public and private law. It is important to recognize, however, that as every individual situation arises which must be examined under the law, there is often an amount of intersectionality between the most specific sub-categories, as we can see in an example of a legal matter, provided below.

1.5.1 International Law vs Domestic Law

International law involves the regulation of relationships between sovereign states, while *domestic law*, on the other hand, confers rights to persons and entities within those individual sovereign states. Domestic law and international law are enforced differently, primarily because international law deals with the issue of sovereignty.

Thus, while international law involves the regulation of the relationship between sovereign states, domestic law confers rights to persons and entities within the sovereign state [56].

1.5.2 Recognition of Sovereignty

Sovereignty refers to the legal power and authority of a governing body to exercise control over a nation or state and the autonomy of that governing body to do so freely and without external pressure, control or influence [57]. In any nation or state, sovereignty is assigned to the person, governing body, or other institution that has the ultimate authority over other people in order to establish a law or change an existing law [58].

Nations and states are also sometimes described as being sovereign themselves. When a nation identifies as a *sovereign nation*, it means that the population or residents of the nation have power over themselves and control over their own government, rather than their government being under the control of an external authority. In this way, sovereignty in domestic law refers to the power of a governmental body to rule without intrusion from outside forces or external influence from other countries.

In international law, sovereignty is the exercise of power by a state [59]. *De jure sovereignty* refers to the legal right of the state to exercise their power and authority. This can be contrasted with *de facto sovereignty*, which refers to the actual factual ability of a state to exercise their power and authority rather than the legal right to do so. While we typically expect *de jure* and de facto sovereignty to exist at the same place, at the same time, and within the same governing organization, a failure of that expectation can become an issue of concern for the determination of sovereignty in international law. Although the twentieth century resulted in greater limitations on sovereignty, it continues to be a major issue in international law, particularly in cases of international human rights violations and regional genocide.

The current notion of national or state sovereignty contains four aspects consisting of: territory; population; authority; and recognition [60]. According to Stephen Krasner—an academic and international relations professor at Stanford University—sovereignty can be understood in four different ways [61]:

1. *Domestic sovereignty* is the actual control over a nation or state exercised by an authority organized within the state.
2. *Interdependence sovereignty* refers to the actual control of movement across state borders.
3. *International legal sovereignty* is formal recognition of sovereignty by other sovereign states.
4. *Westphalian sovereignty* refers to a lack of other authority over a state other than the domestic authority, such as a non-domestic church, political organization, or other external agent [62].

Often, these four aspects all appear together, but this is not necessarily the case. State sovereignty is sometimes confused, or viewed synonymously, with independence—that is the condition of anybody in which at least a portion of its population exercises self-government. Often, independence will also entail sovereignty, but that is not always the case [63]. We can distinguish between sovereignty and independence with the following examples:

1. Independence cannot be transferred as a legal right, whereas sovereignty is legally transferable.
2. Independence can be achieved by a state de facto long after acquiring sovereignty—as in the case of Cambodia and Vietnam.
3. Independence can be suspended when a region becomes subject to an occupation—as in the case of Iraq, whose sovereignty as a nation went uncontested in 2003 while occupied by external forces, as Iraq had not been annexed by neighboring nations.
4. Independence can become completely lost when the sovereignty of a nation or state itself becomes the subject of dispute.

1.5.3 Public Law versus Private Law

As we can distinguish between international law and domestic law, so can we distinguish between public law and private law. The main difference between whether an act is an issue of public law or private law is a question of who is affected.

Public law deals with issues that affect society as a whole, including the regulation of interrelations between the state and the general population. Public law is regulation of the legal system itself, rather than the regulation of individuals. Public law can be further broken down into five major subsections: (1) constitutional law; (2) criminal law; (3) taxation law; (4) administrative law; and (5) all procedural law.

Private law covers the areas of law arising from legal disputes between two or more individuals, including those relating to personal injury, family law matters, private property, real estate, contractual disputes, corporate law, and business relationships.

Legal matters can fall into one or multiple categories, sometimes overlapping public and private legal spheres. For example, a dispute arising from the separation and divorce of a couple with many shared assets [64].

1.5.4 Case Hypothetical: Categories of Law

Person A and Person B have been *Married* for two decades. One year after their marriage, they started a *Business*, which quickly expanded and they ended up incorporating it. Within the next 10 years, they purchase a *Home* and expand their *Family* to include two children, Child A and Child B.

The Business assets are divided into two classes of shares, Class A shares are all held by Person A and Class B shares held by Person B. To ensure that their children will be cared for, they both created *Wills* and together set up *Trusts* for each of the children, in which the *Estate* assets would be held until each child reached the age of 25. As a bonus, all members of the family are covered under the company *Insurance* plan, which includes a large payout if the case of an accidental workplace death.

Following the arrival of Child B, Person A and Person B agree that Person A should take a leave of absence from full-time *Employment* to take care of the children until both children are old enough to attend elementary school during the day. While on leave from work, Person A spends roughly 30 hours per week doing office work to assist Person B in operating their shared Business. The home office was dutifully claimed in their *Taxation* records at a home office, meeting all of the qualifications for that designation.

One day, Person A slips on a pool of water on the floor of the home office and promptly dies. The incident is investigated for *Fraud* by the insurance provider. Person B ends up being charged with *Murder*. He is convicted but *Appeals* the decision based on evidence of *Procedural* error during *Evidence* collection by law enforcement.

Each of the words in bold font in the above case hypothetical, can help to indicate the relevant sub-branch(es) of legal practice. Table 1.2 sorts these keywords and lists the relevant areas of legal practice, either under the Public Law or Private Law category. Through this exercise, we can see that some topics which may arise in the legal realm can intersect with multiple areas of law, in both the public and private spheres of practice.

Some of the major sub-branches and specializations of the legal profession are categorized in Fig. 1.2, being differentiated by international law vs domestic law and by public law vs private law.

1.6 Legal Governance

Legal governance refers to the establishment, execution and interpretation of legal policies, frameworks, processes and rules in a governing body. In other words, this is the intersection of law and politics. As this book is not focused on political issues beyond those directly related to specific cyber laws and cybersecurity, this will be limited to a brief overview of the different systems of government, with the division of jurisdictional power in a constitutional system explained in greater detail.

Historically, there have been many different variations of legal governance throughout our nations and within our local societies. Modern governing structures tend to fall into one of the following four categories: (1) authoritarianism; (2) monarchies; (3) elite government; and (4) popular government.

Table 1.2 Potentially relevant areas of legal practice

Keyword	Areas of Public Law	Areas of Private Law
Married	Personal taxation	Family law Wills and estate law
Business	Corporate taxation	Corporate/commercial law Contract law
Home		Property law Family law
Family		Family law
Wills		Wills and estate law Property law
Trusts		Trusts Wills and estate law
Estate		Wills and estate law Property law
Fraud	Criminal law	Contract law Insurance law
Insurance	Administrative law	Insurance law Personal injury Tort law
Employment		Labor/employment law Family law
Taxation	Personal taxation law Corporate taxation law Criminal law	Corporate/commercial law Wills and estate law
Fraud	Corporate taxation law Criminal law	Corporate/commercial law Insurance law
Murder	Criminal law Constitutional law	Family law Insurance law
Appeals	Administrative law Procedural law	
Procedural	Procedural law Administrative law	
Evidence	Criminal law Constitutional law Evidence law Procedural law	

1.6.1 Authoritarianism

Authoritarianism refers to a state which is characterized by a strong central government that allows people a limited degree of political freedom. However, the political process, as well as all individual freedom, is controlled by the government without any constitutional accountability.

The four primary features of an authoritarian system of governance are:

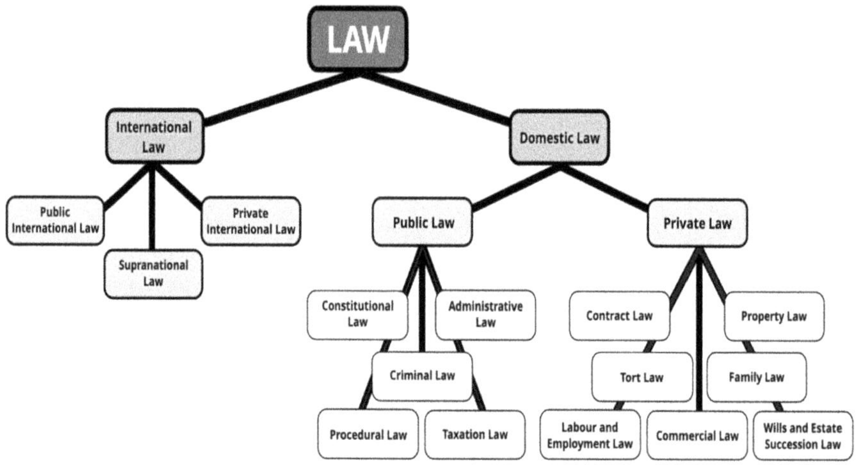

Fig. 1.2 Taxonomy of the Major Areas of Legal Practice

- Limited political freedom with strict government controls imposed on political institutions and groups like legislatures, political parties, and interest groups.
- A controlling regime that justifies itself to the people as a "necessary evil" uniquely capable of coping with "easily recognizable societal problems" such as hunger, poverty, and violent insurgency.
- Strict government-imposed constraints on social freedoms such as suppression of political opponents and anti-regime activity.
- The presence of a ruling executive with vague, shifting, and loosely defined powers.[13]

1.6.1.1 Totalitarianism

Totalitarianism is an authoritarian form of government in which the ruling party recognizes no limitations whatsoever on its power, including exercising near complete control over its citizens' lives and rights and which tolerates no opposition. A single figure often holds power and maintains authority through widespread surveillance of citizens and visitors, restricted access to information through the complete control of mass media, intimidating demonstrations of paramilitary or police power, and suppression of protest, activism, or political opposition by prohibiting the gathering of groups for political purposes which are in opposition to the state [65].

Examples of characteristics that might be present in a totalitarian state include:

- Rule enforced by a single dictator.
- The presence of a single ruling political party.
- Strict censorship, if not total control of the press.

[13] As described by Juan José Linz, Professor Emeritus of Sociology and Political Science at Yale University, in 1964.

- Constant dissemination of pro-government propaganda.
- Mandatory service in the military for all citizens.
- Mandatory population control practices.
- Prohibition of certain religious or political groups and practices.
- Prohibition of any form of public criticism of the government.
- Laws enforced by secret police forces or the military [66].

Typically, the characteristics of a totalitarian state tend to cause people to fear their government. Rather than trying to allay that fear, totalitarian rulers encourage it and use it to ensure the people's cooperation [67].

Early examples of totalitarian states include the Soviet Union under Joseph Stalin, Germany under Adolf Hitler and Italy under Benito Mussolini. According to most authorities, North Korea and the East African state of Eritrea are the world's only two nations recognized as still having totalitarian forms of government [68]. Subtypes of totalitarian governance include: totalitarian states, military dictatorships, and autocracies [69]. We can also see aspects of totalitarianism in some authoritarian and facist governmental systems [70].

1.6.1.2 Dictatorships

A *military dictatorship* is a nation ruled by a single authority with absolute power and no democratic process [71]. The head of state typically comes to power in a time of upheavals, such as high unemployment rates or civil unrest. They usually lead the nation's armed forces, using it to establish their brand of law and order and suppress the people's rights. Dictators dismiss due process, civil liberties, or political freedoms. Dissent or political opposition can be dangerous or even deadly for the country's citizens.

While a *dictatorship* is by definition an autocracy, a dictatorship may also be ruled by an elite group of people, such as a military or religious order. Autocracy can also be compared to oligarchy[14] and democracy.[15] Today, most autocracies exist in the form of absolute monarchies, such as Saudi Arabia, Qatar, and Morocco, and dictatorships, such as North Korea, Cuba, and Zimbabwe [72].

1.6.1.3 Fascism

Fascism is a form of government combining the most extreme aspects of both totalitarianism and authoritarianism. Fascism is characterized by the imposition of dictatorial power, government control of industry and commerce, and the forcible suppression of opposition, often at the hands of the military or a secret police force. Fascism was first seen in Italy during World War I, later spreading to Germany and other European countries during World War II [73].

Today, few governments publicly describe themselves as fascist. Instead, the label is more often used pejoratively by those critical of particular governments or

[14] Rule by a small group of individuals distinguished by their wealth, education or religion.

[15] Rule by a majority of the people.

leaders. The term "neo-fascist," for example, describes governments or individuals espousing radical, far-right political ideologies similar to those of the World War II fascist states [74].

1.6.2 Monarchism

Monarchy is a power system that appoints a person as head of state for life or until abdication. Authority traditionally passes down through a succession line related to one's bloodline and birth order within the ruling royal family, often limited by gender. Today, 45 nations have some form of monarchy, though the concept has become increasingly diluted with the evolution of democratic principles. One of the most well-known examples of a constitutional monarchy is that of Queen Elizabeth II of the United Kingdom, who fulfills a traditional symbolic role in partnership with parliament [75]. There are two types of monarchies: constitutional and absolute.

1.6.2.1 Constitutional Monarchism

Constitutional monarchies limit the scope of power of the monarch within their constitution. In most constitutional monarchies, the political powers of the monarch, if any, are very limited and their duties are mostly ceremonial. Instead, real governmental power is exercised by a parliament or similar legislative body overseen by a prime minister [76].

1.6.2.2 Absolute Monarchism

Absolute monarchies give a monarch unlimited power [77]. Today, 45 nations have some form of monarchy, though the concept has become increasingly diluted with the evolution of democratic principles. In an absolute monarchy, the succession of power is often hereditary, with the throne passing among members of a ruling family. Arising during the Middle Ages, absolute monarchy prevailed in much of western Europe by the sixteenth century [78]. The prevalence of absolute monarchies fell sharply after the French Revolution, which gave rise to the principle of popular sovereignty, or government by the people. Current absolute monarchies include those in Oman, Vatican City, Saudi Arabia, and the United Arab Emirates [79].

1.6.3 Elitism

Elitism tends to favor social systems such as meritocracy, technocracy and plutocracy as opposed to political egalitarianism and populism. Elitists believe only a few have the ability to truly change society, rather than the majority of people who only vote and elect the elites into power. Subtypes of elitism include oligarchies, aristocracies, and theocracies [80].

1.6.3.1 Oligarchy

Oligarchy refers to a government in which a small group of elite individuals, families, or corporations rules over a nation. A specific set of qualities, such as wealth, heredity, and race, are used to give a small group of people power. Oligarchies often have authoritative rulers and an absence of democratic practices or individual rights [81].

1.6.3.2 Aristocracy

Aristocracy is a form of governance in which a small, elite ruling class—the aristocrats—have power over those in lower socioeconomic groups [82]. Members of the aristocracy are usually chosen based on their education, upbringing, and genetic or family history. Aristocracies, which originated in Ancient Greece, often connect wealth and ethnicity with both the ability and right to rule. Aristocracies were the dominant governments during most medieval and modern periods across Europe. Aristocrats led major countries, including Britain, Germany, and Russia, until World War I, when other government forms gained popularity [83].

1.6.3.3 Theocracy

Theocracy refers to a form of government in which a specific religious ideology determines the leadership, laws, and customs. In many instances, there is little to no distinction between scriptural laws and legal codes. Likewise, religious clergy will typically occupy leadership roles, sometimes including the highest office in the nation [84].

1.6.4 Socialism

Socialism is a system that encourages cooperation rather than competition among citizens. Citizens communally own the means of production and distribution of goods and services, while a centralized government manages it. Each person benefits from and contributes to the system according to their individual needs and abilities. Socialist governmental systems can be found in the Scandinavian nations of Denmark, Finland, Iceland, Norway, and Sweden. Subtypes of socialism include communist and social democratic systems of legal governance [85].

1.6.4.1 Communism

Communism is a centralized form of government led by a single party that is often authoritarian in its rule. Inspired by German philosopher Karl Marx, communist states replace private property and a profit-based economy with public ownership and communal control of economic production, such as labor, capital goods, and natural resources. Citizens are part of a classless society that distributes goods and services as needed. The Soviet Union was a one-party, communist state in Northern Eurasia from 1922 to 1991 [86].

Both communism and socialism are political and economic systems that share certain beliefs, including greater equality in the distribution of income. Both communism and socialism advocate public control of the means of production, although socialism allows for the continued existence of capitalism in some parts of the economy. One way communism differs from socialism is that it calls for the transfer of power to the working class by revolutionary rather than gradual means. Contemporary communism is an offshoot of socialism and is sometimes called "revolutionary socialism" for advocating the takeover of governmental powers by the working class through revolution rather than incremental reform. Socialism encompasses a broader spectrum of political beliefs than communism but shares communism's emphasis on a fair (if not necessarily equal) distribution of wealth among citizens, as well as public ownership of the means of production (though not necessarily all of them). In that sense, socialist programs and policies can exist alongside capitalism in a society, which is less likely in a true communist system [87].

1.6.4.2 Social Democracy

Social democracy is a strain of socialism that allows capitalism to exist but attempts to reign in its excesses through regulation, while also addressing inequality through government-run social programs. It gained ground after World War II, in part as a response to the economic failures and brutal governance of the Stalin-era Soviet Union. Countries such as Denmark, Finland, Norway, and Sweden are examples of social democracies, and many social welfare programs might also be seen as social democratic [88] initiatives.

In some countries where socialism has not taken hold as the official form of government, political parties such as Social Democratic Party of Germany and the Labour Party in the United Kingdom exert large influence [89].

1.6.5 Democracy

Democracy is a form of government that allows the people to choose leadership. The primary goal is to govern through fair representation and prevent abuses of power. The result is a system that requires discourse, debate, and compromise to satisfy the broadest possible number of public interests, leading to majority rule. Democracies advocate for fair and free elections, civic participation, human rights protections, and law and order. Democracy often goes hand-in-hand with constitutionalism [90].

1.6.5.1 Direct/Popular Democracy

A *direct democracy* is a type of democracy where the people govern directly. It requires wide participation of citizens in politics. *Popular democracy* is a type of direct democracy based on referendums and other devices of empowerment and concretization of popular will. Direct democracy also includes classical and Athenian democractic models [91].

1.6.5.2 Indirect/Representative Democracy

A *representative democracy* is a form of indirect democracy where sovereignty is held by the people's representatives. A representative democracy can be either liberal—that is, a representative democracy with protection for individual liberty and property by rule of law—it can be illiberal—that is, a representative democracy which has few, if any, limits on the power of the elected representatives or it can be a defensive representative democracy which limits some individual rights and freedoms of the people in order to protect the institutions of the democracy [92].

1.6.5.3 Other Variations of Democracy

There exists a long list of democratic system variations within the field of legal governance. Some of these variations are provided, with definitions, in Table 1.3.

In Fig. 1.3, we can see an illustration of how the systems of legal governance can be subdivided based on the number of leaders holding power over the general population.

1.6.6 Case Hypothetical: Legal Governance

Country X has historically been an *absolute monarchy*, overseen by one or more members of an *oligarchic* family, with title being passed down through a line of succession with each generation. The monarch and relatives were served and cared for by their peers and fellow members of the *aristocratic* class, who would themselves gain power and influence through their position of service in relation to the monarch in power at that time.

At some point, the people of Country X decide that they would like to have more power in the decision-making process and the ability to shape the laws which apply to them. The monarchy—recognizing the legitimacy of the demands of the people of Country X—agrees to a *constitutional monarchy*; maintaining the position of the monarch as head of state while the affairs of the nation itself would be determined by the governing *popular democracy*, using a *parliamentary* structure.

Province Z, in the northern part of Country X, was annexed during the last part of the *absolute monarchy*—before Country X became a *popular democracy* and *constitutional monarchy*. Prior to the annexation, this province was known as Country Y and was governed by an *authoritarian* religious figurehead—as a *theocracy*. The particular religion of Country Y emphasized the need for communal ownership of property, in which property is jointly owned by all members of Country Y. In this way, Country Y was an *authoritarian communist theocracy*.

1.7 Constitutionalism

Constitutionalism, which tends to be a component of democracy governmental systems, divides power between governmental bodies. This could look like a division of jurisdictional power between national and state levels of government, or between the legislature, the executive and the judiciary branches of the democratic governmental body [93].

Table 1.3 Variations of democratic governance

Type of Democracy	**Description**
Anticipatory Democracy	Relies on some degree of disciplined and usually market-informed anticipation of the future, to guide major decisions.
Associative Democracy	Places an emphasis on freedom via voluntary and democratically self-governing associations.
Adversarial Democracy	Emphasizes freedom based on adversarial relationships between individuals and groups, as best expressed in democratic judicial systems.
Cellular Democracy	A system of democratic governance which uses a multi-level bottom-up structure based on either small neighborhood governmental districts or contractual communities.
Consensus Democracy	Proposes rule based on consensus rather than traditional majority rule.
Constitutional Democracy	One which is governed by a constitution.
Defensive Democracy	A democracy in which some individual rights and freedoms are limited in order to protect the institutions of the democracy.
Deliberative Democracy	One in which authentic deliberation, not only voting, is central to legitimate decision-making. It adopts elements of both consensus decision-making and majority rule.
Dominant-Party Democracy	democratic party system where only one political party can realistically become the government, by itself or in a coalition government.
Electoral Democracy	A type of representative democracy which is based on an election system, on electoral vote.
Grassroots Democracy	Emphasizes trust in small decentralized units at the municipal government level, possibly using urban secession to establish the formal legal authority to make decisions made at this local level to be legally binding.
Guided Democracy	A form of democratic government with an increased level of autocracy and in which citizens exercise their political rights without meaningfully affecting the policies, motives, and goals of the government.
Industrial Democracy	A form of workplace democracy involving an arrangement in which workers make decisions and share responsibility and authority in the workplace.
Interactive Democracy	A proposed form of democracy which utilizes information technology to allow citizens to propose new policies, "second" proposals and vote on the resulting laws in a referendum.
Liberal Democracy	A form of representative democracy which values the protection of individual liberty and property by rule of law.
Liquid Democracy	A form of democratic control whereby voting power is vested in individual citizens who may self-select provisional delegates, rather than elected representatives.
Multi-Party Democracy	A two (or more) party system which requires voters to align themselves in large blocs or factions, some of which may be too large to comfortably agree on any overarching principles.

(continued)

Table 1.3 (continued)

Type of Democracy	**Description**
Non-Partisan Democracy	A system of representative government or organization such that universal and periodic elections—conducted by secret ballot—take place without reference to political parties.
Organic Authoritarian Democracy	A system of democracy in which the ruler holds a considerable amount of power, but their rule benefits the people.
Parliamentary Democracy	A democratic system of government where the executive branch of a parliamentary government typically forms a cabinet, and is headed by a prime minister who is considered the head of government.
Participatory Democracy	One which involves more lay citizen participation in decision-making and offers greater political representation than traditional representative democracy. This can include the wider control of proxies given to representatives by those who get directly involved and actually participate in the democratic process.
People's Democracy	A multi-class system of legal governance in which the rule is dominated by the proletariat or working people's class.
Presidential Democracy	A democratic system of government where a head of government is also head of state and leads an executive branch that is separate from the legislative branch.
Radical Democracy	A type of democracy that focuses on the importance of nurturing and tolerating differences and dissent in decision-making processes.
Religious Democracy / Theodemocracy	A form of government where the values of a particular religion have an influence and effect on the laws and rules. This is often found when most of the population is a member of the particular governing religion.
Semi-Direct Democracy	A representative democracy which includes instruments, elements, and/or features reminiscent of a direct democracy.
Sociocracy/Dynamic Social Democracy	A democratic system of legal governance based on consent in decision-making, circle organization, subsidiarity, and double-linked representation

A *constitution*, as a legal document, is a collection of fundamental values, beliefs, and principles which form the legal basis of a government, organization, polity, or other entity and commonly determines how that entity and its members are to be governed. The constitution of a nation typically outlines the key values of the nation and the fundamental rights of the members of that nation.

1.7.1 Division of Jurisdictional Powers

There are three branches of government that are involved in creating, maintaining, and applying our legal structure: the legislative branch—which makes, alters, and revokes laws, the executive branch—which administers and enforces the laws, and the judicial branch—which applies the laws to resolve disputes that cannot be settled outside of the court. The government in power makes and administers both

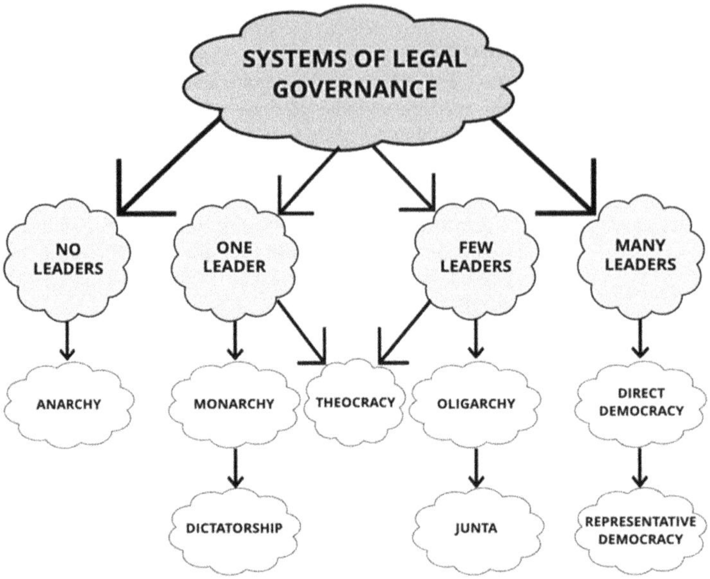

Fig. 1.3 Taxonomy Legal Governance

legislative and executive branches of our laws, and the courts maintain the judicial branch of our legal structure by applying the laws when settling legal disputes. This is the same both federally and provincially, with each level of government being given the power to enact laws and make decisions on specific matters within the jurisdiction of that level of government.

1.7.2 Branches of Legal Governance

The *three branches of legal governance* that we often see in democratic jurisdictions are: the Legislative (or Parliamentary) Branch, the Executive (or Governmental) Branch, and the Judicial Branch (or the Judiciary). The role of each branch, and legal governance as a whole, are illustrated in Fig. 1.4.

The *Legislative Branch*, also called the Parliamentary Branch, of legal governance is responsible for creating and proposing new laws, as well as refining and reviewing existing laws within their respective jurisdiction. The Legislative Branch includes regional legislators, elected members of parliament, house of assembly members, and other popularly-elected government representatives. In order to make new law, the law would need to be proposed and put forward for a vote by members of the Legislative branch.

The *Executive Branch*, or Government Branch, includes the heads of government, cabinet members, ministries, and public servants working in governmental

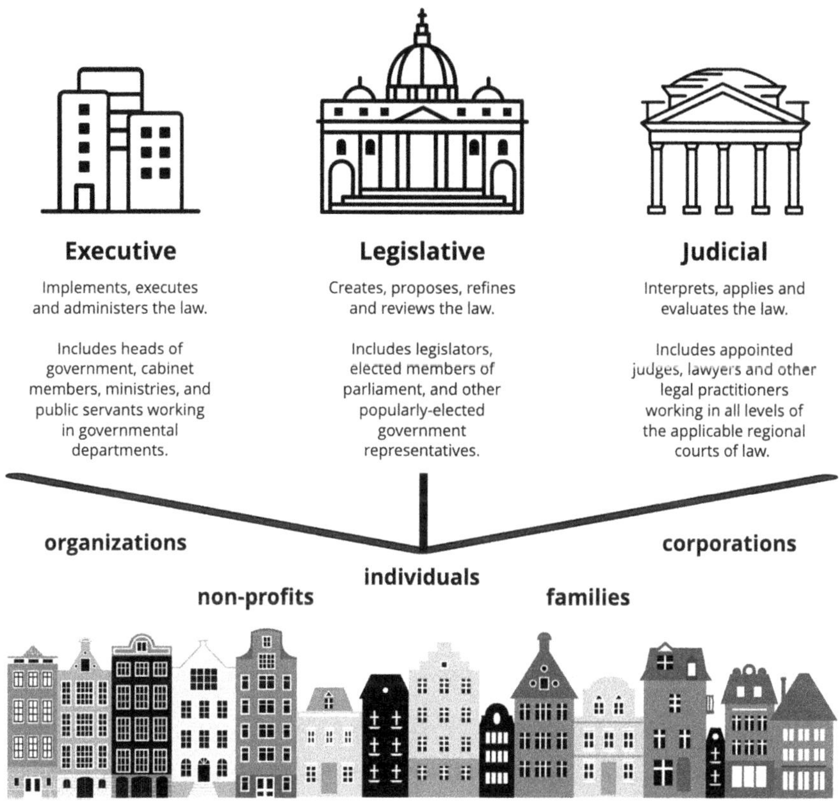

Fig. 1.4 Branches of Legal Governance

departments. The Executive Branch is responsible for implementing, executing, and administering the law.

The *Judicial Branch*, also called the Judiciary, of legal governance interprets, applies, and evaluates the law in its application through the courts. The Judicial Branch includes politically appointed judges, lawyers, and other legal practitioners working in all levels of the applicable regional courts of law.

Together, these three branches work to create and maintain the peace, order, and good governance of their respective jurisdictions [94].

1.8 Summary

In this chapter, we have discussed the foundational purpose and principles upon which our modern legal systems have been built. Starting with the concept of jurisprudence and the philosophy of natural law, we moved through to the analytic and normative legal philosophies which have historically influenced the legal structures and systems of governance in human societies. We have considered the primary sources of law, the concept of legal precedent, and other potential sources of legal influence.

Building on the jurisprudential philosophies and primary sources of law, we then discussed the various systems of law including the common law, civil law, religious law, customary law, and legal pluralism. Within these legal systems, we first distinguished between international and domestic law, followed by public and private law, and branching into specific subtypes of law within the field of legal practice. Finally, we connected the foundations of legal theory to the systems of legal governance which create, enforce, evaluate, and review laws within a specific jurisdiction.

In the next chapter, we will discuss and distinguish the concepts of ownership, property, and possession, as well as the differences between public data, private data, and personal data. We will connect these concepts to those which we have discussed in this chapter, to realize the intersection of (personal) property, (data) privacy, and (cyber)security in our modern legal systems. The answers to the following questions are provided within this chapter:

1. What is the Rule of Law and how is it applied?
2. What influence did Jeremy Bentham have on the area of Jurisprudence?
3. In what ways does Statutory Law differ from Case Law?
4. What are the key differences between the Common Law and the Civil Law legal systems?
5. What is Legal Pluralism?
6. What is the difference between a Constitutional Monarchy and an Absolute Monarchy?
7. Under which source of law would a Constitution be categorized?

References

1. King's Counsel (KC). https://en.wikipedia.org/wiki/Queen%27s_Counsel
2. The office of King's Counsel. http://www.kingscounselandtrust.com/
3. McLintock, A. H. (Ed.). (1966). *An encyclopaedia of New Zealand* (Vol. 3). R. E. Owen, Government Printer.
4. Salmond, J. W. (1907). *Jurisprudence, or, the theory of the law*. Stevens and Haynes.
5. Hobson, C. (1996). *The great chief justice: John Marshall and the rule of law* (p. 57). University Press of Kansas.
6. Black, A. (2009). *A world history of ancient political thought*. Oxford University Press.
7. Cooper, J., et al. (1997). *Complete works by Plato* (p. 1402). Hackett Publishing.
8. Merriam-Webster.com Dictionary, s.v. "aristocracy," https://www.merriam-webster.com/dictionary/aristocracy.
9. Bevir, M. (2010). *The encyclopedia of political theory* (pp. 161–162). Sage.
10. Peerenboom, R. (1993). *Law and morality in ancient China: The silk manuscripts of Huang-Lao* (p. 171). SUNY Press.
11. Keynes, S., & Lapidge, M. (1983). *Alfred the great, Asser's life of king Alfred and other contemporary sources*. Penguin.

12. Keynes, S. (1998). Alfred and the Mercians. In M. A. S. Blackburn & D. N. Dumville (Eds.), *Kings, currency, and alliances: history and coinage of southern England in the ninth century* (pp. 1–46). Boydell & Brewer.
13. Edlin, D. (2006). Judicial review without a constitution. *Polity, 38*, 345–368.
14. Simmons, C. A. (1998). Absent presence: The romantic-era magna Charta and the English constitution. In R. Shippey & T. Utz (Eds.), *Medievalism in the modern world. Essays in Honour of Leslie J. Workman*. Brepols Publishers.
15. United States Senate. (1992). Amendments to the constitution of the United States of America (PDF). In *The constitution of the United States of America: Analysis and interpretation*. US Government Printing Office.
16. Winters, J. A. (2011). *Oligarchy*. Northwestern University, Cambridge University Press.
17. Waldron, J. *The rule of law. The stanford encyclopedia of philosophy* (Summer 2020 Edition), Edward N. Zalta (ed.).
18. Garner, B. A. (2009). *Black's law dictionary* (9th ed.). West. Jurisprudence entry.
19. Shiner, *Philosophy of law*. Cambridge Dictionary of Philosophy.
20. Cicero, De Legibus, bk. 1, sec. 16–17.
21. Barham, F. (1842). Introduction. In *The political works of Marcus Tullius Cicero*. Edmund Spettigue.
22. Cicero, De Legibus, bk. 2, sec. 11.
23. Cicero, M. T., & Keyes, C. W. (1928). *"De re Publica", De Legibus*. Harvard University Press.
24. Aquinas, T. *Treatise on law (summa Theologica, questions 90–97)*, ed. Stanley Parry (Chicago: Henry Regnery Company, 1969), p. 18.
25. Finnis, J. (2020). Natural law theories. In Zalta, E. N. (ed.), *The Stanford encyclopedia of philosophy* (Summer 2020 ed.).
26. Kelsen, H. (2007). *General theory of law and state* (p. 392). The Lawbook Exchange.
27. Murphy, M. (2019). The natural law tradition in ethics. In Zalta, E. N. (ed.), *The stanford encyclopedia of philosophy* (Summer 2019 ed.).
28. Translation: In Latin, Prima Secundæ means "the first of the second" and refers to the first section of the second part of the Summa Theologiæ, which is the "theological summary" as written by Thomas Aquinas.
29. Hart, H. L. A. (1958). Positivism and the separation of law and morals. *Harvard Law Review, 71*, 593, 601–602.
30. Posner, R. A. (2008). *How judges think* (p. 41). Harvard University Press.
31. Moore, M. S. *Critical legal studies*. Cambridge Dictionary of Philosophy
32. Miller, D. (1997). Sir Karl Raimund Popper, C. H., F. B. A. 28 July 1902–17 September 1994.: Elected F.R.S. 1976. *Biographical Memoirs of Fellows of the Royal Society., 43*, 369–409.
33. Stavropoulos, N. (2016). Legal Interpretivism. *PRO, 1*, 23–61.
34. Wexler DB and Winick BJ, 1996, Law in a therapeutic key: Developments in therapeutic jurisprudence.
35. David, B. W. (1999) The development of therapeutic jurisprudence: From theory to practice, 68 Revista Juridica Universidad de Puerto Rico 691–705.
36. Winick, B. J., & Wexler, D. B. (2003). *Judging in a therapeutic key: Therapeutic jurisprudence and the courts*. Carolina Academic Press.
37. Solum, L. B. (2003). *Virtue jurisprudence: A virtue-centered theory of judging*. Georgetown Law Faculty Publications and Other Works. p. 880. https://scholarship.law.georgetown.edu/facpub/880
38. Alexander, L., & Moore, M. Deontological ethics. Edward N. Zalta (ed.) *The stanford encyclopedia of philosophy* (Summer 2021 Edition). URL = https://plato.stanford.edu/archives/sum2021/entries/ethics-deontological/.
39. Kant, I. (1785). *Transition from the common rational knowledge of morals to the philosophical.* § 1 in groundwork of the metaphysic of morals.
40. Bentham, J. (1948). *An introduction to the principles of morals and legislation* (p. 1). Hafner Publishing Company.

41. Marshall, G. (2016). What is binding in a precedent. In *Interpreting precedents* (pp. 503–517). Routledge.
42. Kozel, R. J. (2012). The rule of law and the perils of precedent. *Michigan Law Review First Impressions, 111*, 37.
43. Baude, W. (2020). Precedent and discretion. *The Supreme Court Review, 2019*(1), 313–334.
44. Maltz, E. (1987). The nature of precedent. *NCL Review, 66*, 367.
45. Tetley, W. (1999). Mixed jurisdictions: Common Law v. Civil Law (codified and uncodified). *La L Rev, 60*, 677.
46. Wilson, M., Nagorcka, F., & Stanton, M. (2005). Stranded between partisanship and the truth?: A comparative analysis of legal ethics in the adversarial and inquisitorial systems of justice. *Melbourne University Law Review, 29*(2), 448–477.
47. Merryman, J. H., & Pérez-Perdomo, R. (2020). *The civil law tradition*. Stanford University Press.
48. Huxley, A. (Ed.). (2002). *Religion, law and tradition: Comparative studies in religious law*. Psychology Press.
49. Waldron, J. (2002). One law for all-the logic of cultural accommodation. *Washington and Lee Law Review, 59*, 3.
50. Watson, A. (1984). An approach to customary law. *U Ill L Rev, 561*.
51. Griffiths, J. (1986). What is legal pluralism? *The Journal of Legal Pluralism and Unofficial Law, 18*(24), 1–55.
52. Urscheler, L. H. (2013). Innovation in a hybrid system: The example of Nepal. *European Journal of Comparative Law and Governance, 1*(aop), 1–16.
53. Bary, F. A. (2003). The Legal System of Sri Lanka.
54. Aleck, J. (1991). Beyond recognition: contemporary jurisprudence in the Pacific Islands and the common law tradition. *Queensland U Tech LJ, 7*, 137.
55. Chirayath, L., Sage, C., & Woolcock, M. (2005). Customary law and policy reform: Engaging with the plurality of justice systems.
56. De Mestral, A., & Fox-Decent, E. (2008). Rethinking the relationship between international and domestic law. *McGill LJ, 53*, 573.
57. Philpott, D. (2020). Sovereignty. In Zalta, E. N. (ed.), *The stanford encyclopedia of philosophy* (Fall 2020 ed.), Metaphysics Research Lab, Stanford University.
58. Spruyt, H. (1994). *The sovereign state and its competitors: An analysis of systems change* (pp. 3–7). Princeton University Press.
59. Wallerstein, I. (2004). *World-systems analysis: An introduction* (p. 44). Duke University Press.
60. Biersteker, T., & Weber, C. (1996). *State sovereignty as a social construct. Cambridge studies in international relations. 46*. Cambridge University Press.
61. Stephen, D. (2001). *Krasner, problematic sovereignty: Contested rules and political possibilities*. Columbia University Press.
62. Krasner, S. D. (2001). *Problematic sovereignty: Contested rules and political possibilities* (pp. 6–12). Princeton University Press.
63. Ferreira-Snyman, M. P. (2006). The evolution of state sovereignty: A historical overview. Fundamina: A. *Journal of Legal History, 12*(2), 1–28.
64. Horwitz, M. J. (1981). History of the public/private distinction. *U Pa L Rev, 130*, 1423.
65. Schäfer, M. (2004). *Totalitarianism and political religions*. Psychology Press.
66. Longley, R. *What is totalitarianism? Definition and examples*. ThoughtCo, Feb. 17, 2021. thoughtco.com/totalitarianism-definition-and-examples-5083506.
67. Shorten, R. (2012). *Modernism and totalitarianism: Rethinking the intellectual sources of Nazism and Stalinism, 1945 to the present*. Palgrave.
68. "World Report 2020", Human Rights Watch.
69. An autocracy is a system of government in which one person—an autocrat—holds all political, economic, social, and military power. The autocrat's rule is unlimited and absolute and is not subject to any legal or legislative limitation.

70. Longley, R. *What is totalitarianism? Definition and examples*. ThoughtCo, Feb. 17, 2021, thoughtco.com/totalitarianism-definition-and-examples-5083506.
71. Geddes, B. (2014) Military rule. *Annual Review of Political Science, 17*, 147–162. https://www.annualreviews.org/doi/full/10.1146/annurev-polisci-032211-213418.
72. Longley, R. *What is a military dictatorship? Definition and examples*. ThoughtCo, Feb. 17, 2021. thoughtco.com/military-dictatorship-definition-and-examples-5091896.
73. Eatwell, R. (2011). *Fascism: A history*. Random House.
74. Longley, R. *Totalitarianism, authoritarianism, and fascism*. ThoughtCo, Mar. 29, 2021. thoughtco.com/totalitarianism-authoritarianism-fascism-4147699.
75. Corcos, C. A. (2012). From agnatic succession to absolute primogeniture: The shift to equal rights of succession to thrones and titles in the modern european constitutional monarchy. *Mich St L Rev*, 1587.
76. Harris, N. (2009). *Systems of government monarchy*. Evans Brothers.
77. Locke, J. (1689). *Two treatises of government (everyman)*. Everyman Paperbacks, 1993.
78. Goldie, M., & Wokler, R. (2006). Philosophical kingship and enlightened despotism. In *The Cambridge history of eighteenth-century political thought*. Cambridge University Press.
79. Longley, R. *What is an absolute monarchy? Definition and examples*. ThoughtCo, Feb. 16, 2021. thoughtco.com/absolute-monarchy-definition-and-examples-5111327.
80. Jahn, E. (2015). *International politics: Political issues under debate* (Vol. 1). Springer.
81. Bourguignon, F., & Verdier, T. (2000). Oligarchy, democracy, inequality and growth. *Journal of development Economics, 62*(2), 285–313.
82. Cannadine, D. (1994). *Aspects of aristocracy*. Yale University Press.
83. Longley, R. *What is aristocracy? Definition and examples*. ThoughtCo, Feb. 11, 2021. thoughtco.com/aristocracy-definition-and-examples-5111953.
84. Hirschl, R. (2009). Juristocracy vs. theocracy: Constitutional courts and the containment of sacred law. *Middle East Law and Governance, 1*(2), 129–165.
85. Tay, A. E. S., & Kamenka, E. (1984). Marxism, socialism and the theory of law. *Colum J Transnat'l L, 23*, 217.
86. Pons, S. (2014). *The global revolution: A history of international communism 1917-1991*. OUP Oxford.
87. Přibáň, J. (2005). Political dissent, human rights, and legal transformations: communist and post-communist experiences. *East European Politics and Societies, 19*(4), 553–572.
88. Meyer, T., & Hinchman, L. (2007). The theory of social democracy. *Polity*.
89. Hinnfors, J. (2006). *Reinterpreting social democracy: a history of stability in the British Labour Party and Swedish Social Democratic Party*. Manchester University Press.
90. O'Donnell, G. A. (2001). Democracy, law, and comparative politics. *Studies in Comparative International Development, 36*(1), 7–36.
91. Matsusaka, J. G. (2005). Direct democracy works. *Journal of Economic perspectives, 19*(2), 185–206.
92. Besley, T., & Coate, S. (1997). An economic model of representative democracy. *The Quarterly Journal of Economics, 112*(1), 85–114.
93. Vile, M. J. C. (2012). *Constitutionalism and the separation of powers*. Liberty Fund.
94. Barber, N. W. (2018). *The principles of constitutionalism*. Oxford University Press.

Property and Privacy in Context

2

In this chapter, we will explore the intersecting, albeit unique, concepts of ownership, property, and possession. We will distinguish between public, private, and personal data as seen in the eyes of the law, connecting those concepts to our foundational legal knowledge from the first chapter. At the end of this chapter, we will realize the intersection of (personal) property, (data) privacy, and (cyber) security and how these concepts are dealt with in modern legal systems around the world.

2.1 Perceptions of Property

The concept of private property as a unique entity dates back at least as far as Plato. Prior to the eighteenth century, English speakers generally used the word "property" in reference to estate and land ownership. In England, the concept of "property" came to have a legal definition in the seventeenth century. The issue of determining right to use of enclosed agricultural land in England accompanied efforts in philosophy and political thought and was specifically influenced by the work of the late Thomas Hobbes (1588–1679) [1], James Harrington (1611–1677) [2] and John Locke (1632–1704) [3], among others, in addressing the phenomenon of property and property ownership [4].

In arguing against supporters of absolute monarchy, John Locke conceptualized property as a "natural right" that God had not bestowed exclusively on the monarchy [5]. This has been recognized as the labor theory of property, which states that property is a natural result of labor—in the form of time, effort, and energy—improving upon nature; and thus by virtue of the principle of labor expenditure, the laborer becomes entitled to the benefit of its produce [6].

Influenced by the rise of mercantilism—the economic policy that is designed to maximize the exports and minimize the imports of an economy—Locke argued that private property was antecedent to, and thus independent of, government [7]. Locke

M. Lukings, A. Habibi Lashkari, *Understanding Cybersecurity Law and Digital Privacy*, Future of Business and Finance, https://doi.org/10.1007/978-3-030-88704-9_2

distinguished between "common property, "which referred to common land, and property in consumer and producer goods [8]. The premise for Locke's primary argument for property in land ownership was that it would lead to improved management and cultivation of common land [9].

During the Industrial Revolution in the eighteenth century, the moral philosopher and economist Adam Smith (1723–1790) [10], in contrast to Locke, drew a distinction between the "right to property" as an acquired right, and the natural rights to "liberty and life" [11]. Smith also drew attention to the relationship between employee and employer and identified that property and civil government were symbiotically dependent upon each other, recognizing that "the state of property must always vary with the form of government." Smith further argued that civil government could not exist without property, as the main function of government was to define and safeguard property ownership [12].

In the nineteenth century, the economist and philosopher Karl Marx (1818–1883) [13] provided an influential analysis of the development and history of property formations and their relationship to the technical productive forces of a given period [14]. This conception of private property has been influential in the development of many subsequent economic theories, for communist, socialist, and anarchist political movements, and has led to the widespread association of private property—particularly private property in the means of production—with capitalism [15].

2.2 Ownership, Possession, and Interest

Property law is the application of the law which governs the relationships between individuals and possessions [16]. Indeed, the concepts of property ownership, property possession, property interest all intersect with privacy law in that privacy is the law that allows owners of a thing to exclude others from having use and enjoyment of that thing. We will begin by distinguishing ownership from possession [17].

2.2.1 Distinguishing Ownership from Possession

While many of us informally use the terms "ownership" and "possession" as interchangeable synonyms, each of these terms has a distinct legal definition with different implications in property law. In law, ownership is the absolute right of an owner over the thing that they own, whereas possession involves having physical control of a thing or continuously exercising a claim to the exclusive use of a thing. The primary differences between ownership of property and possession of property are summarized in Table 2.1.

Table 2.1 Ownership versus possession

Ownership	Possession
Ownership is the act, state, or right of owning a thing and the rights and privileges of that ownership.	Possession is the act, state, or right of having the physical custody or use and control of a thing.
Ownership gives the owner the absolute right to possession.	Possession does not give the possessor the right to ownership.
The owner has the absolute rights and legitimate claim to the thing.	The possessor has more claim to the thing than others, except the actual owner of the thing.
Ownership is always with the owner of a property.	Possession can be given to someone else.
No one can interfere with the owner's right to possession, use, and enjoyment of their own property.	Possession of a thing can be overridden by the right to possession of the property by its legal owner.
Ownership can be private (sole), collective, or common.	Possession can be actual, constructive, criminal, etc.
There can be ownership of a thing without possession of that thing.	There can be possession of a thing without ownership of that thing.

2.2.2 Ownership

Ownership, in property law, refers to the set of *legal rights*—held by an individual, group, corporation or government—which grant the legal owner of a property:

1. The *right to possession* of a property.
2. The *privilege of use* of that property.
3. The *right of control* over that property.

These collective rights and privileges—the ability to possess, use, or transfer the property—are jointly referred to as the *legal interest* of the property owner. The legal interest includes the right of the owner to exclude others from the use or enjoyment of the property as well as to assign possession of that property [18].

Property ownership can apply to corporeal and incorporeal things. Corporeal property is that which is tangible, like objects, land, vehicles, books, and other material items. Incorporeal property is that which is intangible, like patents, copyrights, trademarks, intellectual property, and other immaterial things. Ownership can be held by one owner, like a sole proprietorship, or held by multiple owners, such as in a business partnership [19]. The subsets of property ownership can be broken down into specific categories of ownership, which are provided in Table 2.2.

2.2.3 Possession

To possess something is to have continuous *physical control* of the thing *to the exclusion of others*. In law, the continuous exercise of a claim to the *exclusive use* of a property constitutes possession of that property [20]. The exclusive use of a thing

Table 2.2 Categories of ownership

Category	Definition	Example
Corporeal (tangible) ownership	Ownership of something that is tangible in nature.	Land, goods, objects, chattels, household items, physical treasures, etc.
Incorporeal (intangible) ownership	Ownership of something that is intangible in nature.	Copyright, patents, intellectual property, personal reputation, etc.
Sole ownership	Owned by only one legal owner.	Person A owns a car and is the only owner of that car.
Co-ownership	Owned by two or more legal owners.	A business partnership between person A, B, and C.
Legal ownership	The legal claim or title to an asset or property. A person who has legal ownership of a property can transfer the ownership to another party.	Person A is the legal owner of a property, so can transfer ownership of the property, but is not entitled to the use and enjoyment of the property.
Equitable ownership	The benefit of the property that the buyer will use and enjoy. Not true ownership; only the benefit of the property.	Person A is the equitable owner of a property, but not the legal owner, so has the right to use and enjoy the property but is unable to transfer the ownership of the property.
Trust and beneficial ownership	Legal and beneficial ownership belongs to an entity who has the specific property right "use and title" in equity. But the property belongs to some other person.	Property of person A is transferred to trustees to hold the property for the benefit of the beneficiaries. The property is not owned by the trust, but by the trustees themselves.
Vested ownership	By law, the person with vested ownership has the complete and full ownership of the property.	Person A and B share ownership of a property. When one of them dies, the other gets the vested ownership of the property.
Contingent ownership	The owner of the property can claim the property on the fulfillment of some conditions but does not have full claim to the property until any relevant conditions are met.	Person A is the owner of the property but cannot have full claim to the ownership of that property until person A reaches a specified age, or some other condition.
Absolute ownership	Absolute ownership is a free transferable and inheritable property a person can have as his actual right.	Person A owns a property and has a mortgage on that property.
Limited ownership	Limited ownership is the ownership that is not absolute. Such as where the owner enjoys the right to use and enjoy the property for a limited period of time as long as some other person is alive.	Person A has the use of a property, until person B dies. Person A has limited ownership of the property for that time and cannot transfer the ownership of the property.

Table 2.3 Categories of possession

Category	Definition	Example
Corporeal possession	Possession of something that is tangible in nature.	Land, goods, objects, physical treasures, etc.
Incorporeal possession	Possession of something that is intangible in nature.	Copyright, personal reputation, intellectual property, patents, etc.
Direct possession	The person possessing the thing directly possesses the thing. Also called immediate possession.	Person A buys a book and keeps the book. Person A has direct possession of the book.
Indirect possession	Possession of a thing through a mediator, agent, or another party. Also called mediate possession.	Person A buys a book and lends it to person B. person A has indirect possession of the book via person B.
Constructive possession	Having temporary authority over a thing but without having actual legal ownership or possession of that thing. Possession in law, but not in fact.	Person A orders a pizza to be delivered. Person B delivers the pizza to person A. while transporting the pizza, person B has constructive possession.
Adverse possession	The possession of a property for a sufficient time period to become acknowledged as the legal owner of the property.	Person A exercises continuous use of an unused piece of land, a driveway, a field, or other private land. Person A may claim ownership of the property through adverse possession.
De facto possession	De facto is Latin for "in fact." De facto possession is that which exists in reality even if it is not legally recognized.	A common-law spouse can be considered to be a de facto husband or wife if they live as if they were a married couple even though they are not legally married.
De jure possession	De jure is Latin for "in law." De jure possession is legally recognized possession of property regardless of whether that property exists in reality or not. This is also known as juridical possession—Possession in the eyes of the law.	Person A owns a house that was previously rented to, and occupied by, person B. person A does not live in the house or use the house but still intends to have possession of the house rather than abandon it completely.

means that the person who has the possession of the thing also has the right to exclude any or all others from the use or enjoyment of that thing [21]. Table 2.3 details the main categories for classifying possession of property.

2.2.4 Interest

To have a potential claim to the ownership of a property is to have an *ownership interest* in that property. Ownership interest refers to any stake a party owns in any property, company, real estate, product, or any other thing. If there is only one owning party then only this party has ownership interest. If there are several parties involved, then the ownership interest is either divided equally or according to the amount invested by each party. For example, if you have an ownership interest in an investment property with other investors, then you would be entitled to an appropriate share of the profits generated by the property [22].

When the right, interest, or title to the present or future possession of a property can be transferred by its holder to any other party, it is called a *vested interest* with respect to that owner. The right to a vested property cannot be taken away by any third party, regardless of who is in possession of the property at the time that it is vested [23].

While determining proprietary interests can quickly evolve into a complex webs of competing interests, we can break down some of the more basic categories of interest in property in Table 2.4.

Table 2.4 Categories of interest

Category	Definition	Example
Legal interest	The right to possess or use property by the legal owner of that property.	Person A owns a house. Person A is the legal owner of the property and has legal interest in the property.
Beneficial interest	The interest in the economic benefit of a property, which entitles the beneficial owner of a property to some portion of the financial gains received from the property.	Person A is the sole legal owner of a property which is held in trust for the benefit of person B. person B has a beneficial interest in the property.
Vested interest	An interest that does not have to meet any conditions to take effect.	Person A leaves property to person B upon their death. Once person A dies, person B has the vested interest.
Contingent interest	An interest that does not take effect until a condition (contingency) has been met.	Person A has contingent interest in a thing and that interest will not vest until person A has reached a certain age.
Future interest	A legal right to property ownership that does not include the right to present possession or enjoyment of the property.	Person A has possession of a house until their death, at which time the house will go to person B. person B has a future interest in the house.
Interest in reversion	A reversion occurs when the ownership of a granted estate transfers back to the grantor upon the death of the grantee.	Person A owns a house and grants it to person B "for life." upon the death of person B, the property reverts to person A. person A has the reversion.
Interest in remainder	A future interest in a third party that vests upon the natural conclusion of the grant to the original grantee. It is the interest in the property that is "left over", or remains, after the original grantee is finished possessing it.	Person A owns a house and grants the house to person B "for life", and then to person C. person C then has interest in the remainder of the property.
Executory interest	A future interest held by a third-party transferee, which either cuts off another's interest or begins some time after the natural termination of a preceding estate. Executory interest vests upon any condition subsequent except the natural termination of the original grantee's rights.	Person A grants property to person B so long as person B uses the property for a specific purpose. If person B does not use it for the specified purpose then the property vests to person C. here we can say that person C has an executory interest in the property.

2.2.5 Case Hypothetical: Ownership, Possession, and Interest

This hypothetical involves an interaction between a customer, Person A, the store owner, Entrepreneur B, the store employee, Employee C, the author of the book, Author X, and the publishing company, Company Z. We can divide the interaction into five different parts.

Example One
Person A goes to a bookstore, owned by Entrepreneur B, to purchase some new reading material. Walking down the first aisle, Person A finds a hat on the floor, presumably left behind by a previous customer. Person A picks up the hat off the floor, intending to drop it off at the front of the store on the way out.

At this point:

- Person A has *direct corporeal possession* of the hat.
- Person A does not have *legal ownership* of the hat.

Example Two
Continuing to browse the aisles of the store, Person A comes across an intriguing book about which they have read many positive reviews. Person A would like to purchase the book, so Person A picks up the book and carries it, along with the hat, down the rest of the aisle to the next row of shelves.

At this point:

- Person A has *constructive possession* of the book and the hat.
- Person A does not have *legal ownership* of the book or the hat.
- Entrepreneur B, the store owner, has a *beneficial interest* in the book. As the book must be purchased for Entrepreneur B to have a *vested interest* in the proceeds from the book, Entrepreneur B's *interest* in the book is a *contingent interest*, as it requires the book to be purchased, at which point Entrepreneur B has a *vested interest.*

Example Three
Person A brings the hat and the book to the front of the store and hands both items to the employee of the store, Employee C. Person A asks to buy the book and explains to Employee C that the hat was found on the floor.

At this point:

- Person A has *contingent ownership* of the book but that ownership is contingent on Person A paying for the book.
- Person A does not have *direct corporeal possession* of either the book or the hat.
- Person A has a *future interest* in the book.

- Entrepreneur B continues to have a *beneficial interest* in the book.
- Employee C has *direct corporeal possession* of both the book and the hat but does not have *ownership* of, or *interest* in, either the book or the hat.

Example Four

Person A pays for the book and slides it into their bag. Person A then asks Employee C about the store policy on lost and found items. Employee C explains that the *legal owner* of the hat will have 72 hours to claim the lost property, at which time, if the *legal owner* has not come forward to claim their *legal interest* in the hat, then the hat would become available for the individual who found it, that being Person A.

At this point:

- Person A has the *direct corporeal possession* of the book.
- Person A has *contingent interest* in the hat, which will become a *vested interest* if the person who has the *legal ownership* and *legal interest* in the hat does not return to collect the hat within 72 hours.
- Employee C has *direct corporeal possession* of the hat. This is also a *constructive possession* because Employee C only has temporary possession of the hat until it is collected by the owner or is claimed by Person A as the finder.

Example Five

With regard to the book itself, the contents of the book are the *intangible intellectual property* of the author, Author X. In order to publish the book, Author X transfers the *equitable ownership* of the intellectual property and grants the use of that property to the publishing company, Company Z, which prints and circulates the books for a percentage of the income made from the book sales.

With respect to the book:

- Person A has the *sole corporeal possession* and *corporeal ownership* of that specific book.
- Company Z has the *legal interest* in the book and a *beneficial interest* in a portion of the proceeds made from the sales of the book.
- Company Z also has an *equitable ownership* in the book.
- Author X has a *beneficial interest in remainder* of the proceeds made through the sale of the book, after the percentage owed to Company Z has been paid.
- Author X also has *equitable ownership* of the book.

2.3 Property and Privacy

Property, as a concept in law and political economics, is any physical or intangible entity that is owned by a person, jointly by a group of people, or a legal entity such as a corporation or society [24]. Property can also be one or more components or a greater thing, such as the pieces that make up a person's estate. Depending on the nature of the property, the owner of the property has the right to consume, sell, rent, mortgage, transfer, exchange, or destroy their property, as well as the right to exclude others from doing these things. Property can be either moveable or immovable property and tangible or intangible property [25].

Recall that property ownership is a relationship between two or more individuals and a thing, where at least one of the individuals holds a bundle of legal rights over the thing. In that case, the individual holding the rights would be the owner of the property. There are three broad forms of property ownership: private property; public property; and collective, or cooperative, property [26]. All of these topics will be discussed in this section.

2.3.1 Classifications of Property

Real property or *immovable property* refers to the physical property consisting of land and all structures—also called fixtures or improvements—integrated with or affixed to that land, including crops, buildings, machinery, wells, dams, ponds, natural resources, mines, canals, and roads, among other things [27]. The term "real property" arises from the now-discontinued "form of action" system for handling legal claims, which distinguished between real property disputes and personal property disputes [28].

Personal property or *movable property* was, and continues to be, all property that is not real property. In common law legal systems, personal property is also called chattels or personality [29]. In civil law systems, personal property is often called movable property or movables—that is, any property that can be moved from one location to another [30]. Personal property can be contrasted with real property or immovable property, that being, land and the fixtures attached to the land [31]. Personal property can be subdivided into two categories: tangible personal property and intangible personal property [32].

Tangible personal property includes physical things that can be moved, touched, or felt and includes physical objects like household items, furniture, books, and other moveable physical things [33]. Tangible property is often what people think of when we discuss personal possessions [34].

In contrast to tangible property, *intangible personal property* is a moveable property that lacks a physical substance—that is, it cannot be physically picked up and moved, touched, or felt—but which still represents something of value [35]. This can include patents, copyrighted material, franchises, registered trademarks, trade names, software, research data, and other non-physical assets [36]. In the illustration in Fig. 2.1, we can see how the different types of property are classified.

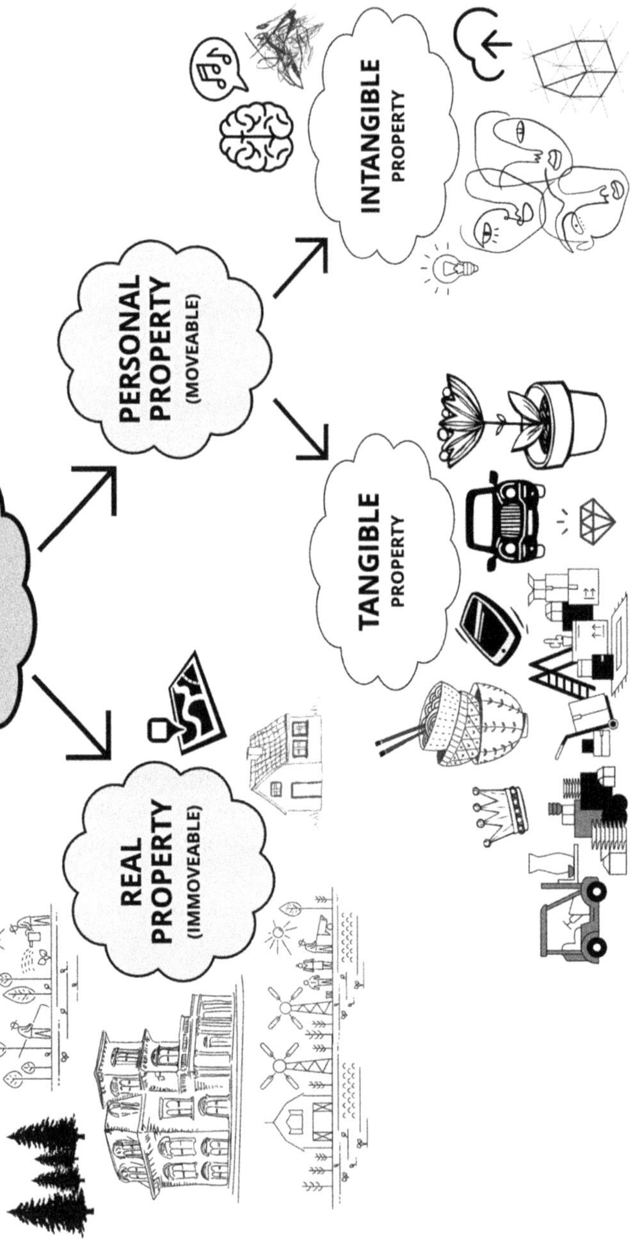

Fig. 2.1 Classifications of property

2.3.2 Private Property Versus Public Property

Private property is a legal designation for property which is owned by non-governmental legal entities. Private property is distinguished from public property, which is owned by a state entity, and from collective or cooperative property, which is owned by a group of non-governmental entities. The distinction between private and personal property varies depending on individual political philosophy, as a concept in law, private property is defined and enforced by the political system of the particular country.

Public property is common property that is dedicated to public use. In the modern representative democracy, public property is said to be either collectively owned by the people of a state, or held in trust by the government for the common benefit of the people. In many of the Commonwealth countries, public property is considered to be owned by the Crown [37].

2.3.3 Privacy

Privacy, in a very broad sense, is the right to be let alone, or freedom from interference or intrusion. We can extend privacy to property in that the owner of property has the right to exclude others from the use, enjoyment, profit, etc. of their personal property. Information privacy is the right to have some control over how your personal information is collected and used [38].

2.3.4 Differentiating Personal from Private

Personal information is information that cannot be used to identify you, such as your age, gender, sexuality, country of residence, how many siblings you have, favorite pizza topping, etc. Private information, on the other hand, is information that can be used to identify you as a specific individual, such as your name, street address, date of birth, names of family members, email, phone number, driver's license number, health card information, etc.

The fundamental difference between these two categories of information is that, while personal information does tell others about you, it cannot be used for identity theft or fraud. Private information is much more specific to you as an individual and can be used for both identity theft and identity fraud [39].

For example, in Canada, the definition of personal information includes data about an "identifiable individual". That is, information that on its own or combined with other pieces of data can identify you as a specific individual [40]. The exact definition for personal information differs slightly between different statutory laws. For example, the *Privacy Act* and the *Personal Information Protection and Electronic Documents Act* are both Canadian federal legislation (so statutory law) but the definition of personal information differs slightly between these two statutory laws.

Generally, personal information about an individual includes:

- Race, national or ethnic origin.
- Religion.
- Age and marital status.
- Medical, education, or employment history.
- Financial information.
- DNA.
- Identifying numbers such as a social insurance number of driver's license number.
- Views or opinions about an individual as an employee.

In general, the individual data that is not considered to be personal information tends to include:

- Information that is not about an individual, because the connection with a person is too weak or far-removed.
- Information about an organization or a business.
- Information that has been rendered anonymous, provided that it is not possible to link that data back to an identifiable person.
- Certain information about public servants such as their name, position, and title.
- The business contact information for a person that is collected, used or disclosed by an organization for the sole purpose of communicating with that person in relation to their employment, business, or profession.
- Governmental information [41].

In Table 2.5, we summarize the main features of personal information, as it is defined within the scope of the *General Data Protection Regulation* (GDPR) of the European Union, as well as other consumer privacy regulations.

Table 2.5 Determining what is personal

Any information that is...	(a) Objective. (b) Subjective, OR. (c) Sensitive.
Relating to...	(a) An individual. (b) A particular person, OR. (c) Impacting a certain person.
Who can be identified or identifiable...	(a) Directly OR. (b) Indirectly.
As a natural person who is...	(a) A human. (b) Living, AND. (c) Not deceased.
And includes data that...	(a) Is provided by the electronic devices we use, AND. (b) Can be used to identify a specific person when combined with unique identifiers and other information.

2.3.5 Legislative Example: Canadian Consumer Privacy Protection

Canada's *Personal Information Protection and Electronic Documents Act*—commonly known as the PIPEDA—was implemented as a means to help grow consumer trust in electronic commerce and the digital economy. It was created as a response to international consensus regarding the need to promote fairness in the handling of personal information in the private sector more generally, rather than just in certain sectors, such as those already covered in the existing federal *Privacy Act* for governmental bodies [42].

The PIPEDA applies specifically to: private-sector organizations; which are operating either fully or partially in Canada; and, that collect, use, or disclose personal information in the course of commercial activities. It also applies to all businesses that operate in Canada and handle personal information that crosses provincial or national borders, regardless of the province or territory in which they are based, including provinces with substantially similar legislation, and to federally regulated organizations that conduct business in Canada, such as airports, aircrafts and airlines, banks, transportation companies, telecommunications, offshore drilling, radio, and televisions, etc.

Private-sector organizations that fit into this category are bound by the provisions of the *Personal Information Protection and Electronic Documents Act* to apply the given privacy principles to protect the consumer information exchanged during the commercial activity. These provisions aim to protect the privacy of those individuals, specific subsets/targeted groups of individuals, or organizations from whom the personal information has been gathered [43].

Figure 2.2 illustrates the data collection and exchange relationships that can often be found in private sector corporations within the course of normal commercial activities. It is these trusted relationships between commercial organizations and consumers which the provisions in the *Personal Information Protection and Electronic Documents Act* aim to protect and strengthen.

For the purposes of the provisions given in the PIPEDA, the law defines a "*commercial activity*" as any particular transaction, act, or conduct, or any *regular course of conduct* that is of a *commercial nature*, including the selling, bartering, or leasing of donor, membership or other fundraising lists [44].

The definition for "*personal information*" under the PIPEDA includes any factual or subjective information, whether recorded or not, about an *identifiable individual* and gathered during the course of *commercial activity*. The provisions do not apply to the contact information for a business, including an employee's name, title, business address, and the telephone number or email addresses that are used for the purpose of communicating with that person solely in relation to their employment or business [42].

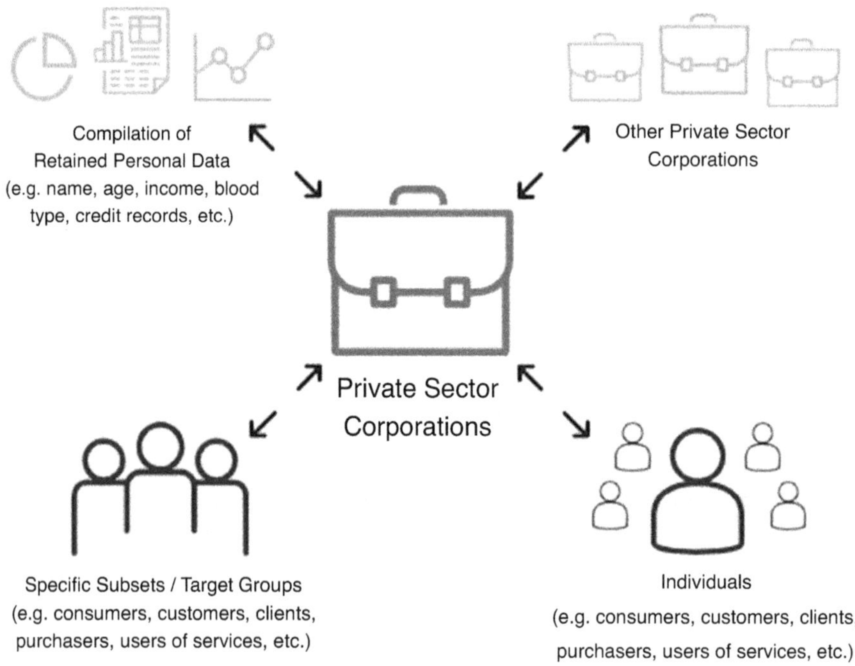

Fig. 2.2 Consumer privacy in private sector corporations

2.3.6 Case Hypothetical: Consumer Privacy Protection

As an example of how personal and private data regulations may apply in the real world, we can use the jurisdiction of a specific common law country to show how the relevant consumer privacy protection laws would apply. It is important to keep in mind that specific consumer privacy protection laws will differ in their nuances between nations or jurisdictions. As there is not an accepted uniform international standard, we will use Canada as the jurisdiction for this particular hypothetical.

Hypothetical Tech Company ("HTC") is a private sector corporation engaged in commercial activity by providing an online-based web conferencing service to customers within Canada. The service offered by HTC enables online communication, allowing its users to see and hear each other, share documents, conduct meetings, do online presentations, collaborate on material in real-time, and generally exchange data between users from the comfort of their own homes. HTC does not charge for access to the basic features of their service but does have a user fee to access some extra features. HTC makes additional income through revenue gained from offering advertising space on certain publicly accessible areas of their user interface.

As a commercial organization operating within the Canadian jurisdiction, HTC must operate according to the provisions specified in the *Personal Information Protection and Electronic Documents Act*—commonly shortened to PIPEDA—

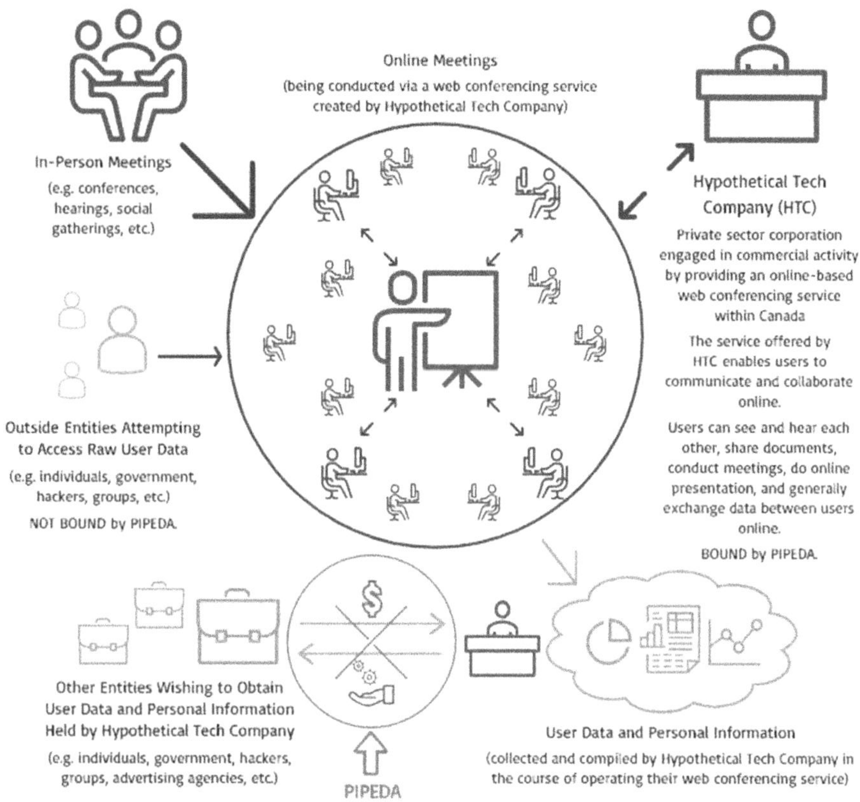

Fig. 2.3 Consumer privacy protection hypothetical

regarding their collection, use, and disclosure of user data and personal information obtained during the course of operating their web conferencing service. This example is illustrated in Fig. 2.3.

The parties who are NOT bound by the PIPEDA in this scenario are: (1) the individual users of the web conferencing service; (2) outside entities attempting to access the information without consent; and (3) government institutions.

2.4 The Intersection of Property, Privacy, and Cybersecurity Law

We are living in an era that has been marked by rapid technological development, advancing data-use research, and an increasingly hyper-connective global infrastructure. Cyberspace is playing an undeniably fundamental role in our day-to-day lives and in business operations around the world, and yet human error still accounts for 95% of all data breaches. This makes it crucial for corporations, organizations, and governments to address and mitigate any potential threats to cybersecurity before such a breach occurs. As the online world around us changes and grows, it is necessary for our laws to evolve to remain effective in this rapidly developing landscape [45].

Cybersecurity refers to the body of technologies, processes, and practices designed to protect and defending computers, servers, mobile devices, electronic systems, networks, and data from malicious attacks, information disclosure, theft of—or damage to—their hardware, software, or electronic data, as well as from the disruption or misdirection of the services they provide.

Cybersecurity laws—including data protection and privacy legislation—are laws that aim to safeguard information technology and computer systems from privacy breaches and unauthorized activity as well as to compel corporations and organizations to protect their online infrastructure from cyberattacks. Potential cyberattacks include activities like security breaches by malware, attacks, unauthorized access to confidential or private information, access to intellectual property, protected information, personal information, metadata, etc. Unfortunately, there will always be antagonistic parties acting in hostile ways. The current threat to data stored in, or transmitted by, electronic mobile devices is at an all-time high which means that the list of people, not just hackers and crackers, that could potentially threaten the data kept by all organizations is long and diverse [46].

2.4.1 Criminal Law/Statutory Law

Statutory law is a formally written law which is deliberately created and passed by a governing legislative body. That could be a federal, state, or provincially based legislature or other governing body. These statutes are often codified, meaning that they are numbered, collected, and indexed in one place. Statutory law includes Acts, Statutes, Legislation, Code, Charters, Constitutions, etc. Different jurisdictions and levels of government can have their own indexed collections of statutes and codes which apply to matters within the scope of that jurisdiction. While statutes make up the written body of law, statutory law refers to the resulting body of law itself, which is made up of the individual statutes [47].

As in our topic of cybersecurity, data protection, and privacy legislation, there are criminal offences encoded in the legal structures of many countries, some of which may also fall into the category of tort law in a common law system. The same issue could be dealt with in a common law system through a civil lawsuit. The reasons for charging someone under criminal law may differ from the reasons for suing someone in tort under the common law. It is worth noting that to sue someone can result in a direct benefit to the complainant, whereas a criminal charge does not. As well, it becomes more difficult to benefit from suing someone in tort after they have already been criminally convicted of the same offence.

2.4.2 Tort Law/Common Law

Salmond defined tort law in his work entitled *The Law of Torts*. According to Salmond, a "tort is a civil wrong for which the remedy is a common law action for unliquidated damages, and which is not exclusively the breach of a contract or the breach of a trust, or other merely equitable obligation [48]." The field of tort law provides compensation for people who have been injured or whose property has been damaged by the wrongdoing of others. A tort consists of a wrongful act or injury that leads to physical, emotional, or financial damage to a person in which another person could be held legally responsible. Common law torts are primarily judge-made law, with roots in the English tort system. All torts require proof of fault in order to determine legal responsibility, however, fault is measured differently for the different types of tort [49].

There are two main branches of torts: intentional torts and unintentional torts. An intentional tort is when a person intends to achieve a particular outcome that results in injury to people or damage to property, whereas an unintentional tort such as negligence, occurs when there has been a lack of duty of care or foreseeability that results in injury to people or damage to property. Some intentional torts include actions like assault, battery, false arrest, false imprisonment, nuisance, trespass, and intentional infliction of mental distress. For negligence to be found, there must be an established duty of care, a violation of the standard of care, actual causation of the damage, reasonable foreseeability of the harm, and harm must have actually occurred [50].

The reasons for charging someone under the criminal law may differ from the reasons for suing someone in tort under the common law through the civil courts. It is worth noting that to sue someone can result in a direct benefit to the complainant, whereas a criminal charge does not directly benefit the complainant. As well, it becomes more difficult to benefit from suing someone in tort after they have already been criminally convicted of the same offence.

2.4.3 Case Hypothetical: Intersection of Criminal and Tort Law

Person A and Person B both live in the same country and within the same legal jurisdiction. Person A is a malicious party who would like to steal the identity of Person B in order to use that individual's excellent credit history and financial background to make large purchases.

In order to do this, Person A acquires and utilizes illegal hacking tools to gain access to the personal computer of Person B, on which much of their personal information is stored, including the first and last name, mailing address, social insurance number, driver's license, birth date, etc. of Person B. Person A then uses this information to apply for large sums of credit under the name of Person B, maxing out the credit limits almost immediately after they are approved.

Person B discovers this issue when the bank contacts them with regard to an unusual series of large purchases which have resulted in the bank freezing Person

B's main bank account. Person B employs a private investigator to look into the identity theft and quickly learns that the theft was done by Person A.

Under the federal body of *statutory law* for the jurisdiction in which Person A and Person B both reside, identify theft, fraud, and hacking are all *criminal law* offences. As well, the body of *tort law* for that jurisdiction provides for a tort of "intrusion upon seclusion," which provides compensatory damages to individuals who have had their privacy intentionally breached by another person. The tort of intrusion upon seclusion has been previously determined by a judge, also within that jurisdiction, to apply to acts of intrusion on a personal computer with the intention of breaching the privacy of another person.

In this matter, Person B has a number of options available.

Option One—Criminal:

- Person B can report the hacking, privacy breach, identity theft, and fraud to the law enforcement within that jurisdiction to try to criminally charge Person A under the statutory laws—specifically the body of statutory criminal laws.
- Person A would be the Defendant / Accused in the criminal case.
- Person B would be a Witness / Victim in the criminal case.
- The criminal charge would be brought against Person A by the government, the "Crown," or the state on behalf of the public.
- Person A could be fined, penalized, or imprisoned.
- Person B would not personally benefit from the criminal charge against Person A other than in their knowledge that justice is being served against Person A.
- The purpose served by the criminal court in this case would be to deter and denounce the actions of Person A.

Option Two—Civil:

- Person B can use the common law precedent in tort law to bring a civil lawsuit against Person A for their breach of privacy as "intrusion upon seclusion" in hacking into Person B's personal computer.
- Person A would be the Respondent in the civil lawsuit.
- Person B would be the Applicant in the civil lawsuit.
- The civil lawsuit would be brought forward against Person A by Person B as the Applicant on their own behalf.
- Person B would receive the remedy or relief prescribed by the court, likely in the form of monetary damages, that being, financial compensation for the damage caused by Person A to Person B.
- The purpose served by the civil court in this case would be to provide damages, financial relief, or another remedy to Person B as compensation for damage caused or inflicted by Person A.

If Person B decides to use the Criminal Law option, Person B would be relying on the statutory laws of their jurisdiction, specifically the body of statutory criminal laws. Person A could be criminally charged in relation to the possession of hacking

Table 2.6 Criminal versus Civil Law

Features	Option One: Criminal	Option Two: Civil
Category of law	Public law / criminal law	Private law / civil law
Jurisdiction	Federal	Provincial
Type of court	Criminal / Federal Court of law	Civil / provincial court
Source(s) of law	Statutory law / criminal provisions	Common law / legal precedents
Role of person A	Defendant / accused	Respondent
Role of person B	Witness / victim	Applicant / appellant
Outcomes for person A	Criminal charge / record Fines / penalties Imprisonment	Payment of damages (to person B) Other civil remedies or relief
Outcomes for person B	Knowledge of justice being served	Receipt of damages (from person A) Other civil remedies or relief

tools, hacking itself, identity theft, and identity fraud. The outcome of this option could either result in fines and penalties, jail time, or a combination of both. The benefit to Person B would be to see justice served against Person A for their criminal activities. We can summarize these outcomes to highlight the differences between a criminal law case and a civil tort law case for Persons A and B in Table 2.6.

2.5 Summary

In this chapter, we have discussed the historical perspectives of property, possession, and ownership. We have distinguished between property possession, property ownership, and property interest in the relationship between an individual entity and a thing. We have classified the different subtypes of property, differentiating based on private, public, and personal.

Finally, we have outlined the intersection of property law with cybersecurity law, equating private property with private data and personal privacy with data privacy. This brings us to the introduction of the legal landscape as it relates to current cybersecurity capabilities and concerns, as well as issues of data privacy, data governance, and data sovereignty. We connected the cybersecurity topic to the three branches of law with which there is the greatest intersection: statutory law, criminal law, and tort law.

In the next chapter, we will describe the different types of cybercriminal activities: those which are cyber-enabled, cyber-dependent, or computer/cyber-supported. We will contextualize the nature of cybercrime, the growing prevalence of online reliance, and the categorization of cybercrime in the law. The answers to the following questions are provided within this chapter:

1. How does legal Ownership differ from legal Possession?
2. Why is Interest in Property important?

3. What is the difference between Personal Information and Private Information?
4. What are three things that could fall under the classification of Intangible Personal Property?
5. What is Real Property?

References

1. Williams, G. *Thomas Hobbes: Moral and political philosophy*. Internet Encyclopedia of Philosophy.
2. Cotton, J. (1991). *James Harrington's political thought and its context*. Garland Publisher.
3. Hirschmann, N. J. (2009). *Gender, class, and freedom in modern political theory* (p. 79). Princeton.
4. Sreenivasan, G. (1995). *The limits of Lockean rights in property*. Oxford University Press.
5. Tuckness, A. Locke's political philosophy. In E. N. Zalta (Ed.) *The stanford encyclopedia of philosophy (winter 2020 edition)*. Available online at: https://plato.stanford.edu/archives/win2020/entries/locke-political.
6. Locke, J. (1963). *Works, 10 volumes, London, 1823; reprinted*. Scientia Verlag.
7. Tully, J. (1980). *A discourse on property: John Locke and his adversaries*. Cambridge University Press.
8. Udi, J. (2015). Locke and the fundamental right to preservation: On the convergence of charity and property rights. *The Review of Politics, 77*(2), 191–215.
9. Proast, J. (1999a). In M. Goldie (Ed.), *The argument of the letter concerning toleration briefly considered and answered, in the reception of Locke's politics* (Vol. 5). Pickering & Chatto.
10. Neil MacCormick, Adam Smith on Law, 15 Val. U. L. Rev. 243 (1981). Available at: https://scholar.valpo.edu/vulr/vol15/iss2/2.
11. Smith, A. (2002). *The wealth of nations*. Oxford, England: Bibliomania.com ltd. [web.] retrieved from the Library of Congress, https://lccn.loc.gov/2002564559.
12. Hill, L. (2007). Adam Smith, Adam Ferguson and Karl Marx on the division of labour. *Journal of Classical Sociology, 7*(3), 339–366.
13. Hobsbawm, E. (2004). *Marx, Karl Heinrich*. Oxford Dictionary of National Biography.
14. Oakley, A. (1984). *Marx's Critique of political economy: 1844 to 1860 archived 10 September 2015 at the Wayback machine* (p. 51). Routledge.
15. Moradi, M. (2020). *Analysis of private property, Karl Marx*. https://doi.org/10.13140/RG.2.2.15530.77765.
16. Alexander, G., & Donahue, Jr. Charles (2018, January 25). *Property law. Encyclopedia Britannica*. https://www.britannica.com/topic/property-law
17. Austin, L. M. "Property and the rule of law" (2014) 20:2 Legal Theory 79.
18. Clarke, A., & Kohler, P. (2005). *Property law: commentary and materials*. Cambridge University Press.
19. Rose, C. M. (1985). Possession as the origin of property. *The University of Chicago Law Review, 52*(1), 73–88.
20. Rudmin, F. W., & Berry, J. W. (1987). Semantics of ownership: A free-recall study of property. *The Psychological Record, 37*(2), 257–268.
21. Callies, D. L., & Breemer, J. D. (2000). The right to exclude others from private property: A fundamental constitutional right. *Wash UJL & Pol'y, 3*, 39.
22. Katz, L. (2008). Exclusion and exclusivity in property law. *University of Toronto Law Journal, 58*(3), 275–315.
23. Newman, C. M. (2016). Vested use-privileges in property and copyright. *Harv JL & Tech, 30*, 75.
24. Baron, J. B. (2013). Rescuing the bundle-of-rights metaphor in property law. *University of Cincinnati Law Review, 82*, 57.

25. von Benda-Beckmann, F., von Benda-Beckmann, K., & Wiber, M. G. (2006). The properties of property. *Changing Properties of Property, 40*, 1–39.
26. Alexander, G. S. (2011). Governance property. *University of Pennsylvania Law Review, 160*, 1853.
27. Niles, R. D. (1933). The rationale of the law of fixtures: English cases. *NYULQ Review, 11*, 560.
28. Hetland, J. R. (1965). Real property and real property security: The Well-being of the law. *California Law Review, 53*, 151.
29. O'Keefe, K. M. (1983). The classification issue and the law of fixtures: A chattel by any other name.... *J. St. Tax'n, 2*, 37.
30. Rahmatian, A. (2008). A comparison of German moveable property law and English personal property law. *Journal of Comparative Law, 3*, 197.
31. Niles, R. D. (1934). The intention test in the law of fixtures. *NYULQ Review, 12*, 66.
32. Moore, A. D. (1998). Intangible property: Privacy, power, and information control. *American Philosophical Quarterly, 35*(4), 365–378.
33. Carnahan, W. (1934). Tangible property and the conflict of Laws. *University of Dayton Law Review, 2*, 345.
34. Arezzo, E. (2007). Struggling around the natural divide: The protection of tangible and intangible indigenous property. *Cardozo Arts & Entertainment Law, 25*, 367.
35. Child, J. W. (1990). The moral foundations of intangible property. *The Monist, 73*(4), 578–600.
36. Hardy, I. T. (2000). Not so different: Tangible, intangible, digital, and analog works and their comparison for copyright purposes. *University of Dayton Law Review, 26*, 211.
37. Horwitz, M. J. (1981). History of the public/private distinction. *U Pa L Rev, 130*, 1423.
38. DeCew, J. W. (1986). The scope of privacy in law and ethics. *Law and Philosophy, 5*(2), 145–173.
39. Lemley, M. A. (1999). Private property. *Stanford Law Review, 52*, 1545.
40. Al-Fedaghi, S. (2018). Privacy things: Systematic approach to privacy and personal identifiable information. *International Journal of Computer Science and Information Security (IJCSIS), 16* (2).
41. Gratton, E. (2013). If personal information is privacy's gatekeeper, then risk of harm is the key: A proposed method for determining what counts as personal information. *Alb LJ Sci & Tech, 24*, 105.
42. Personal Information Protection and Electronic Documents Act, SC 2000, c 5, https://canlii.ca/t/541b8
43. Austin, L. M. (2006). Reviewing pipeda: Control, privacy and the limits of fair information practices. *Can Bus LJ, 44*, 21.
44. Personal Information Protection and Electronic Documents Act (SC 2000, c 5).
45. Shackelford, S. J. (2016). Protecting intellectual property and privacy in the digital age: the use of national cybersecurity strategies to mitigate cyber risk. *Chap. L. Rev., 19*, 445.
46. Kosseff, J. (2017). Defining cybersecurity law. *Iowa L Rev, 103*, 985.
47. Kosseff, J. (2016). Positive cybersecurity law: Creating a consistent and incentive-based system. *Chap L Rev, 19*, 401.
48. Salmond, J. W. (1907). *The law of torts*. Stevens and Haynes.
49. Lunney, M., & Oliphant, K. (2008). *Tort law: text and materials*. Oxford University Press.
50. Malone, W. S. (1970). Ruminations on the Role of Fault in the History of the Common Law of Torts. *La. L. Rev., 31*, 1.

Cybersecurity and Cybercrimes 3

Cybersecurity law is not simply the application of legal systems to the protection of private data; it also includes using our legal systems to address criminal activity that is conducted using networked technologies—otherwise known as cybercrime. This chapter will outline the types of cybersecurity laws needed to address issues such as interpersonal privacy, criminal copyright infringement, data breaches, network attacks, and other computer-related activities of a criminally malicious nature.

In this chapter, we will differentiate cybercriminal activities based on whether they are: cyber-enabled, cyber-dependent, or computer/cyber-supported. In each of the four categories, we will break down the common specific criminal offences and the treatment of these offences under global legal systems. We will also discuss the issue of national security offences committed using technologies—otherwise known as cyberterrorism—and the jurisdictional complexities of navigating these issues within our respective systems. In each of the four categories, we will break down the common specific criminal offences and the treatment of these offences under global legal systems.

3.1 Categorizing Cybercrimes

There are four categories for activities that can fall under the label of "cybercrime": (1) cyber-enabled crimes; (2) cyber-dependent crimes; (3) computer/cyber-supported crimes; and (4) national security offences, also known as "cyberterrorism." Within each of these larger categories, we can further break down the specific subtypes of criminal activities which fall under each one [1].

M. Lukings, A. Habibi Lashkari, *Understanding Cybersecurity Law and Digital Privacy*, Future of Business and Finance, https://doi.org/10.1007/978-3-030-88704-9_3

3.1.1 Cyber-Enabled Offences (On/Offline)

Cyber-enabled crimes are crimes that can be committed with or without the use of technology, but which are increased in their scale or reach by the use of computers, computer networks, and other technology. Cyber-enabled crimes can include activities like cyber-stalking, fraud, extortion, child pornography, various trafficking offences, and cybercriminal-for-hire services. These types of crimes have also been identified as "technology-as-instrument" cybercrime offences [1].

Some of the traditional in-person crimes which have expanded into cyber-enabled crimes include: electronic phishing, theft, and fraud; illegal distribution of intimate images and sexual cybercrimes; cyberbullying and online harassment; child pornography and grooming for the purpose of sexual exploitation; and some types of organized crime, such as trafficking in persons and illegal online market-based activities in which transactions are completed through dark networks [2].

3.1.1.1 Electronic Theft, Fraud, and Phishing

Identity theft and *identity fraud* tend to go hand-in-hand. Identity theft is provided as "obtaining or possessing another person's identity information with the intent to use it to commit an indictable offence." Identity fraud involves fraudulently impersonating someone "with the intent of gaining an advantage, obtaining property, causing disadvantage to another, or to avoid arrest or prosecution". This can include pretending to be another person or using that other person's identity, personal information, signature, legal name, user name, password, etc. to intentionally accomplish a goal that is an indictable offence, like fraud. Phishing is sometimes used as a method of gaining the necessary personal identification information from a target [3].

Phishing is a type of cybercriminal activity in which a target (or targets) of an identity theft or fraud are contacted by email, telephone, or text message by someone posing as a legitimate institution to lure those individuals into providing private data such as personally identifiable information, banking, and credit card details, and passwords. This is often, but not always, related to identity theft and/or fraud [4].

Criminal copyright infringement is a specific type of electronic theft that involves circumventing a technological protection measure [5].

3.1.1.2 Intimate Images and Sexual Cybercrimes

In the modern age of high-speed information sharing, privacy and the ability to control the information which is publicly shared about yourself has become increasingly imperative. Sexual cybercrimes include offences like the distribution of intimate images and other visual recordings; non-consensual pornography or revenge porn; cyberbullying and online harassment creation, distribution, or other interaction with child pornography; Engaging in these types of illegal activities can result in very serious legal consequences. Not only can an offence of this nature result in jail time and a criminal record, but the malicious actor may also be hit with a costly civil lawsuit on top of the criminal charges.

An *intimate image* is "a visual recording of a person made by any means, such as a photograph, film or video recording: (a) in which the person is nude, is exposing his or her genital organs or anal region or her breasts or is engaged in explicit sexual activity; (b) in respect of which, at the time of the recording, there were circumstances that gave rise to a reasonable expectation of privacy; and (c) in respect of which the person depicted retains a reasonable expectation of privacy at the time the offence is committed [6]."

With relation to intimate images, the intersection with *private acts* occurs where images or other visual recordings taken in which the person has a "reasonable expectation of privacy" [7]. These are not limited to images depicting sexual activity or nudity.

Illegal distribution of intimate images occurs when a person distributes an intimate image, in that, if he or she knowingly publishes, transmits, sells, advertises or otherwise distributes or makes the image available to a person other than the person depicted in the image. This is sometimes also called the "non-consensual distribution of intimate images" or, more simply, "revenge porn" [8].

Non-consensual pornography, or *revenge porn*, occurs when intimate images, which are taken consensually, are then uploaded to the internet or otherwise distributed for nefarious or malicious purposes or to otherwise cause harm to the individual depicted in the visual recordings [9]. While also involving the production and publication of intimate images, child pornography constitutes a criminal offence on its own, distinct from the illegal distribution of intimate images.

Voyeurism is the practice of gaining sexual pleasure from watching others when they are naked or engaged in sexual, intimate, or otherwise private activity. Surveillance, as a form of voyeurism, can be defined as besetting or watching the dwelling-house, or place where the other person, or anyone known to them, resides, works, carries on business or happens to be. This would suggest that the offender must have the victim under physical surveillance and leaves a potential gap where the offender may be monitoring the victim remotely or using other forms of surveillance like monitoring emails, text messages, and other communications or using geolocation services to track or record the movements of a person [2].

To accommodate for this gap, we can define *digital surveillance* as a subset of surveillance which is based on the idea that a person should have some control over the personal information which is shared and made publicly available about them and the right to restrict access to one's personal information, including that which is collected and/or stored digitally [10].

The prevalence of digital communication has created nearly limitless possibilities for the rapid, large-scale sharing of private communications, intimate images, and personal information. Not only can the intrusion upon your personal life feel harmful and disruptive to your personal and professional reputation, but the use of visual recordings of intimate images has also been weaponized as a tool for criminal acts of extortion and cyberbullying, and has quickly become a contributing factor to an increase of suicides and suicide attempts amongst vulnerable populations [11].

3.1.1.3 Cyberbullying and Online Harassment

Cyberbullying is the use of technology (like the internet, social media, text messaging, etc.) to harass, threaten, intimidate, embarrass or otherwise harmfully target another person, specific group, or other identifiable entity. Through the use of online tools and social media applications, access to the internet can be used to turn a small threat within an interpersonal dispute into a viral media publication; downloaded, viewed, and retransmitted to millions of people around the world [12].

3.1.1.4 Child Sexual Exploitation, Grooming, and Abuse Material

The rapid expansion of the Internet and the increase in our normalization of advanced digital technology lies parallel to the explosion of the child pornography market. Child sexual abuse material, commonly known as child pornography, is readily available through networked technology, including social networking websites, file-sharing sites, photo-sharing sites, gaming devices, and mobile apps. In many countries, federal law prohibits the production, distribution, importation, reception, or possession of any image of child sexual abuse unfortunately, no area of the world is immune from individuals who seek to sexually exploit children online [13]. Online child sexual exploitation can include:

1. *Child sexual abuse material.*
   Actual, but also fictitious, written depictions of child sexual abuse, audio, video, and images, also known as child pornography
2. *Self-generated materials and sexting.*
   Youth-generated explicit images/videos on the Internet, which are often further distributed without consent
3. *Sextortion (or sexual extortion).*
   Use of coercion and threats to extort child sexual exploitation images/videos from youth (either by other youth or adult offenders)
4. *Grooming and luring.*
   Use of applications and platforms to connect with children and youth for the purpose of sexually exploiting them
5. *Live child sexual abuse streaming.*
   Viewing of child sexual abuse in real-time often involves the offender directing the abuse
6. *Made-to-order content.*
   Ordering videos/images to suit offenders' preferences.

Offenders can also connect on Internet forums and networks to share their interests, desires, and experiences abusing children, in addition to selling, sharing, and trading images. These online communities have promoted communication and collaboration between child pornography offenders, thereby fostering a larger relationship premised on a shared sexual interest in children. This has the effect of eroding the shame that typically would accompany this behavior, as well as desensitizing those involved to the physical and psychological damage caused to the child victims [14].

In many child pornography cases, the abuse is not a singular event, but rather a series of events constituting ongoing victimization. This can progress over months or years, as it is common for producers of child pornography to groom their victims—essentially cultivate a relationship with the child—and gradually sexualize the contact over time. This grooming process fosters a false sense of trust and authority over a child which serves to desensitize or break down their resistance to sexual abuse [15].

Victims of distributed child sexual abuse material are victimized not just from the sexual abuse inflicted upon them to produce child pornography, but also experience revictimization in that their images can be continuously traded and viewed by others worldwide. Once an image is on the Internet, it is virtually irretrievable; continuing to circulate indefinitely. The knowledge of the existence of a permanent record of personal sexual abuse and exploitation can have a huge impact on the lives of child victims. Many victims of child pornography go on to experience feelings of helplessness, fear, humiliation, lack of control, and other symptoms which are indicative of post-traumatic stress [16].

The continuous production and distribution of child pornography has created a demand for new and more shocking images, perpetuating the continued victimization and abuse of children, as well as the demand for new child victims [17]. According to research done by the United States Department of Justice, unfortunately, emerging trends seem to reveal an overall increase in the number of images depicting sadistic and violent child sexual abuse, and an increase in the number of images depicting very young children, including toddlers and infants [18].

3.1.1.5 Example in Law: US Federal Laws on Child Pornography

> Unfortunately, we've also seen a historic rise in the distribution of child pornography, in the number of images being shared online, and in the level of violence associated with child exploitation and sexual abuse crimes. Tragically, the only place we've seen a decrease is in the age of victims. This is—quite simply—unacceptable [19].

Images of child pornography are not protected under First Amendment rights and are illegal contraband under federal law in the USA. Federal law prohibits the production, distribution, reception, and possession of an image of child pornography using or affecting any means or facility of interstate or foreign commerce. Within Title 18 of the United States Code, there are six federal legal provisions relating to activities involved in child pornography, both online and offline:

1. *Section 2256* of Title 18, United States Code defines *child pornography* as any *visual depiction* of *sexually explicit conduct* involving a *minor*.
   Visual depictions include photographs, videos, digital or computer-generated images indistinguishable from an actual minor, and images created, adapted, or modified, but appear to depict an identifiable, actual minor. Undeveloped film, undeveloped videotape, and electronically stored data that can be converted into a visual image of child pornography are also deemed illegal visual depictions under federal law.

The legal definition of *sexually explicit conduct* does not require that an image depict a child engaging in sexual activity to be deemed to be sexually explicit. This means that a picture of a naked child may constitute illegal child pornography if it is sufficiently sexually suggestive.

A *minor* is defined as someone under 18 years of age regardless of the age of consent for sexual activity in a given state. This means that any depiction of a minor under 18 years of age engaging in sexually explicit conduct is illegal.

2. *Section 2251* of Title 18, United States Code makes it illegal to persuade, induce, entice, or coerce a minor to engage in sexually explicit conduct for purposes of producing visual depictions of that conduct. Any individual who attempts or conspires to commit a child pornography offense is also subject to prosecution *under federal law*.
3. *Section 2251A* of Title 18, United States Code specifically prohibits *any parent, legal guardian* or *other person* in *custody or control of a minor* under the age of 18, to buy, sell, or transfer *custody* of that minor for purposes of producing child pornography.
4. *Section 2252* of Title 18, United States Code prohibits certain activities relating to material involving the sexual exploitation of minors including the possession, distribution, and receipt of child pornography. It specifies that the *federal legal jurisdiction* is to be implicated if the child pornography offense occurred in interstate or foreign commerce. Also, federal jurisdiction almost always applies when the Internet is used to commit a child pornography violation. Even if the child sexual abuse material itself did not travel across state or international borders, federal law may still be implicated if the materials, such as the computer used to download the image originated or previously traveled in interstate or foreign commerce.
5. *Section 2252A* of Title 18, United States Code criminalizes certain activities relating to material constituting or containing child pornography.
6. *Section 2260* of Title 18, United States Code prohibits any persons *outside of the United States* to knowingly produce, receive, transport, ship, or distribute child pornography with the *intent to import* or *transmit* the visual depiction into the USA [20].

Convicted federal child pornography offenders in the United States can face severe statutory penalties. For example, a first time offender convicted of producing child pornography under Section 2251 can face financial penalties and between 15 years to 30 years in prison. A first-time offender convicted of transporting child pornography in interstate or foreign commerce under Section 2252, can also be fined and receive between 5 years to 20 years in prison. Convicted offenders may face harsher penalties if: (1) the images are violent, sadistic, or masochistic in nature; (2) the minor was sexually abused; or (3) the offender has prior convictions for child sexual exploitation. In these circumstances, an offender may face up to life imprisonment if convicted in the USA. As well as being prosecuted under the United States' federal child pornography laws, an offender can also be prosecuted under state child pornography laws instead of, or in addition to, the federal laws we have just outlined [21].

3.1.1.6 Case Hypothetical: Cyber-Enabled Murder-for-Hire

Person A is a malicious party who wishes to inflict harm on Person B but Person A does not want to be responsible for inflicting the harm directly. Instead, Person A decides to subcontract the work of harming Person B, via a murder-for-hire arrangement. As Person A is unfamiliar with the local guild of assassins, Person A accesses the DarkNet to anonymously find and respond to an ad—posted on a DarkWeb forum—offering murder-for-hire services with guaranteed anonymity, in exchange for lump-sum payment via cryptocurrency transfers.

This arrangement is suitable for Person A, so Person A responds to the ad and hires the assassin—Person C—over the DarkNet, agreeing to pay two lump sums of money to Person C—the first payment being a 50% deposit and the second payment to be transferred once confirmation of the murder of Person B by Person C has been received by Person A. To ensure the delivery of services, Person A makes a deposit of 50% of the lump sum to Person C using cryptocoin, for further anonymity.

This is an example of a cyber-enabled offence because Person A can certainly find a way to connect with and hire an assassin in person or otherwise, but the ease of online access to the criminal underworld has enabled Person A to simply log onto the DarkNet to find a suitable assassin. In this way, the crime being committed is not dependent on Person A having cyber access—as internet access is not a necessary requirement for hiring an assassin for a contractual murder—rather, it is a traditional crime which is enabled by the online access of Person A.

3.1.2 Cyber-Dependent Offences (Online)

Cyber-dependent crimes are those which can only be committed using a computer, a computer network, or other information technology. Examples of cyber-dependent crimes include hacking offences—such as unauthorized access, modification, impairment and/or interception of data—and attacking offences—including activities like DoS and DDoS attacks, criminal botnet operations, and malicious software (malware). Cyber-dependent crimes seek to compromise the confidentiality, integrity, and availability of network systems and data. Malware, as a branch of hacking and attacking tools, can be further broken down into subtypes of malware, which will be discussed below. These types of offences are examples of "true cybercrimes" in that they would not exist at all without the use of a computer and the target itself is typically one or more computers or the networks between them. These can also be distinguished as "technology-as-target" cybercrime offences [22].

The Cyber Kill Chain® framework was developed by Lockheed Martin, as part of the Intelligence Driven Defense® model for the identification and prevention of cyber intrusions activity.[1] The model identifies what the adversaries must complete in order to achieve their objective. The seven steps of the Cyber Kill Chain® enhance visibility into an attack and enrich an analyst's understanding of an adversary's tactics, techniques, and procedures. The seven steps of a cyberattack are identified by Lockheed Martin as:

1. *Reconnaissance*—Harvesting email addresses, conference information, etc.
2. *Weaponization*—Coupling exploit with backdoor into deliverable payload.
3. *Delivery*—Delivering the weaponized bundle to the victim via email, web, USB, etc.
4. *Exploitation*—Exploiting a vulnerability to execute code on a victim's system.
5. *Installation*—Installing malware on the asset.
6. *Command and Control* (C2)—Command channel for remote manipulation of the victim.
7. *Actions of Objectives*—With full access and control, intruders accomplish their objectives.

3.1.2.1 Hacking

Hacking is a broad term that refers to someone exploiting a computer system or private network through a computer to gain access to digital files or systems without permission. Hackers use brute force, security exploits, social engineering, and other means to gain and maintain access to systems without proper authorization. In law, hacking refers to the unauthorized access to, control of, and/or wilful interception of, personal information, private communication, and other private data over computer network systems for some illicit purpose. The activity of hacking can be broken down into five categories: (1) unauthorized access; (2) modification of data; (3) impairment of data; (4) interception of data; and (5) misuse of assets.

Unauthorized access refers to a person gaining logical or physical access or entry to a network, application, data, website, program, server, service, or other system, without obtaining the proper permission or credentials to do so. This is often done by using someone else's account or other methods that constitute a manner of access not intended by the system owner. Unauthorized access could also occur if a user attempts to access an area of a system they should not be accessing. When attempting to access that area, they would be denied access and possibly see an unauthorized access message [23].

Some system administrators set up alerts to let them know when there is an unauthorized access attempt, so that they may investigate the reason. These alerts help stop hackers from gaining access to a secure or confidential system. Many secure systems may also lock an account with too many failed login attempts. Gaining unauthorized access to any account or service is considered illegal in all parts of the world.

[1] https://www.lockheedmartin.com/en-us/capabilities/cyber/cyber-kill-chain.html

Modification of data refers to the act of changing, inserting, removing, and/or otherwise altering data without authorization to do so. The term "data modification" also covers the introduction of malware or spyware onto a computer, electronic vandalism, and theft of information [1].

Impairment of data is when the transmission or communication of data is disrupted. There are three types of transmission impairments: data attenuation impairment, delay distortion impairment, and noise impairment. *Data attenuation impairment* refers to an impairment that is caused by the degradation of signal strength over a transmission link and is often impacted by distance. *Delay distortion impairment* occurs when a receiver clock deviates from an incoming transmission signal at random, causing an incoming signal to potentially arrive significantly earlier or later than intended. *Noise impairment* occurs when an unwanted signal is inserted between transmission and reception. Examples of noise impairments include thermal noise, intermodulation noise, cross talk, and impulse noise [23].

Interception of data occurs when data is intercepted during transmission, allowing a hacker to gain access to data being transmitted between machines. This can also allow unauthorized users to access applications, network systems, and environments. Most attacks aiming to intercept data are intended to breach confidentiality with regard to private data. Interception of data is sometimes done using a specific type of software, called a packet sniffer, which examines data packets as they are sent around a network, or across the internet. The information gathered through these examinations is then sent back to the hacker. In other cases, interception of data can be part of the process of installing malware to execute a planned cyberattack.

National laws tend to vary in their criminalization of the *misuse of devices* [24]. Some countries have laws that cover the possession, creation, distribution, and use of computer misuse tools, while other countries that have cybercrime laws criminalize some, but not all, of these activities [25].

3.1.2.2 Attacking

A *cyber attack* is any attempt—using one or more computers against a single or multiple computers or networks—to expose, alter, disable, destroy, steal or gain information through unauthorized access to or make unauthorized use of an asset, often in the form of protected computers or networks. These attacks, when correctly executed, can maliciously disable computers, steal data and information, or use a breached computer as a launch point, or zombie, for other attacks [26].

Cyber attacks can be active or passive. An *active attack* attempts to alter system resources or affect their operation, while a *passive attack* attempts to learn or make use of information from the system but does not affect system resources, such as by wiretapping or the installation of keystroke software [27].

An attack can be perpetrated by an insider or from outside the organization. An *inside attack* is an attack initiated by an entity inside the security perimeter, also called an "insider". An example of this could be an "insider" or internal entity that has the authorization to access system resources but uses those resources in a way that was not approved by those who granted the initial authorization. Conversely, an *outside attack* is initiated from outside of the security perimeter, by an unauthorized or illegitimate user of the system, referred to as an "outsider." Potential outside attackers have ranged from amateur pranksters to organized criminals, international terrorists, and hostile government entities [28].

The *Common Attack Pattern Enumeration and Classification* (CAPEC) was established by the U.S. Department of Homeland Security as part of the Software Assurance strategic initiative of the United States' Office of Cybersecurity and Communications [29]. Initially released in 2007, the CAPEC List has continued to evolve with public participation and openly sourced contributions to form a standard mechanism for identifying, collecting, refining, and sharing attack patterns among the cybersecurity community. CAPEC [29] divides cyberterror attack patterns into nine distinct categories: (1) engaging in deceptive interactions; (2) abusing existing functionality; (3) manipulating data structures; (4) manipulating system resources; (5) injecting unexpected items; (6) employing probabilistic techniques; (7) manipulating timing and state; (8) collecting and analyzing information; and (9) subverting access control.[2]

Engaging in Deceptive Interactions

These types of attacks are focused on malicious interactions with a target in an attempt to deceive the target and convince the target that it is interacting with some other principal and as such take actions based on the level of trust that exists between the target and the other principal. These types of attacks assume that some piece of content or functionality is associated with an identity and that the content/functionality is trusted by the target because of this association. Often identified by the term "spoofing," these types of attacks rely on the falsification of the content and/or identity in such a way that the target will incorrectly trust the legitimacy of the content.

For example, in a *content spoofing* attack, an adversary modifies content to make it contain something other than what the original content producer intended while keeping the apparent source of the content unchanged. Other examples include identity spoofing, resource location spoofing, and action spoofing [30].

Abusing Existing Functionality

In this type of attack, an adversary uses or manipulates one or more functions of an application in order to achieve a malicious objective not originally intended by the application, or to deplete a resource to the point that the target's functionality is affected. This is a broad class of attacks wherein the adversary is able to alter the intended result or purpose of the functionality and thereby affect application behavior or information integrity. Outcomes can range from information exposure, vandalism, degrading or denial of service, as well as execution of arbitrary code on the target machine.

---

[2]Reference: https://capec.mitre.org/data/definitions/1000.html

For example, a *denial-of-service attack*—or DoS attack—occurs when an adversary either temporarily or indefinitely disrupts the services of a host connected to the internet, which makes the legitimate users unable to access information systems, devices, and other network resources. In a DoS attack, the attacker typically uses one computer and one internet connection to flood the target. *Distributed denial of service* attacks—or DDoS attacks—are similar to DoS attacks, but much larger. Whereas in a DoS attack, the attacker typically uses one computer and one internet connection to flood the target, a DDoS attack uses multiple computers and multiple internet connections to heavily disrupt network traffic. DDoS attacks can result in devastating consequences for the target, including unauthorized data access, email spamming, data theft, and massive data leaks. These types of attacks can be incredibly large-scale, global attacks when they are distributed through botnets. Other examples of abusing existing functionality as a type of cyber attack include interface manipulation, flooding, excessive allocation, resource leak exposure, functionality misuse, communication channel manipulation, sustained client engagement, protocol manipulation, and functionality bypass [31].

Manipulating Data Structures

Attack patterns in this category aim to manipulate and exploit specific characteristics of system data structures in order to violate the intended usage and protections of these structures. This is done in such a way that it yields either improper access to the associated system data or violations of the security properties of the system itself due to vulnerabilities in how the system processes and manages the data structures. Often, vulnerabilities and therefore exploitability of these data structures exist due to ambiguity and assumptions in their design and prescribed handling.

For example, *buffer manipulation* involves an adversary who manipulates the interaction between an application with a buffer in an attempt to read or modify data to which they should not have access. Other examples include shared resource manipulation, pointer manipulation, and input data manipulation.

Manipulating System Resources

The types of attack patterns within this category focus on the ability of the adversary to manipulate one or more resources in order to achieve a desired outcome. This is a broad class of attacks wherein the attacker is able to change some aspect of a resource's state or availability and thereby affect system behavior or information integrity. Examples of resources include files, applications, libraries, infrastructure, and configuration information. Outcomes can range from vandalism and reduction in service to the execution of arbitrary code on the target machine.

For example, a *file manipulation* attack occurs when an adversary modifies file contents or attributes—such as extensions or names—of files in a manner to cause incorrect processing by an application. Other examples include infrastructure manipulation, configuration or environment manipulation, software integrity attack, modification during manufacture, manipulation during distribution, hardware integrity attack, malicious logic insertion, contaminate resource, and obstruction [32].

Injecting Unexpected Items

Attack patterns within this category focus on the ability to control or disrupt the behavior of a target either through crafted data submitted via an interface for data input, or the installation and execution of malicious code on the target system. The former happens when an adversary adds material to their input that is interpreted by the application causing the targeted application to perform steps unintended by the application manager or causing the application to enter an unstable state. Attacks of this type differ from Data Structure Attacks in that the latter attacks subvert the underlying structures that hold user-provided data, either pre-empting interpretation of the input (in the case of Buffer Overflows) or resulting in values that the targeted application is unable to handle correctly (in the case of Integer Overflows). In Injection attacks, the input is interpreted by the application, but the attacker has included instructions to the interpreting functions that the target application then follows.

For example, *code injection* is when an adversary exploits a weakness on the target to force arbitrary code to be retrieved locally, or from a remote location, and executed as an attack. Other examples include parameter injection, code inclusion, resource injection, code injection, command injection, local execution of code, object injection, traffic injection, and hardware fault injection [33].

Employing Probabilistic Techniques

An attacker utilizes probabilistic techniques to explore and overcome security properties of the target that are based on an assumption of strength due to the extremely low mathematical probability that an attacker would be able to identify and exploit the very rare specific conditions under which those security properties do not hold.

For example, a *brute force* attack is one in which some asset—such as information, functionality, or identity—is protected by a finite secret value. The attacker attempts to gain access to this asset by using trial-and-error to exhaustively explore all the possible secret values in the hope of finding the secret value—or a value that is functionally equivalent—that will unlock the asset. Another example of this type of attack is called fuzzing [34].

Manipulating Timing and State

An attacker exploits weaknesses in timing or state maintaining functions to perform actions that would otherwise be prevented by the execution flow of the target code and processes. An example of a state attack might include manipulation of an application's information to change the apparent credentials or similar information, possibly allowing the application to access material it would not normally be allowed to access. A common example of a timing attack is a test-action race condition where some state information is tested and, if it passes, an action is performed. If the attacker can change the state between the time that the application performs the test and the time the action is performed, then they might be able to manipulate the outcome of the action to malicious ends.

For example, a *forced deadlock* is an attack in which an adversary triggers and exploits a deadlock condition in the target software to cause a denial of service. Other examples of this type of attack include leveraging race conditions and manipulating state.

Collecting and Analyzing Information

Attack patterns within this category focus on the gathering, collection, and theft of information by an adversary. The adversary may collect this information through a variety of methods including active querying as well as passive observation. By exploiting weaknesses in the design or configuration of the target and its communications, an adversary is able to get the target to reveal more information than intended. Information retrieved may aid the adversary in making inferences about potential weaknesses, vulnerabilities, or techniques that assist the adversary's objectives. This information may include details regarding the configuration or capabilities of the target, clues as to the timing or nature of activities, or otherwise sensitive information. Often this sort of attack is undertaken in preparation for some other type of attack, although the collection of information by itself may in some cases be the end goal of the adversary.

For example, a *reverse engineering* attack is one in which an adversary discovers the structure, function, and composition of an object, resource, or system by using a variety of analysis techniques to effectively determine how the analyzed entity was constructed or how it operates. Other examples include excavation, interception, footprinting, protocol analysis, fingerprinting, and information elicitation [35].

Subverting Access Control

An attacker actively targets exploitation of weaknesses, limitations, and assumptions in the mechanisms a target utilizes to manage identity and authentication as well as manage access to its resources or authorize functionality. Such exploitation can lead to the complete subversion of any trust the target system may have in the identity of any entity with which it interacts, or the complete subversion of any control the target has over its data or functionality. Weaknesses targeted by subversion of authorization controls are often due to three primary factors: (1) a fundamental dependence on authentication mechanisms being effective; (2) a lack of effective control over the separation of privilege between various entities; and (3) assumptions and overconfidence in the strength or rigor of the implemented authorization mechanisms.

For example, *authentication abuse* occurs when an attacker obtains unauthorized access to an application, service, or device either through knowledge of the inherent weaknesses of an authentication mechanism or by exploiting a flaw in the authentication scheme's implementation. Other examples include the exploitation of trusted identifiers, exploiting trust in client, adversary in the middle, authentication bypass, privilege abuse, privilege escalation, bypassing physical security, physical theft, and the use of known domain credentials [36].

3.1.2.3 Malware Categories

Malware, or "malicious software" is a general term for some types of software-based hacking and attacking tools including adware, ransomware, spyware, trojans, viruses, worms, and other types of harmful software. The differentiating factor between malware and software is that malware must be intentionally malicious. This distinguishes malware from software that unintentionally causes harm, but is not created or intended to be used for malicious purposes [32].

Included below are some of the more common types of malware and other tools that hackers and attackers use to penetrate digital systems and wreak targetted or widespread havoc on them include: viruses; worms; logic bombs; mobile codes; trojans; back/trap-doors; rootkits; ransomware; bots and botnets; spammers; spyware; and adware. Next, we will define each of these terms for the benefit of clarity.

Viruses are a type of malware that is similar to a flu virus in that it is designed to spread outwardly from one program to another and it has the ability to self-replicate. When a virus type of malware is executed on a machine, it replicates itself by modifying other computer programs, boot sectors, or documents; inserting its own malicious code. Once the virus has spread between computers, the computers which have succumbed to the virus are referred to as an "infected system."

A *worm*, unlike a computer virus, is a standalone malware program that replicates itself in order to spread to other computers. It often uses a computer network to spread itself, relying on security failures on the target computer to access it. Then it will use this machine as a host to scan and infect other computers in the attacked network.

A *logic bomb* is a piece of code, intentionally inserted into a software system, that is intended to set off a malicious function when certain specified conditions are met. The term "logic bomb" is based on the idea that the code in the logic bomb "explodes" when it becomes triggered by a specific event. The code can be inserted into the computer's existing software or into other forms of malware such as viruses, worms or Trojan horses. It then lies dormant, and typically undetectable, until the trigger occurs. Triggers for logic bombs could be a specified date or time, or it could be an action, such as a particular record being deleted from a system or the launching of an infected software application. Unlike other forms of malware that aim to break into a secure system, logic bomb attacks tend to be motivated with the intention of cyber-sabotage from a person within an organization who has access to sensitive data.

Mobile code refers to an external code that is transmitted and executed on a remote machine and encompasses programs that can be executed on multiple host machines separate from the machine on which they originated. Mobile code can be a program—or parts of a program—that is: (1) obtained from a remote source; (2) moved from the source computer to one or more target computers; and (3) removed executed on local systems; and (4) without explicit installation or execution by the recipient target. A mobile code can be transferred over a network through storage media, or embedded in emails, documents, or websites.

Unlike traditional code, mobile code is not explicitly installed on the local host; indeed, most users are not even aware the mobile code has been downloaded, much less executed. Because they are easily distributed and run without the permission of the host, mobile code is often used in a malicious context to cause different degrees of damage to computer systems. Common examples of mobile code include Java Applet, JavaScript, Flash players, and other embedded macros.

A *trojan*—also referred to as a trojan horse or trojan virus—is a type of malware that downloads onto a computer disguised as a legitimate program. A trojan is unique in that it appears to be a bona fide application or file to deceive the user into unwittingly loading and executing the malware. Once installed, the trojan can perform the action for which it was designed. Trojans can be found on file-sharing sites, in email attachments, spoofed messages, infected websites, hacked Wi-Fi networks, and others.

Some of the subtypes of trojan viruses include backdoors, trapdoors, rootkits, downloaders, infostealers, mailfinders, bankers, flooders, and others. The name of the trojan subtype is often indicative of the function of the virus. For example, a downloader is a type of trojan horse malware that downloads and installs files and/or malicious programs. Another common example is the flooder trojan, which enables an attacker to send massive amounts of data to a specific target, inundating their system.

Backdoors and *trapdoors* are a type of malware that is used to create a hidden entrance to a computer system by exploiting software vulnerabilities. The back or trapdoor entrance can be used to bypass existing security safeguards, allowing an outside user access to the target device without the knowledge or permission of the primary user and without leaving any determinable traces for the system to detect. Backdoors and trapdoors are often used by hackers or other external parties to gain access to a target machine for things like digital surveillance, data theft, cryptojacking, cybersabotage, and for initiating other types of malware attacks.

A *rootkit* is a collection of tools that allows remote administrative access to, and control over, a computer while also disguising the presence of the tools on the target computer. Rootkits are often associated with a type of malware that provides root-level, privileged access to a computer, while effectively hiding its existence and actions from primary user detection. Activities that commonly rely on rootkits include data theft, file removal or deletion, privilege escalation, anti-malware and/or antivirus software deactivation, digital surveillance, to damage user-mode applications, or to simply gain external remote control over a target computer. Some specific subtypes of rootkit malware are: application rootkits; bootloader rootkits; kernel rootkits; firmware rootkits; and virtualized rootkits.

Ransomware is a subset of malicious software that is used to lock, or disable user access to, a computer or network system. Depending on the type of ransomware, either the entire operating system or individual files are encrypted. The malicious actors can then demand a ransom to be paid in exchange for the release of the computer or system back to the primary user. This is done using asymmetric encryption—a cryptography technique that uses a pair of keys to encrypt and decrypt a file. Ransomware can be categorized into two groups: locker ransomware—in which the basic computer functions are affected—and Crypto ransomware—in which individual files are encrypted.

A bot is an application, software, or process that has been created expressly for the purpose of automating repetitive tasks. Bots perform automated, repetitive, pre-defined tasks and typically imitate or replace human user behavior. Beneficial bots are used to carry out useful tasks, however, bad bots—also known as malware bots—are considered to be among the most unpleasant and difficult to manage threats to cybersecurity. Bots can be used to steal sensitive data, to infect a computer with malware, as a launching point for DDoS attacks, and much more.

Botnets are groups of connected computers or devices that perform a number of repetitive tasks. Over a period of time, malicious attackers can take over multiple computers, creating a network of zombie computers. When a botnet becomes infected by malware, the network falls under the control of the attacking party. These computers are then used to launch a large-scale malicious attack. Users might never realize that their computers are part of a botnet because the footprint left by a botnet is so small and easily overlooked. Some examples of common botnet subtypes include spambots, chatterbots, file-sharing bots, credential stuffing bots, DoS/DDoS bots, vulnerability scanner bots, click fraud bots, and traffic monitoring bots.

A *spammer* is a standalone utility that can be used to send massive amounts of unsolicited commercial electronic messages to different addresses. Spammers usually fake email message headers and use anonymous SMTP servers to send emails. While the use of such tools is illegal in several countries, these programs are not inherently destructive.

Spam can include more than just fraudulent and unsolicited commercial electronic messages. Examples of spam attempts can include messages related to lottery scams, phishing, or computer viruses. Subsets of spam include comment spam, trackback spam, negative SEO attacks, spiders, bots, DoS/DDoS attacks, and typical commercial electronic email spam. Spammers often target potential buyers of specific goods and services which they seek to promote. These can then be divided into categories of adult content, health, information technology, personal finance, political/philosophical, and education/training opportunities.

Spyware is a subset of malware that is specifically designed to steal information about online activities, frequently visited sites, the types of things that are downloaded by the user, usernames and passwords, security questions and answers, banking and payment information, and emails—both sent and received—via the targeted computer. Spyware relies on the exploitation of security vulnerabilities and often also includes phishing and the use of trojans. Spyware can have a number of different objectives but is most often used for fraudulent financial gain.

Spyware is highly versatile and can be used to perform a number of illicit functions including creating targeted pop-up advertisements, capturing personal banking login details, taking screenshots of the sites you visit, and even logging the keys you type. As an example, Keylogger is a type of spyware that can be used to track and log the specific keys used on a keyboard, effectively capturing any information which was typed or otherwise inputted into the computer via the keyboard—watching and recording everything entered by the user.

Adware, also known as advertising-supported software, generates revenue for its developers by automatically generating advertisements on your screen, typically within a web browser. This normally contextualizes as a software that displays unwanted, sometimes irritating, pop-up ads which can appear on a computer, mobile, or other networked devices. Adware normally comes in software and other programs which are downloaded from the internet and usually in the form of freeware or shareware. The adware self-installs onto the targeted device without the knowledge of the user.

Adware can be designed to analyze the location, type, and content of the Internet sites which have been visited, and then generate targeted advertising which is relevant to the topics or the types of goods or services featured in, or relating to, the content of the websites which are frequented by that user. The adware itself can be either harmless and harmful. Harmless adware can be found in legitimate programs which allow users to give informed and express consent to ads and promotions. This can help to offset the costs for the developer, enabling the developer to offer—or share—their software to others without charging the software users directly. Harmful adware presents the risk of Potentially Unwanted Applications (PUAs)—or Potentially Unwanted Programs (PUPs)—being unknowingly installed onto a computer. This includes the installation of any program for which the primary user has not given express informed consent.

Possession of hacking tools refers to the possession of any tools which are designed or adapted primarily to commit either computer/network "hacking" or computer/network "mischief" while knowing that the device or software has been used, or is intended to be used, for those purposes. This also includes making, selling, importing, distributing, or making available such a device.

3.1.2.4 Example in Law: UK Unauthorized Access and Modification

The United Kingdom's *Computer Misuse Act 1990* and *Data Protection Act 2018* protect personal data held by organizations from unauthorized access and modification.

Computer Misuse Act 1990

Unauthorized access, in the *Computer Misuse Act 1990*, occurs when an individual enters a computer system without permission—what we also know as hacking—and also includes unauthorized access to computer materials with the intent to commit a further crime.

Modification refers to modifying or deleting data, and also includes the introduction of malware or spyware onto a computer, electronic vandalism, and theft of information.

Examples of unauthorized access and modification include the deliberate or reckless impairment of a computer's operation, the prevention or hindering of access to computer material by a legitimate user, or the impairment of the operation or reliability of computer-held material. For a charge to be made under the *Computer Misuse Act*, the offender must know that the act was unauthorized.

Definitions

It is important to note that the *Computer Misuse Act 1990* does not provide a definition of a "computer" because rapid changes in technology would mean any definition would soon become out of date. Instead, as the United Kingdom has a common law-based legal system, the definition of a "computer"—for lack of a provided legislative definition—can be inferred from previous cases as a legal precedent. For example, in the case of *Director of Public Prosecutions (DPP) v McKeown and Jones*, Lord Hoffman defined a computer as "a device for storing, processing and retrieving information [37]."

We can also look to definitions provided by the *Council of Europe Cybercrime Convention 2001* (the Budapest Convention), which defined computer system and computer data as follows:

Computer system refers to any device or a group of interconnected or related devices, one or more of which, pursuant to a program, performs automatic processing of data.

Computer data is any representation of facts, information, or concepts in a form suitable for processing in a computer system, including a program suitable to cause a computer system to perform a function [38].

Jurisdiction

Under sect. 3.4 of the *Computer Misuse Act*, liability for the offences provided under sections 3.1, 3.3, or 3ZA requires proof of at least one "significant link" with the "home country" concerned, that being, England and Wales. A "significant link" could include:

- The accused is in the home country at the time of the offence.
- The target of the CMA offence is in the home country.
- The technological activity which has facilitated the offending may have passed through a server based in the home country.

As defined in sect. 3.5, in relation to an offence under Section 3ZA, any of the following is also a "significant link" with domestic jurisdiction:

- That the accused was in the home country concerned at the time when s/he committed the unauthorized act (or caused it to be done).

- That the unauthorized act was done in relation to a computer in the home country concerned.
- That the unauthorized act caused, or created a significant risk of, serious damage of a material kind (within the meaning of that section) in the home country concerned.

As defined in sect. 3.6, the extended extra-territorial jurisdiction arrangements also apply to conspiracy or attempts to commit offences under the *Computer Misuse Act 1990* and therefore will supersede the usual rule for conspiracy charges.

As well, the United Kingdom's *Data Protection Act 2018* defines personal data as any information relating to an identified or identifiable living individual.

Offences

The five specific offences covered under the *Computer Misuse Act* are provided in Sections 1, 2, and 3 of the Act. They are:

Section 1—Unauthorized access to computer material.

Maximum penalty on indictment = 2 years imprisonment.

Section 2—Unauthorized access with intent to commit or facilitate commission of further offences.

Maximum penalty on indictment = 5 years imprisonment.

Section 3—Unauthorised acts with intent to impair, or with recklessness as to impairing the operation of a computer.

Maximum sentence on indictment = 10 years' imprisonment.

Section 3ZA—Unauthorised acts causing, or creating risk of, serious damage.

Maximum sentence on indictment = 14 years, unless the offence caused or created a significant risk of serious damage to human welfare or national security, as defined in Sect. 3.3 (a) and (b), in which case a person guilty of the offence is liable to imprisonment for life.

Section 3A—Making, supplying or obtaining articles for use in offence under Section 1, 3 or 3ZA.

Maximum sentence on indictment = 2 years' imprisonment.

Data Protection Act 2018

The *Data Protection Act 2018* creates a number of offences in relation to the control and access to data:

Section 119: Creates offences relating to the obstruction of inspections of personal data by the Information Commissioner.

Section 132: Creates an offence for persons who are currently or have previously been the Information Commissioner, a member of the Information Commissioner's staff, or an agent of the Information Commissioner from disclosing information obtained in the course of, or for the purposes of, the discharging of the Information Commissioner's functions unless made with lawful authority.

Section 144: Creates an offence for a person to intentionally or recklessly make a false statement in response to an information notice.

Section 148: Creates an offence where the Information Commissioner has given an information notice or an assessment notice requiring access to information, a document, equipment, or other material, it is an offence to destroy or otherwise dispose of, conceal, block or (where relevant) falsify it, with the intention of preventing the Commissioner from viewing or being provided with or directed to it.

Section 170: Creates an offence of the deliberate or reckless obtaining, disclosing, procuring, and retention of personal data without the consent of the data controller.

Section 171: Creates a new offence of knowingly or recklessly re-identifying information that has been de-identified without the consent of the controller who de-identified the data. This responds to concerns about the security of de-identified data held in online files. For example, recommendations in the Review of Data Security, Consent and Opt-Outs by the National Data Guardian for Health and Care called for the Government to introduce stronger sanctions to protect de-identified patient data.

Section 173: Creates an offence of the alteration of personal data to prevent disclosure following the exercise of a subject access right. The relevant subject access rights are set out in subsection (2).

Section 184: Creates an offence for an employer to require employees or contractors, or for a person to require another person who provides goods, facilities, or services, to provide certain records obtained via subject access requests as a condition of their employment or contract. It is also an offence for a provider of goods, facilities, or services to the public to request such records from another as a condition for providing a service.

Together, the *Computer Misuse Act 1990* and the *Data Protection Act 2018* work to protect computers and computer systems from unauthorized access, modification, impairment, and data privacy breaches.

3.1.2.5 Case Hypothetical: Cyber-Dependent Botnet/DDoS Attack

Person A has taken to a life of cybercrime. Person A has decided, for whatever reason, to wreak havoc on a network service provider (the target). Person A does this using a combination of malware, botnets, and DDoS attack modules.

In our case, Person A is an unauthorized party, acting maliciously, who intentionally infects a network of computers with malware. This malware infection creates a "botnet" (robot network). The infected network (botnet) of computers, now under the control of Person A (the unauthorized party) works in tandem to execute planned DDoS (distributed denial-of-service) attacks on the targeted network. The target experiences a disruption to their network traffic and services as a result of the heavy influx of requests from the botnet. This disruption of service prevents the authorized parties from having access to the network, further disrupting the traffic and potentially resulting in devastating consequences, including unauthorized data access, widespread email spamming, data theft, and massive organizational leaks. This scenario is illustrated in Fig. 3.1 below.

In this hypothetical example, Person A could be charged for the following:

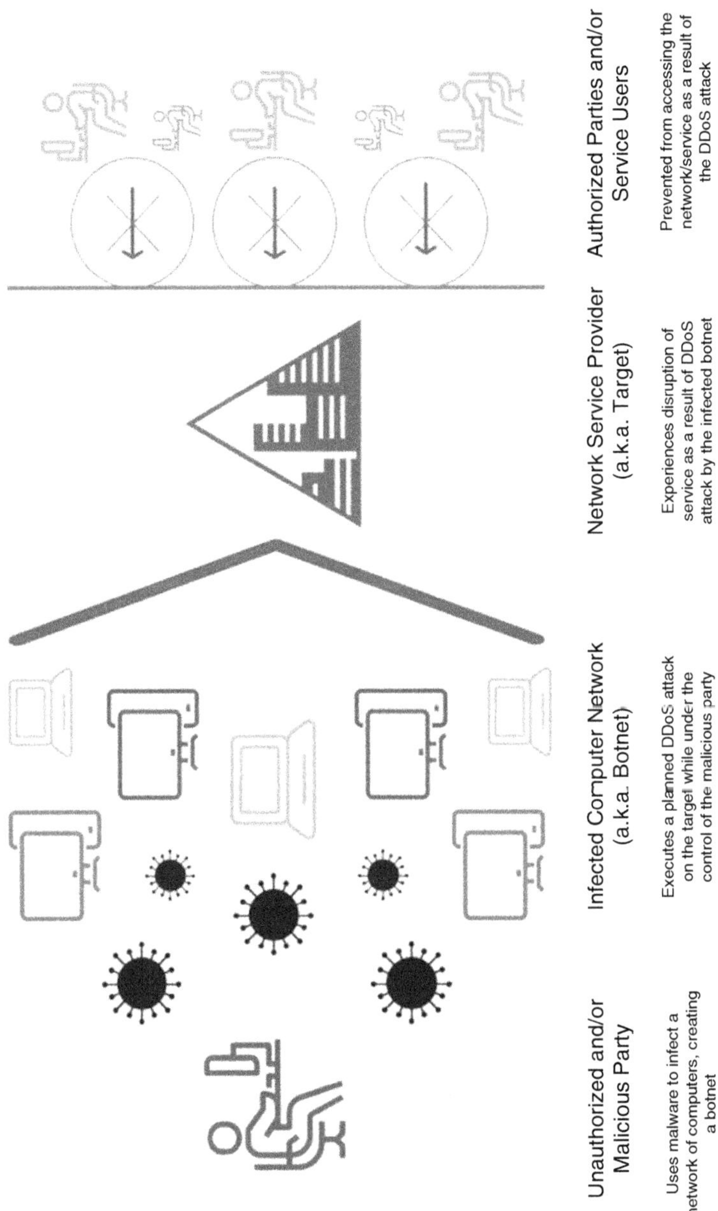

Fig. 3.1 Botnet cyber attack hypothetical

1. *Mischief* for the malware and DDoS attacks.
2. If the crime is considered to be a national security offence, then Person A could be charged for *cyberterrorism*.
3. If private communications were intercepted, then Person A could be charged for *interception*.
4. If Person A continues to possess the tools used to do the hacking, malware, and DDoS attacks, then Person A could be charged with *possession of tools*.
5. If electronic theft involving criminal copyright infringement occurs, then Person A could also be charged for *copyright infringement*.

What we can see from this hypothetical example of a malware/DDoS attack, is that criminal charges involving cyber-specific criminal activities can very quickly escalate and these charges can rack up very serious consequences.

3.1.3 Computer/Cyber-Supported Offences

In addition to what we typically consider to be cybercrime, there are also *computer crimes* and *cyber-supported crimes* which cover the use of computers by criminals for communication and document and data storage. Essentially, *computer/cyber-supported crimes* are those in which the use of the computer or network is only incidental to the actual commission of the crime, but which may still be legally relevant for evidentiary purposes. As an example, data recorded on a computer or over a network could be an integral part of an investigation for murder, which would make that murder a "computer-supported" crime. Other terms for this type of activity include: "computer crime," "computer-related crime," "high-tech crime," "cyber-crime," and "Internet crime" and are often used interchangeably by law enforcement and media, as well as in the context of public engagement [1].

3.1.3.1 Example in Law: Aggravating Factors for Sentencing in the US

In law, when an individual commits a criminal offence, they are charged with that specific offence. As we know that computer-supported crimes only involve the use of a computer or networked system as tertiary and not directly related to the commission of the offence, there is no specific legal example for an offence that covers the tertiary use of a computer or networked device which not directly related to the offence of the crime. In such a case, the person who committed the offence would be charged with the offence which was directly committed, rather than tertiary details. This is clarified more in the hypothetical example below.

However, while computer-supported offences are not direct criminal offences themselves, there are situations in which the tertiary use of a computer during or following the commission of a crime could become an aggravating factor to be considered in the sentencing phase of criminal convictions. In this phase, the court considers all relevant factors to the specific crime and the person who committed the crime and adjusts the sentence accordingly.

Factors that can adjust the sentence of an offender are either aggravating factors or mitigating factors. *Aggravating factors* include context, evidence, or other information that increases the severity of the crime as well as the severity of the eventual sentence. Conversely, *mitigating factors* are those which may serve to reduce the perceived severity of the offence and therefore also the severity of the sentence.

Offenders who used their knowledge or ability, with regard to computers or networked systems, could risk their knowledge being determined as a "special skill" by the court, which is an aggravating factor in sentencing for criminal offences.

We can look to the United States for an example of how cyber-specific abilities could be interpreted as aggravating factors in sentencing. Under the United States Federal Sentencing Guidelines (the "USSG"), if the defendant in a criminal offence "uses a special skill that significantly facilitates the commission or concealment of the offence, the 2-level adjustment in subsection 3B1.3 may apply.[3]

"Unlike the abuse of trust adjustment, an adjustment solely for the use of a special skill may not be applied in addition to an adjustment under ss. 3B1.3 ("Aggravating Role"). The guidelines define a "special skill" as one not possessed by the general public and that usually requires substantial education, training, or licensing."[4] In a comment provided with ss. 3B1.3 of the Guidelines, the following examples are listed: lawyers, pilots, doctors, accountants, chemists, and demolition experts.

Does having knowledge of computers count as an aggravating factor to the commission and sentencing of a criminal offence? Maybe.

In the following US cases, the defendant's computer knowledge and ability as a form of "special skill" which could be used in the commission of an offence *were upheld* by the court:

A. A case in which the defendant had an associate's degree in graphic design, specialized knowledge, and the ability to manipulate drawings in AutoCAD and used those skills to steal data and attempt to sell it to his former employer's competitors.[5]
B. A case in which the defendant had "skills in civil engineering, radio technology, and computer technology... legitimate skills [he] turned to criminal purposes."[6]
C. A case in which the defendant, a computer consultant, had specialized knowledge of an airline reservations program and trained others within a travel agency on that program.[7]
D. A case in which the defendant held several degrees and professional licenses, "completed numerous computer and network training courses ... [and] has been employed in the IT field since 1991."[8]

[3]United States Sentencing Guidelines, §3B1.3.

[4]United States Sentencing Guidelines, §3B1.3, comment. (n.4).

[5]United States v. Lange, 312 F.3d 263, 270 (seventh Cir. 2002).

[6]United States v. Campa, 529 F.3d 980, 1017–18 (11th Cir. 2008).

[7]United States v. O'Brien, 435 F.3d 36, 42 (first Cir. 2006).

[8]United States v. Kyereme, 371 F. App'x 292, 293–94 (3d Cir. 2010).

E. A case in which the defendant, with no special training in electronics—but an "impressive knowledge of electronics"—installed electronic equipment into ATMs that allowed him to access account numbers and withdraw money.[9]
F. A case in which the defendant possessed computer skills that were self-taught and hacked into website order logs, rewrote scripts, and downloaded validity checks for credit card numbers to further access device fraud, as "[a] court can reasonably infer requisite education from the nature and extent of the skill possessed."[10]
G. A case in which the defendant had self-taught knowledge of computer systems and used that knowledge to facilitate the offences of computer fraud, possession of a stolen vehicle, conspiracy to commit computer and wire fraud, and interception of communications. The court upheld the adjustment based on the defendant's "extraordinary knowledge" of computers but also cautioned—in a footnote—that, "only where a defendant's computer skills are particularly sophisticated do they correspond to the Sentencing Commission's examples of 'special skills'. Courts should be particularly cautious in imposing special skills adjustments where substantial education, training or licensing is not involved."[11]
H. A case in which the defendant, after learning from a high school vocational program, built his own computer systems and modified consoles while trafficking in circumvention technology, noting that circuit precedent required self-taught skills to be "particularly sophisticated."[12]

In the following US cases, the court *did not recognize* the defendant's computer knowledge and ability as a form of "special skill" which could be used in the commission of an offence.

A. A case in which the defendant created a website identical to the Honolulu marathon's website, registered a similar domain name, and sold fake registrations for the marathon. This adjustment was reversed by the court—citing the footnote in the Peterson case—because the defendant was "a video rental store operator who copied a website .... [whose] level of sophistication was nothing like Petersen's."[13]
B. A case in which the defendant's use of Adobe Page Marker and a computer scanner to create counterfeit currency was found by the court to be "easily duplicated by members of the general public with a minimum of difficulty."[14]
C. A case—involving failure to register a bitcoin business and drug conspiracy—in which the defendant did not "come close to the 'expert hacker' in Peterson" and

[9] United States v. Lavin, 27 F.3d 40, 41 (2d Cir. 1994).
[10] United States v. Prochner, 417 F.3d 54, 61 (first Cir. 2005).
[11] United States v. Petersen, 98 F.3d 502 (ninth Cir. 1996).
[12] United States v. Reichert, 747 F.3d 445, 454–55 (sixth Cir. 2014).
[13] United States v. Lee, 296 F.3d 792, 797–99 (ninth Cir. 2002).
[14] United States v. Godman, 223 F.3d 320, 322–23 (sixth Cir. 2000).

lacked education, training, or licensing in the skills at issue—even though the defendant was described as "a very intelligent computer skills set-type person" that had a working knowledge of the "darknet marketplace."[15]

3.1.3.2 Case Hypothetical: Computer/Cyber-Supported Offence

Person A enjoys dirt biking and occasionally dabbles in poetry to pass the time. In dirt biking, Person A takes solace in the thrill of the ride, sometimes taking on obstacles and jumps for that extra rush of excitement. For an emotional outlet, Person A uses creative writing—specifically poetry—as a means to reduce the negative impact of potential incidents stemming from impulsive decision-making by providing a period of reflection through the written word. Person A is committed to their poetic works and hopes to receive a contract to publish a small book of poetry. In the meantime, Person A resolves to simply type up any completed poems to be saved on a folder on the desktop computer in Person A's living room. These two hobbies—dirt biking and creative poetry writing—take up most of Person A's spare time; however, from time to time, Person A does partake in a more nefarious hobby: stalking and kidnapping children.

While Person A does make a solid effort to avoid the overwhelming impulse to kidnap children by staying involved with dirt biking and creative writing, this is not a perfect solution and, unfortunately, every now and then Person A still craves the rush of a good kidnapping. On one such occasion, Person A decides that enough time has passed since the last kidnapping and uses this as a reason to justify choosing a new target to stalk and kidnap. After reflecting on personal preferences, ease of access, and physical difficulty, Person A decides to target and kidnap Child X, for purposes that are irrelevant to the facts of this case.

To this end, Person A devises an intricate plan to stalk, observe, and gradually collect information about the regular routine of Child X, to best determine the ideal time and place for the actual kidnapping to occur. As Person A enjoys doing these activities in person and feels less likely to be caught by law enforcement if there is not an online record or browser history connecting Person A to the crime, no technology is used during the course of stalking, observation, or information gathering. Rather than technology, Person A carries a notebook and a pen to detail any useful information gathered. To temporarily store the child post-kidnapping, Person A has refurbished a small windowless room in the basement of Person A's house.

After a sufficient amount of time has passed and Person A feels that enough information has been gathered about the comings and goings of Child X, Person A decides that the time for the kidnapping has arrived. In preparation for the occasion, Person A prints out a street map from the internet, marking the target location on the printed page in blue pen.

On the chosen day and at the chosen location, Person A successfully intercepts, transports, and confines Child X, shoring the child in the refurbished basement room

[15] States v. Lord, 915 F.3d 1009, 1024–25 (fifth Cir. 2019).

which was prepared for this purpose. Once the child is confined to the room, Person A decides to unwind with a few drinks and a pen and paper to write some new reflective poetry. The creative juices are flowing, and in no time at all Person A has completed five new poetic masterpieces. Person A feels great about such an accomplishment, rejoices in the victory, and sets about typing up the newly-crafted poems, saving them to the same folder as always.

Days pass by. Weeks pass by. After a couple of months, when the initial investigation into the disappearance of Child X has settled down a bit, Person A begins to feel bored with having Child X around. Although Person A is a fan of stalking and kidnapping, Person A does not want to start adding murder to the already-questionable list of enjoyed hobbies. However, Person A is unsure how to get rid of the child. Always a keen problem-solver, and feeling slightly inebriated, Person A decides to release Child X back into nature, as one might do with a fostered wild raccoon or other wild outdoor creature. To that end, Person A drives Child X outside the city limits, and into the surrounding countryside, leaving Child X in a heavily-treed forest at the end of a gravel road, just off the main highway.

Unbeknownst to Person A, prior to being kidnapped, Child X had been an avid participant in a local outdoor wilderness survival group for 4 years. While unable to effectively apply those skills while confined to the small windowless basement room, Child X is highly skilled in navigation and wilderness survival, easily creating a temporary shelter and foraging for edible forest plants. Within only a few days, Child X returns to the city, informs law enforcement of the kidnapping, and provides enough descriptive information for the police to narrow down the location where Child X was confined to a residential street consisting of four houses. Based on the physical description of the suspect—also provided by Child X—the police believe that the crime was committed by either Person A or by Person B— a neighbor living two houses down the street from Person A. As a result, both Person A and Person B are identified as prime suspects in the kidnapping case.

The police obtain a search warrant which gives them the ability to enter and search the private properties of Person A and Person B. The warrant also gives the police the power to seize any possible evidence found during the search. During the dual property searches, police seize all desktop computers found in the homes of Person A and Person B and start the process of forensic analysis for corroborating evidence.

Officer Q is a law enforcement officer with the local police department who specializes in digital forensics and evidence collection. While browsing through the computer files of Person A for potential clues, Officer Q stumbles upon Person A's personal folder of creative writing. As an avid reader of the written word, a connoisseur of new-age rap, and a decades-long fan of poetry, Officer Q casually reads through the poems, mentally commending Person A for their talent in rhyming and lyrical prosody.

When Officer Q comes upon the most recently typed group of poems, Officer Q discovers a reference in one of the poems which features the given name of Child X. In another poem in the same set, Officer Q reads of Person A's recent feeling of relief and satisfaction after having completed some foreboding task, which is described by Person A as "the bad day". Growing suspicious, Officer Q opens the document settings and, sure enough, the date on which this set of poems were typed matches the timeline established by the police in relation to the kidnapping of Child X.

Officer Q extends the search of Person A's computer, looking through the browser history, search data, photos, and other media. Finally, Officer Q opens the print queue history and finds the map which was printed out by Person A prior to the kidnapping. This map is localized to the area in which Child X was known to have been immediately prior to their disappearance. Officer Q alerts the rest of the investigation team.

Person A is quickly arrested and formally charged by law enforcement with kidnapping, forcible confinement, and a handful of other related offences. The collective works of poetry and the map saved in the print queue are both admitted by the prosecution as material evidence in the criminal court.

In this scenario, the crime itself was neither dependent upon, or enabled by, Person A's use of the computer and networked printer. Instead, the computer and printer acted as supporting tools within the entirety of the scope of the offence, providing contextual evidence of a link between Person A and the commission of the crime. IFor this reason, this hypothetical scenario acts as an example of a computer/cyber-supported crime. While the use of the computer was not a necessary requirement or an enabling factor for Person A to stalk and kidnap Child X, it provided the much-needed evidentiary link between the alleged suspect and the criminal kidnapping and confinement offence.

3.1.4 National (Cyber)Security Offences

National cybersecurity offences, also informally referred to as "*cyberterrorism*," are umbrella terms for the commission of an indictable offence for the benefit of, at the direction of, or in association with, an organization that commits a terrorist activity or otherwise engages in terrorism, either domestic or international. International legal considerations in relation to cyber laws, including international criminal laws, will be covered in much greater detail in section 5.4 of this book, but a general overview will be provided here as well [39].

> Cyberterrorism is the convergence of terrorism and cyberspace [40].

To understand the potential threat of cyberterrorism, two factors must be considered:

(a) Whether there are targets that are vulnerable to an attack that could lead to violence or severe harm, and.
(b) Whether there are actors with the capability and motivation (or intention) to carry out these attacks on vulnerable targets.

3.1.4.1 Attack Vulnerability of Target

Several studies have shown that critical infrastructures can be vulnerable to cyberterrorist attacks. Unfortunately, although many of the known weaknesses in computerized systems can be corrected, it is effectively impossible to completely eliminate all vulnerabilities. This is because, even if the technology itself offers good security, the technology itself can be frequently configured or used in ways that would make it open to attack. For bigger targets, there is also always the possibility of using insiders, either acting alone or with other cyberterrorists, misusing their access capabilities [32].

3.1.4.2 Capability and Motivation of Attacker

If we accept that critical infrastructures are vulnerable to a cyberterrorist attack, then the question becomes whether there are malicious actors with the *capability and motivation* to carry out such an operation. While many hackers have the knowledge, skills, and tools to attack computer systems, they generally lack the motivation to cause violence or severe economic or social harm. Conversely, terrorists who are motivated to cause violence seem to lack the capability or motivation to cause that degree of damage in cyberspace [41].

Levels of Cyberterror Capability

The Center for the Study of Terrorism and Irregular Warfare at the Naval Postgraduate School in Monterey, California—the Monterey group—issued a report titled "Cyberterror: Prospects and Implications," with the goal of improving articulation of the demand side of terrorism. Specifically, they assessed the prospects of terrorist organizations pursuing cyberterrorism. They concluded that the barrier to entry for anything beyond annoying hacks is quite high and that terrorists generally lack the wherewithal and human capital needed to mount a meaningful operation.

In their "Cyberterror: Prospects and Implications" report, the Monterey group defined three levels of cyberterror capability:

- *Simple-Unstructured:* The capability to conduct basic hacks against individual systems using tools created by someone else. The organization possesses little target analysis, command, and control, or learning capability.
- *Advanced-Structured:* The capability to conduct more sophisticated attacks against multiple systems or networks and possibly, to modify or create basic hacking tools. The organization possesses an elementary target analysis, command and control, and learning capability.
- *Complex-Coordinated:* The capability for coordinated attacks capable of causing mass disruption against integrated, heterogeneous defenses (including cryptography). Ability to create sophisticated hacking tools. Highly capable target analysis, command, and control, and organization learning capability.

The Monterey group also estimated that to start from scratch would take 2–4 years to reach the advanced-structured level and 6–10 years to reach the complex-coordinated level, although some groups might get there in just a few years or turn to outsourcing or sponsorship to extend their capability [40].

3.1.4.3 Categories of Cyberterrorism

National security offences, in broad terms, tend to fall into one, or more, of the following five subtypes of cyberterrorism activity. They are: (1) incursion; (2) destruction; (3) disinformation; (4) denial of service; and (5) defacement of websites [42].

Incursion refers to a hostile entry, invasion, or attack of territory. In this specific digital context, it would refer to unauthorized access and invasion attacks targeting computer information systems, infrastructures, computer networks, or personal electronic devices.

Destruction is an umbrella term for the process of destroying digital data to the point where it becomes completely unreadable, unaccessible, or able to be used for unauthorized purposes. A subtype of destruction-based attack is a destruction-of-service (DeOS) attack, a form of cyberattack that targets an organization's entire online presence as well as their ability to recover from the attack afterward. Just one false claim alleging a company breach, or a conspiracy theory targeting the practices of a specific company can set off a chain reaction, growing anxiety amongst shareholders, fostering tension for customers, and putting the reputation and future success of the targeted company, group, individual, or other entity in jeopardy.

Disinformation refers to the intentional dissemination of false information, with an end goal of misleading, confusing, or manipulating an audience. A recent example of this can be seen in the fake hacktivist groups organized by state actors during the last United States federal election, which lead to a violent insurrection culminating in an unprecedented assault on the United States Capitol on January 6, 2021. Another recent, ongoing, topical example of a disinformation attack campaign involves the pharmaceutical companies Pfizer, Moderna, and Johnson & Johnson, all of whom have been battling disinformation campaigns surrounding their rollout of COVID-19 vaccines. The rumors—based on larger disinformation campaigns—have worked to spread doubt in the effectiveness of the COVID-19 vaccines produced by these three companies and to challenge the widespread perception that these vaccines can be safely administered. It should be noted, of course, that the research at this juncture suggests that all three of these vaccines are, in fact, safe and effective, and should absolutely be taken, if given the opportunity.[16]

Distributed Denial of service (DDoS) attacks are a type of cyberattack in which the malicious actor seeks to shut down a machine or network, making it inaccessible or unavailable to its intended users by temporarily or indefinitely disrupting the services of a host connected to the Internet. DDoS attacks often target the web servers of high-profile organizations such as banks, large corporations, commercial organizations, media companies, and/or governmental and trade organizations.

[16] Seriously. Read it again. These vaccines are safe, effective, and should absolutely be taken if given the opportunity.

Defacement of websites is a subset of cyberattacks in which malicious parties penetrate a website and replace the site content with their own messages. These defacements often convey political or religious messages, profanity or other inappropriate content that could embarrass website owners and tarnish the reputation and public perception of online organizations, or may simply convey a notice that the website has been hacked by a specific hacker group for some purpose.

3.1.4.4 Example in Law: Canada's Anti-Terrorism Laws

Criminal Code of Canada (RSC, 1985, c C-46), s. 83.01(1) provides definitions relevant to Canada's specific anti-terrorism laws. In this section, definitions are provided as follows:

"Canadian" means a Canadian citizen, a permanent resident within the meaning of subsection 2(1) of the *Immigration and Refugee Protection Act* or a body corporate incorporated and continued under the laws of Canada or a province.

"entity" means a person, group, trust, partnership or fund or an unincorporated association or organization.

"listed entity" means an entity on a list established by the Governor in Council under section 83.05.

"terrorist activity" means...

(a) an act or omission that is committed in or outside Canada and that, if committed in Canada, is one of the following offences:
   - (i) The offences referred to in subsection 7(2) that implement the Convention for the Suppression of Unlawful Seizure of Aircraft, signed at The Hague on December 16, 1970.
   - (ii) The offences referred to in subsection 7(2) that implement the Convention for the Suppression of Unlawful Acts against the Safety of Civil Aviation, signed at Montreal on September 23, 1971.
   - (iii) The offences referred to in subsection 7(3) that implement the Convention on the Prevention and Punishment of Crimes against Internationally Protected Persons, including Diplomatic Agents, adopted by the General Assembly of the United Nations on December 14, 1973.
   - (iv) The offences referred to in subsection 7(3.1) that implement the International Convention against the Taking of Hostages, adopted by the General Assembly of the United Nations on December 17, 1979.
   - (v) The offences referred to in subsection 7(2.21) that implement the Convention on the Physical Protection of Nuclear Material, done at Vienna and New York on March 3, 1980, as amended by the Amendment to the Convention on the Physical Protection of Nuclear Material, done at Vienna on July 8, 2005, and the International Convention for the Suppression of Acts of Nuclear Terrorism, done at New York on September 14, 2005.
   - (vi) The offences referred to in subsection 7(2) that implement the Protocol for the Suppression of Unlawful Acts of Violence at Airports Serving International Civil Aviation, supplementary to the Convention for the

Suppression of Unlawful Acts against the Safety of Civil Aviation, signed at Montreal on February 24, 1988.

(vii) The offences referred to in subsection 7(2.1) that implement the Convention for the Suppression of Unlawful Acts against the Safety of Maritime Navigation, done at Rome on March 10, 1988.

(viii) The offences referred to in subsection 7(2.1) or (2.2) that implement the Protocol for the Suppression of Unlawful Acts against the Safety of Fixed Platforms Located on the Continental Shelf, done at Rome on March 10, 1988.

(ix) The offences referred to in subsection 7(3.72) that implement the International Convention for the Suppression of Terrorist Bombings, adopted by the General Assembly of the United Nations on December 15, 1997.

(x) The offences referred to in subsection 7(3.73) that implement the International Convention for the Suppression of the Financing of Terrorism, adopted by the General Assembly of the United Nations on December 9, 1999, or.

(b) An act or omission, in or outside Canada,
   (i) That is committed.
      A. In whole or in part for a political, religious, or ideological purpose, objective or cause, and.
      B. In whole or in part with the intention of intimidating the public, or a segment of the public, with regard to its security, including its economic security, or compelling a person, a government or a domestic or an international organization to do or to refrain from doing any act, whether the public or the person, government or organization is inside or outside Canada, and.
   (ii) That intentionally.
      A. Causes death or serious bodily harm to a person by the use of violence.
      B. Endangers a person's life.
      C. Causes a serious risk to the health or safety of the public or any segment of the public.
      D. Causes substantial property damage, whether to public or private property, if causing such damage is likely to result in the conduct or harm referred to in any of clauses (A) to (C), or.
      E. Causes serious interference with or serious disruption of an essential service, facility or system, whether public or private, other than as a result of advocacy, protest, dissent, or stoppage of work that is not intended to result in the conduct or harm referred to in any of clauses (A) to (C).

... and includes a conspiracy, attempt or threat to commit any such act or omission, or being an accessory after the fact or counselling in relation to any such act or omission, but, for greater certainty, does not include an act or omission that is committed during an armed conflict and that, at the time and in the place of its commission, is in accordance with customary international law or conventional international law applicable to the conflict, or the activities undertaken by military forces of a state in the exercise of their official duties, to the extent that those activities are governed by other rules of international law. (*activité terroriste*).

"terrorist group" means:

(a) An entity that has as one of its purposes or activities facilitating or carrying out any terrorist activity, or.
(b) A listed entity,

and includes an association of such entities.

(1.1) For greater certainty, the expression of a political, religious, or ideological thought, belief or opinion does not come within paragraph (b) of the definition of *terrorist activity* in subsection (1) unless it constitutes an act or omission that satisfies the criteria of that paragraph.

(1.2) For greater certainty, a suicide bombing is an act that comes within paragraph (a) or (b) of the definition *terrorist activity* in subsection (1) if it satisfies the criteria of that paragraph.

(2) For the purposes of this Part, facilitation shall be construed in accordance with subsection 83.19(2) [43].

3.1.4.5 Case Hypothetical: National Security Offences/Cyberterrorism

In analyzing national security and offences relating to cyberterrorism, it is first necessary to determine whether the attack was targeted, coordinated, and persistent, or it was diffuse, opportunistic, and random. The second item of analysis requires the determination of whether the attack actually succeeded in "terrorizing" the intended target.

For example, first imagine that there is a power blackout affecting your entire neighborhood. After 30 minutes, the lights briefly come back on for a moment—everyone is relieved—and then the lights go out again. In this scenario, there are numerous possible explanations for the cause of the blackout and, in most cases, those affected might never find out the underlying reason after the incident has been resolved.

If we were to compare the neighborhood blackout hypothetical to a blackout that is localized to the apartment of a specific person, the perceived threat, experience of "terror" and the psychological impact will be vastly different than that experienced in the neighborhood blackout. Imagine that, instead of a neighborhood, the target is an individual who experiences a sudden localized power blackout but is unable to locate the problem or restore the power to their apartment. Suddenly the power is restored and the lights go back on. After ten minutes, the power switches off again, and then back on. This continues. First at ten minutes intervals for half an hour, then 9-minute intervals for half an hour, then 8 minutes, then 7... and so on.

How would you feel by the time the power was going off and back on again every minute?

Analytically, the only two differences between these two hypotheticals that are important to us are: (a) the distance between the attacker and the intended target, and (b) the psychological resonance effect emanating from the attack—that is, how terrifying the experience is perceived to be by the target or targets of the attack. When we extend this to the level of national security offences, the same principles of determining the distance between the attacker and the target and psychological resonance of the attack for the target are magnified.

3.2 Growing Prevalence of Cybercrime

Where the Internet and its related technologies have been fundamental in reshaping global societies and economies, they have changed the criminal landscape fundamentally. Online marketplaces, anonymous forums, and Internet-connected devices provide the same opportunities and benefits for serious and organized criminal networks as they do for legitimate businesses. Through new and evolving information technologies, criminals are expanding their reach to commit entirely new crimes and old crimes in new and creative ways [44].

The vast popularity and ever-increasing interconnectedness of our mobile devices have made them an especially attractive target for criminal exploitation, with malware increasingly being developed to target vulnerabilities found within our mobile operating systems. Mobile device features, including text messaging and downloadable applications, can be used to deploy malware and gain unauthorized remote access to those same mobile platforms. This can be done for a variety of illicit purposes including, but not at all limited to: interception or theft of personal data; obtaining GPS coordinates; cyber-surveillance; revenge porn; and cyberstalking [45].

Widespread months-long lockdowns of cities around the world during the COVID-19 pandemic have shown that we are more dependent on our ties with technology than ever before. With this reliance must come an increase in legal protective measures to prevent malicious actors from causing widespread harm to individuals, businesses, organizations, and governments [46].

Widely available, ready-made malware and other hacking tools provide both professional and amateur criminals with new and simplified ways to steal information and financially impact businesses and individuals. Criminal activities in cyberspace are complex and often transnational, where potential evidence can be transient or spread across multiple legal jurisdictions. As so many facets of our daily lives move to online and cloud-based forums, such online criminal activity should be a growing concern for everyone. Addressing these challenges requires both domestic and international cooperation and legislative engagement with public and private sector organizations.

3.3 Categorizing Cybercrimes in the Law

In Table 3.1, we can see how the different varieties of cybercriminal activities are classified and categorized to gain a better understanding of the intricate landscape of cybersecurity laws within the global domain.

In Fig. 3.2, we can see the classifications and categories of cybercriminal activity arranged as a visual taxonomy.

Table 3.1 Classifications and categories of cybercriminal offences

Classification	Offence	Method
Cyber-enabled	Digital/electronic theft	Online or enabled by a computer or network system
Cyber-enabled	Copyright infringement	Online or enabled by a computer or network system
Cyber-enabled	Identity theft	Online or enabled by a computer or network system
Cyber-enabled	Identity fraud	Online or enabled by a computer or network system
Cyber-enabled	Phishing	Online or enabled by a computer or network system
Cyber-enabled	Revenge porn	Online or enabled by a computer or network system
Cyber-enabled	Extortion	Online or enabled by a computer or network system
Cyber-enabled	Voyeurism	Online or enabled by a computer or network system
Cyber-enabled	Child sexual exploitation	Online or enabled by a computer or network system
Cyber-enabled	Child abuse material	Online or enabled by a computer or network system
Cyber-enabled	Cyberbullying	Online or enabled by a computer or network system
Cyber-enabled	Online harassment	Online or enabled by a computer or network system
Cyber-enabled	Traditional crime; online	Online or enabled by a computer or network system
Cyber-enabled	Money laundering	Online or enabled by a computer or network system
Cyber-enabled	Trafficking in persons	Online or enabled by a computer or network system
Cyber-enabled	Trafficking in illegal items	Online or enabled by a computer or network system
Cyber-dependent	Unauthorized access	Hacking
Cyber-dependent	Modification of data	Hacking
Cyber-dependent	Impairment of data	Hacking
Cyber-dependent	Interception of data	Hacking
Cyber-dependent	Misuse of devices	Hacking
Cyber-dependent	Engaging in deceptive interactions	Attacking
Cyber-dependent	Abusing existing functionality	Attacking

(continued)

Table 3.1 (continued)

Classification	Offence	Method
Cyber-dependent	Manipulating data structures	Attacking
Cyber-dependent	Manipulating system resources	Attacking
Cyber-dependent	Manipulating timing and state	Attacking
Cyber-dependent	Injecting unexpected items	Attacking
Cyber-dependent	Employing probabilistic techniques	Attacking
Cyber-dependent	Collecting and analyzing information	Attacking
Cyber-dependent	Subverting access control	Attacking
Computer / Cyber-supported	Any offence which is neither cyber-enabled nor cyber-dependent	Incidental involvement of computer system or network which is connected, but neither necessary nor enabling, to the commission of the offence
Cyberterrorism	Incursion	Hacking/attacking
Cyberterrorism	Destruction	Hacking/attacking
Cyberterrorism	Disinformation	Hacking/attacking
Cyberterrorism	Denial of service	Hacking/attacking
Cyberterrorism	Defacement of websites	Hacking/attacking

3.4 Summary

In this chapter, we have discussed the four categories of cybercrime: (1) cyber-enabled; (2) cyber-dependent; (3) computer or cyber-supported; and (4) national security offences, or cyberterrorism. In each of those categories, we have broken down the specific types of digital criminal activity and described each of them. Finally, we outlined the growing prevalence of cybercrime within our modern and increasingly digital societies. The answers to the following questions are provided within this chapter:

1. What are the four main categories of cybercrime?
2. How do cyber-enabled crimes differ from cyber-dependant or cyber-supported crimes?
3. What are three examples of Malware?
4. What is a spamming botnet attack?
5. What distinguishes Cyberterrorism from other cybercriminal activities?
6. What is the importance of the DarkNet with regard to cybersecurity and data privacy law?

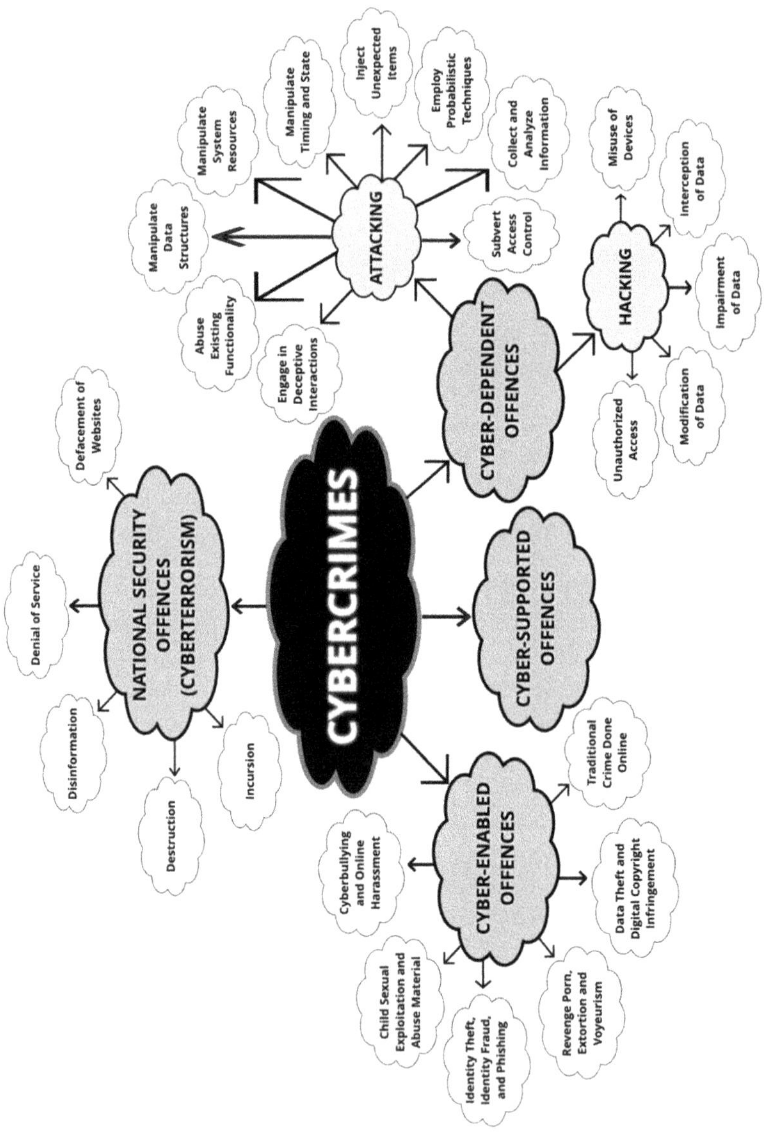

Fig. 3.2 Cybercrime taxonomy tree

References

1. Clough, J., & Einstein, A. (2015). Principles of cybercrime.
2. Ram, C. (2016). Jonathan Clough, Principles of Cybercrime, (Cambridge: Cambridge University Press, 2015). *Canadian Journal of Law and Technology, 14*(1).
3. Jamieson, R., Land, L. P. W., Winchester, D., Stephens, G., Steel, A., Maurushat, A., & Sarre, R. (2012). Addressing identity crime in crime management information systems: Definitions, classification, and empirics. *Computer Law & Security Review, 28*(4), 381–395.
4. Jahankhani, H., Al-Nemrat, A., & Hosseinian-Far, A. (2014). Cybercrime classification and characteristics. In *Cyber crime and cyber terrorism investigator's handbook* (pp. 149–164). Syngress.
5. Urbas, G. (2015). *Cybercrime legislation, cases and commentary*. LexisNexis Butterworths.
6. Criminal Code of Canada (RSC, 1985, c C-46), s 162.1(2).
7. Aikenhead, M. (2018). A reasonable expectation of sexual privacy in the digital age. *Dalhousie LJ, 41*, 273.
8. Popham, J., McCluskey, M., Ouellet, M., & Gallupe, O. (2020). Exploring police-reported cybercrime in Canada: Variation and correlates. *Policing: An International Journal.*
9. Marcum, C. D., & Higgins, G. E. (2019). Cybercrime. In *Handbook on crime and deviance* (pp. 459–475). Springer.
10. Loader, B. D., & Thomas, D. (Eds.). (2013). *Cybercrime: Security and surveillance in the information age*. Routledge.
11. Briandana, R., Oktavianingtyas, I., & Marta, R. F. (2020). Cybercrime in online dating site: Pornography business in the virtual world.
12. Al-Garadi, M. A., Varathan, K. D., & Ravana, S. D. (2016). Cybercrime detection in online communications: The experimental case of cyberbullying detection in the Twitter network. *Computers in Human Behavior, 63*, 433–443.
13. Buono, L. (2014, June). Fighting cybercrime through prevention, outreach and awareness raising. In ERA Forum (Vol. 15, No. 1, pp. 1-8). Springer .
14. Aiken, M., Mc Mahon, C., Haughton, C., O'Neill, L., & O'Carroll, E. (2016). A consideration of the social impact of cybercrime: Examples from hacking, piracy, and child abuse material online. *Contemporary Social Science, 11*(4), 373–391.
15. Lee, H. E., Ermakova, T., Ververis, V., & Fabian, B. (2020). Detecting child sexual abuse material: A comprehensive survey. *Forensic Science International: Digital Investigation, 34*, 301022.
16. Aiken, M., Moran, M., & Berry, M. J. (2011, September). Child abuse material and the Internet: Cyberpsychology of online child related sex offending. In *29th meeting of the INTERPOL Specialist Group on Crimes against Children, Lyons, France, September* (pp. 5–7).
17. ECPAT International. (2018, April). *Trends in online child sexual abuse material*. ECPAT International.
18. United States Department of Justice. (2020). "Subject Areas" and "Citizen's Guide to U.-S. Federal Child Exploitation Laws" in About the Criminal Division: Child Exploitation and Obscenity Section, United States Department of Justice. https://www.justice.gov/criminal-ceos/citizens-guide-us-federal-child-exploitation-and-obscenity-laws
19. Attorney General Eric Holder Jr. Speaks at the National Strategy Conference on Combating Child Exploitation in San Jose, California, May 19, 2011.
20. Title 18, U.S.C., §—
21. Moise, A. C. (2017). The legal regulation of cybercrime in the United States of America legislation. *Journal of Advanced Research in Law and Economics (JARLE), 8*(27), 1576–1578.
22. Maimon, D., & Louderback, E. R. (2019). Cyber-dependent crimes: An interdisciplinary review. *Annual Review of Criminology, 2*, 191–216.
23. Clough, J. (2011, March). Data theft? Cybercrime and the increasing criminalization of access to data. In Criminal Law Forum (Vol. 22, No. 1, pp. 145-170). Springer.

24. Li, F., Clarke, N., Papadaki, M., & Dowland, P. (2011). Misuse detection for mobile devices using behaviour profiling. *International Journal of Cyber Warfare and Terrorism (IJCWT), 1* (1), 41–53.
25. Comprehensive study on cybercrime. Support section, organized crime branch, division for treaty affairs, United Nations Office on Drugs and Crime (UNODC), 2013. https://www.unodc.org/documents/organized-crime/UNODC_CCPCJ_EG.4_2013/UNODC_CCPCJ_EG4_2013_2_E.pdf.
26. Hathaway, O. A., Crootof, R., Levitz, P., Nix, H., Nowlan, A., Perdue, W., & Spiegel, J. (2012). The law of cyber-attack. *California Law Review*, 817–885.
27. Ganeshkumar, K., Arivazhagan, D., & Sundaram, S. (2013). Strategies of cybercrime: Viruses and security sphere. *Journal of Academia and Industrial Research (JAIR), 2*(7), 397–401.
28. Huang, K., Siegel, M., & Madnick, S. (2018). Systematically understanding the cyber attack business: A survey. *ACM Computing Surveys (CSUR), 51*(4), 1–36.
29. Common Attack Pattern Enumeration and Classification (CAPEC), https://capec.mitre.org/index.html
30. Sharma, P., Doshi, D., & Prajapati, M. M. (2016, November). Cybercrime: Internal security threat. In *2016 international conference on ICT in business industry & government (ICTBIG)* (pp. 1–4). IEEE.
31. Brenner, S. W. (2012). Cybercrime and the law: Challenges, issues, and outcomes. UPNE.
32. Sabillon, R., Cano, J. J., Cavaller Reyes, V., & Serra Ruiz, J. (2016). Cybercrime and cybercriminals: A comprehensive study. *International Journal of Computer Networks and Communications Security, 4*(6).
33. Provos, N., Rajab, M. A., & Mavrommatis, P. (2009). Cybercrime 2.0: When the cloud turns dark. *Communications of the ACM, 52*(4), 42–47.
34. An, J., & Kim, H. W. (2018). A data analytics approach to the cybercrime underground economy. *IEEE Access, 6*, 26636–26652.
35. Smith, G. S. (2015). Management models for international cybercrime. *Journal of Financial Crime.*
36. Al Abdulwahid, A., Clarke, N., Furnell, S., Stengel, I., & Reich, C. (2015, April). The current use of authentication technologies: an investigative review. In *2015 International Conference on Cloud Computing (ICCC)* (pp. 1–8). IEEE.
37. Director of Public Prosecutions (DPP) v McKeown and Jones [1997] 2 Cr. App. R. 155, HL, at page 163.
38. Council of Europe, Convention on Cybercrime, 23 November 2001. Available at: https://www.refworld.org/docid/47fdfb202.html
39. Marsili, M. (2019). The war on cyberterrorism. *Democracy and Security, 15*(2), 172–199.
40. Denning, E. Dorothy, testimony before the special oversight panel on committee on armed services US house of representatives, "cyber terrorism", 23 may 2000. *URL.*: http://www.cs.georgetown.edu/~denning/infosec/cyberterror.html. https://web.archive.org/web/20140310162011/http://www.cs.georgetown.edu/~denning/infosec/cyberterror.html
41. Brewster, B., Kemp, B., Galehbakhtiari, S., & Akhgar, B. (2015). Cybercrime: attack motivations and implications for big data and national security. In *Application of big data for national security* (pp. 108–127). Butterworth-Heinemann.
42. Al Mazari, A., Anjariny, A. H., Habib, S. A., & Nyakwende, E. (2018). Cyber terrorism taxonomies: Definition, targets, patterns, risk factors, and mitigation strategies. In *Cyber security and threats: Concepts, methodologies, tools, and applications* (pp. 608–621). IGI Global.
43. Criminal Code (RSC, 1985, c C-46).
44. Greer, B. (2017). The growth of cybercrime in the United States. *Growth.*
45. Tountas, S. W. (2003). Carnivore: Is the regulation of wireless technology a legally viable option to curtail the growth of cybercrime. *Wash UJL & Pol'y, 11*, 351.
46. Naidoo, R. (2020). A multi-level influence model of COVID-19 themed cybercrime. *European Journal of Information Systems, 29*(3), 306–321.

Global Relevance

4

In 2020, with the dawn of a new decade ahead of us—the 2020s—many of us looked back at the end of 2019 and the start of 2020 as a turning point; an opportunity for a fresh start. At that point in time, we had no idea of the dramatic social, educational, and occupational changes that this year would have in store for us all. While the new decade has not yet been the vibrant beacon of social and technological advancement that we may have hoped for, our global entry into 2020 has undoubtedly been a rollercoaster. From widespread mandatory isolation, necessarily remote workspaces and increased civilian interaction with public health authorities, to the necessarily rapid introduction of digital communication technologies to populations who had previously been able to avoid developing a dependence on digital technology as a primary form of social interaction. All of these factors, and more, have contributed to the massive inundation of public reliance on digital communication technology and its corresponding infrastructure around the globe.

Much of this increase in technological reliance has long been foreseen; anticipated by researchers, academics, and the especially tech-savvy folks among us. What was not anticipated, however, was the sudden increase in the speed at which we have all had to adapt to these new realities. This past year, in particular, has necessitated a review and revitalization of our existing privacy, data protection, cybersecurity, and cybercrime laws in keeping with the ongoing effort to expand, revise, or otherwise rewrite the relevant legislation to accommodate for our rapidly-evolving global, national, and localized cybersecurity concerns.

With 2021 being a year of rapid, unprecedented, large-scale global change, the many necessarily proposed alterations to our current cybersecurity-related laws have quickly shifted to the forefront of national security discussion. While some of the existing laws have adequately covered personal privacy and related provisions and detailed the legal provisions for criminal offences, there remains an increasingly ominous lack of comprehensive cybersecurity-specific legislation and cybercrime-specific criminal law provisions under our existing many existing national legal structures. When so many features and daily facets of our lives are digitally

M. Lukings, A. Habibi Lashkari, *Understanding Cybersecurity Law and Digital Privacy*, Future of Business and Finance, https://doi.org/10.1007/978-3-030-88704-9_4

connected to a larger network upon which our daily activities and interactions have become reliant, the idea that our national security and digital infrastructure may be at risk of exploitation or malicious interference is highly concerning.

This past year, in the era of the global COVID-19 pandemic, has helped to effectively highlight many of the legislative gaps and other areas in need of improvement within our current national legislative scheme. One possible explanation for this gap is the reality that the speed of technological development increased far too quickly, when compared with the adaptation of our federal legislation, to allow for the construction of adequately tailored legal accommodations. Posited from an adjusted position, another explanation of the same result is that the legislation did not adapt quickly enough to keep up with the inevitable (and arguably foreseeable) advances in data technology and digital communication that we have seen and continue to see.

Fortunately, we are not alone. Indeed, many other countries are experiencing the same push to revise and re-evaluate legislative structures which had, until very recently, been adequately effective at regulating privacy relations and general data protection. In this chapter, we will outline the relevant national privacy and cybersecurity-related laws currently in effect in Canada, Australia, the United Kingdom, and the United States, as examples of cybersecurity-related legal provisions in common law countries.

4.1 Review of Canadian Cybersecurity Laws

Countries that follow the common law legal system, including Canada, the United Kingdom, Australia, and the United States are considered to be "common law countries." The basis for the common law legal system relies upon a body of customary law; the body of unwritten laws based on legal precedents established by the courts in previous judicial decisions.

In addition to being common law countries, Canada, the United Kingdom, Australia, and the United States each have specific statutory provisions which apply to identity theft and fraud, copyright infringement, patents and intellectual property, commercial electronic messages, and general criminal provisions. We can start by reviewing the current laws in Canada before outing the laws in effect in Australia, the United Kingdom, and the United States, respectively.

4.1.1 Regulating Governmental Relationships

The *Privacy Act* and the *Access to Information Act* were both implemented by the Canadian federal government in 1985 and have acted as a starting point for more recent legislation and privacy laws, including those pertaining to the cyber sector. These Acts work together to provide a legislative framework for personal data collection, use, retention, disclosure, and individual access within the federal public sector.

4.1.1.1 Privacy Act (RSC 1985, c P-21)

The *Privacy Act* regulates governmental bodies' access to the information of individuals. The *Privacy Act* is the legal framework governing personal information in the federal public sector. It explains how personal information must be protected in the relationships between individuals and the federal government [1].

4.1.1.2 Access to Information Act (RSC 1985, c A-1)

The *Access to Information Act*, in contrast, serves to provide a method for individuals to access their own personal information as held by those governmental bodies. The fundamental key to the *Access to Information Act* is the "right of access." This legislation is overseen by the Information Commissioner of Canada [2].

4.1.2 Regulating Businesses, Organizations, and Commercial Enterprises

The commercial marketplace, including private businesses, corporations, and organizations, must abide by the provisions established in the *Personal Information Protection and Electronic Documents Act* and by the rules regulating the use of commercial electronic messages in *Canada's Anti-Spam Legislation*.

4.1.2.1 PIPEDA (SC 2000, c 5)

The *Personal Information Protection and Electronic Documents Act,* otherwise known as PIPEDA, officially became law in 2000 as a means to help grow consumer trust in both electronic commerce and the digital economy.

The PIPEDA applies specifically to private-sector organizations; which are operating either fully or partially in Canada; and that collect, use, or disclose personal information in the course of commercial activities. For the purposes of this legislation, the law defines a commercial activity as any particular transaction, act, or conduct, or any regular course of conduct that is of a commercial character, including the selling, bartering or leasing of donor, membership or other fundraising lists.

Private-sector organizations that fit into this category are bound by the provisions of the *Personal Information Protection and Electronic Documents Act* to apply the provided privacy principles to protect consumer information exchanged during commercial activities. These provisions aim to protect the privacy of those individuals, specific subsets, and targeted groups of individuals, or organizations from whom the personal information has been gathered.

Exemptions to PIPEDA arise when a province already has its own privacy legislation. Those provinces are currently: Alberta, British Columbia, and Quebec. PIPEDA provisions can also be applied specifically to personal health information collected or handled in the provinces of: Ontario, New Brunswick, Newfoundland and Labrador, and Nova Scotia. These exemptions to PIPEDA apply only where the commercial activity actually took place within the relevant province [3].

4.1.2.2 Canada's Anti-Spam Legislation (SC 2010, c 23)

Canada's Anti-Spam Legislation (CASL), is the federal law that addresses spam and other electronic threats. It established the rules for sending commercial electronic messages and the installation of computer programs. As defined in CASL, "spam" refers to unwanted or unsolicited commercial electronic messages received over the internet. As defined, a "commercial electronic message" is an electronically received message that encourages participation in a commercial activity, such as an email that contains a coupon or tells customers about a promotion or sale.

CASL aims to protect consumers and businesses from the misuse of digital technology, including spamming and other non-consensual activities. It applies to all electronic messages sent by businesses and organizations in connection with a "commercial activity"—that is, electronic messages sent in hopes of encouraging engagement from the consumer, with the ultimate purpose being to make a profit. The key distinguishing feature of this legislation is the requirement that Canadian (and global) organizations that send commercial electronic messages within, from, or to Canada must receive express consent from recipients prior to sending those messages [4].

This strategy goes much further than regulating the bulk, unsolicited email communications, which we know as spam. *Canada's Anti-Spam Legislation* creates an "express consent-based regime" that applies to almost all electronic messages which are sent for any commercial purpose. There are five full exemptions to the CASL requirements, a few specified categories of implied consent, and a partial exemption for third-party referral messages.

The legislation has penalties for non-compliance with anti-spam provisions. When the CASL requirements are not followed, corporate directors, officers, and agents can be held liable for corporations, and corporations can be held liable for the actions of their employees. For corporations, fines can be up to $100,000 for the first offence and $250,000 for repeat offences. For individuals, fines can be $10,000 for a first offence and $25,000 for subsequent offences. Penalties for violating the legislation can be as severe as $1 million for individuals and $10 million for businesses.

4.1.3 Regulating Interpersonal Relationships and Criminal Activities

Criminal law provisions in Canada are governed by federal legislation in the *Criminal Code of Canada* which outlines the relevant criminal offences, features required to make a criminal offence, the procedures, possible defences, and sentencing rules for the criminal courts. Civil courts are guided by tort law and presidential common law, rather than overarching federal legislation.

4.1.3.1 Criminal Code (RSC (1985), c C-46)

The *Criminal Code of Canada* provides the Canadian criminal justice system with the applicable laws, offences, defences, procedures, and penalties for those who are charged and convicted of a criminal offence. Malicious parties participating in cybercriminal activity can be divided into cyber-enabled crimes and cyber-supported crimes.

Cyber/computer-enabled activities with corresponding *Criminal Code* provisions include hacking, possession of "hacking tools," denial-of-service attacks, distributed denial of service attacks, botnets, malware, phishing, identity theft and identity fraud, and criminal copyright infringement.

Cyber/computer-supported activities can be thought of as traditional crimes which are committed through a cyber medium. For example, child trafficking is a criminal offence regardless of the medium over which the exchange is made or the forum used for the transaction. If a child trafficking offence is committed through the use of DarkNets, encrypted or anonymous networks, or otherwise supported by cyber technology, then the crime is a cyber-supported crime [5].

4.1.3.2 Protecting Canadians from Online Crime Act (SC 2014, c 31)

The *Protecting Canadians from Online Crime Act* came into force on March 10, 2015, and was intended to address the problem of cyberbullying after the high-profile suicide deaths of Rehtaeh Parsons and Amanda Todd. This Act, among other things, amended the *Criminal Code* to create a new offence for the non-consensual distribution of intimate images.

This is given under s. 162.1(1) where "everyone who knowingly publishes, distributes, transmits, sells, makes available or advertises an intimate image of a person knowing that the person depicted in the image did not give their consent to that conduct, or being reckless as to whether or not that person gave their consent to that conduct is guilty of an indictable offence and liable to imprisonment for a term of not more than five years; or of an offence punishable on summary conviction" [6].

4.1.3.3 Common Law and Civil Tort Law

In January 2012, the case of *Jones v Tsige* (2012 ONCA 32) became a landmark case in the Ontario Court of Appeal for recognizing the "new" privacy tort of "intrusion upon seclusion," which allows victims of such privacy breaches to have the right to sue the privacy breacher in civil court for invasion of privacy. In this case, the Ontario Court of Appeal found that the Canadian common law was required to evolve in order to effectively respond to more modern privacy issues. This includes those which have arisen from technological changes and the constantly evolving need to reassess how personal information is collected, stored, protected, and made accessible in electronic form.

Jones v Tsige involved a bank employee who accessed and reviewed another employee's personal bank accounts on 174 occasions over a 4-year period. When the victim became aware of this, she sued the defendant. The victim claimed that by improperly accessing and reviewing her bank accounts the defendant committed the tort of invasion of privacy. In response, the defendant argued that Ontario does not recognize the invasion of privacy as a tort.

Following a thorough review of the case law and previous legal commentary related to the "invasion of privacy" tort, Ontario Court of Appeal Justice Sharpe concluded that "Ontario has already accepted the existence of a tort claim for appropriation of personality and, at the very least, remains open to the proposition that a tort action will lie for an intrusion upon seclusion" [7].

The *Canadian Charter of Rights and Freedoms* protects the right to privacy under s. 8. Although the *Charter* cannot apply in a civil case, the Court considered the idea that the common law should evolve and develop consistently with *Charter* values to be most effective in our modern circumstances. Justice Sharpe noted that the existing case law establishes that personal privacy is worthy of constitutional protection and that it is integral to the relationship between individuals and the rest of society. He then combined this explicit *Charter* recognition with the idea that the common law should evolve and develop consistently with *Charter* values. In Justice Sharpe's view, there was already ample support to recognize a civil action for damages (aka: a lawsuit) for "intrusion upon seclusion" as a tort. He described it as follows:

> *...the tort includes physical intrusions into private places as well as listening or looking, with or without mechanical aids, into the plaintiff's private affairs. Of particular relevance to this appeal, is the observation that other non-physical forms of investigation or examination into private concerns may be actionable. These include opening private and personal mail or examining a private bank account.*
> — ONCA Justice Sharpe [7]

And just like that, the common law tort of "intrusion upon seclusion" was born.

This common law tort, in conjunction with the provisions given in the *Protecting Canadians from Online Crime Act*, the *Criminal Code of Canada*, *Canada's Anti-Spam Legislation* (CASL), the *Personal Information Protection and Electronic Documents Act* (PIPEDA), the *Access to Information Act*, and the *Privacy Act*, make up the majority of Canada's currently existing data privacy and cybersecurity-related federal legislation.

4.2 Review of Australian Cybersecurity Laws

In Australia, the legislative powers are divided between the national government (called the Commonwealth) and the six States (New South Wales, Queensland, South Australia, Tasmania, Victoria, and Western Australia) and three Territories (Australian Capital Territory, Northern Territory, and Norfolk Island) within the greater nation.

4.2.1 Regulating Governmental, Business, and Organizational Relationships

Within the Australian Commonwealth, cybersecurity laws for government and corporations are guided by the *Privacy Act 1988*, the *Privacy Amendment 2012*, and the *Privacy Regulation 2013*. The 13 Australian Privacy Principles included in the *Privacy Act* legislation are to be applied in guiding the development of privacy protocols in these organizations. The use of commercial electronic messages is regulated by the *Spam Act 2003*.

4.2.1.1 Privacy Act 1988 (Cth)

Australia's *Privacy Act 1988* is the foundational piece of Australian legislation that protects the handling of personal information, including the collection, use, storage, and disclosure of personal information in the federal public sector and the private sector. The *Privacy Act* and the 13 Australian Privacy Principles apply to all organizations which carry out business in Australia which include actively collecting personal information.

Other statutory provisions also affect privacy and separate privacy regimes apply to state and territory public sectors. This department assists the Attorney-General to administer the *Privacy Act*. The *Privacy Act* is supported by the *Privacy Amendment (Enhancing Privacy Protection) Act 2012*, and the *Privacy Regulation 2013*.

The Notifiable Data Breaches scheme was implemented as part of the *Privacy Act* in February 2018. This scheme requires notification to all affected individuals and to the Office of the Australian Information Commissioner (OAIC) when a party who is subject to the *Privacy Act* experiences a data breach of personal information which poses a likely risk of serious harm to the affected individuals [8].

4.2.1.2 Australian Privacy Principles (APPs)

With the enacting of the *Privacy Amendment (Enhancing Privacy Protection) Act 2012*, the *Privacy Act* outlines 13 Australian Privacy Principles (APPs) which apply to government agencies and to private sector organizations with an annual turnover of $3 million or more. The APPs are "principles-based" with the aim of protecting individual privacy while simultaneously not overburdening agencies and organizations with inflexible, and potentially expensive, prescriptivist rules.

The Australian Privacy Principles deal with all stages of the processing of personal information. They set out the standards for the collection, use, disclosure, quality, and security of personal information, and they provide obligations concerning access to, and correction of, an individual's own personal information for agencies and organizations which are subject to the *Privacy Act*.

This is overseen by the Office of the Australian Information Commissioner—the independent national regulator for privacy and freedom of information which promotes and upholds the right of individuals to access government-held information and have their personal information protected—within the Australian Government. The 13 Australian Privacy Principles are summarized on the OAIC website as:

- *Principle 1—Open and transparent management of personal information*
  This ensures that APP entities manage personal information in an open and transparent way and includes having a clearly expressed and up-to-date APP privacy policy.
- *Principle 2—Anonymity and pseudonymity*
  Requires APP entities to give individuals the option of not identifying themselves, or of using a pseudonym. Limited exceptions apply.

- *Principle 3—Collection of solicited personal information*
  Outlines when an APP entity can collect personal information that is solicited. It applies higher standards to the collection of "'sensitive"' information.
- *Principle 4—Dealing with unsolicited personal information*
  Outlines how APP entities must deal with unsolicited personal information.
- *Principle 5—Notification of the collection of personal information*
  Outlines when and in what circumstances an APP entity that collects personal information must notify an individual of certain matters.
- *Principle 6—Use or disclosure of personal information*
  Outlines the circumstances in which an APP entity may use or disclose personal information that it holds.
- *Principle 7—Direct marketing*
  An organization may only use or disclose personal information for direct marketing purposes if certain conditions are met.
- *Principle 8—Cross-border disclosure of personal information*
  Outlines the steps an APP entity must take to protect personal information before it is disclosed overseas.
- *Principle 9—Adoption, use, or disclosure of government related identifiers*
  Outlines the limited circumstances when an organization may adopt a government-related identifier of an individual as its own identifier, or use or disclose a government-related identifier of an individual.
- *Principle 10—Quality of personal information*
  An APP entity must take reasonable steps to ensure the personal information it collects is accurate, up to date, and complete. An entity must also take reasonable steps to ensure the personal information it uses or discloses is accurate, up to date, complete and relevant, having regard to the purpose of the use or disclosure.
- *Principle 11—Security of personal information*
  An APP entity must take reasonable steps to protect personal information it holds from misuse, interference, and loss, and from unauthorized access, modification, or disclosure. An entity has obligations to destroy or de-identify personal information in certain circumstances.
- *Principle 12—Access to personal information*
  Outlines an APP entity's obligations when an individual requests to be given access to personal information held about them by the entity. This includes a requirement to provide access unless a specific exception applies.
- *Principle 13—Correction of personal information*
  Outlines an APP entity's obligations in relation to correcting the personal information it holds about individuals [9].

The OAIC is responsible for investigating breaches of the APPs and credit reporting provisions. The OAIC has the power to accept enforceable undertakings, seek civil penalties in the case of serious or repeated breaches of privacy, and conduct assessments of privacy performances for both Australian Government agencies and businesses.

4.2.1.3 Australian Government Agencies Privacy Code 2017

The *Australian Government Agencies Privacy Code* was registered in October 2017 and went into effect on July 1, 2018. It applies to all Australian governmental agencies who are subject to the *Privacy Act 1988* (except for Ministers) and sets out the specific requirements and key practical steps that must be taken in order to comply with the Australian Privacy Principles.

In effect, the *Australian Government Agencies Privacy Code 2017* enhances existing privacy capability within agencies, builds greater transparency in information handling practices, and fosters a culture of respect for privacy and the value of personal information. It requires government agencies to move towards a "best practice" approach to privacy governance in order to help to create a consistent, high standard of personal information collection and management across all Australian government agencies.

We can summarize the thirteen Australian Privacy Principles in the form of a table, as below in Table 4.1.

4.2.1.4 Spam Act 2003 (Cth)

The *Spam Act 2003* was passed by the Australian Parliament in 2003 to regulate commercial e-mail and other types of commercial electronic messages. The Act restricts the prevalence of spam, particularly email spam and some types of phone spam, as well as the harvesting of email addresses.

Specifically, the *Spam Act 2003* provides that unsolicited commercial electronic messages must not be sent unless they are "designated commercial electronic messages." As well, the messages must include information about the individual or organization who authorized the sending of the messages and must also contain a functional unsubscribe (or "opt-out") option. In addition, address-harvesting software, or electronic address lists produced using address-harvesting software, must not be supplied, acquired, or used [10].

The legal remedies given for breaches of the *Spam Act 2003* are predominantly civil penalties, punitive fines, and injunctions.

4.2.2 Regulating Interpersonal Relationships and Criminal Activities

Most of the criminal law provisions in Australia are created and administered by the six individual States (New South Wales, Queensland, South Australia, Tasmania, Victoria, and Western Australia) and three Territories (Australian Capital Territory, Northern Territory, and Norfolk Island) of Australia. However, there is a body of criminal law, including the *Criminal Code Act 1995*, which is made and administered by the federal government.

4.2.2.1 Crimes Act 1914 (Cth)

Australia's *Crimes Act 1914* is one of the first recognizable compilations of federal criminal law since federation in 1901. The *Crimes Act 1914* deals with the most

Table 4.1 Australian privacy principles

APP number	Name of principle	Purposive description
Principle One	Open and transparent management of personal information	This ensures that APP entities manage personal information in an open and transparent way and includes having a clearly expressed and up-to-date APP privacy policy.
Principle Two	Anonymity and pseudonymity	Requires APP entities to give individuals the option of not identifying themselves, or of using a pseudonym. Limited exceptions apply.
Principle Three	Collection of solicited personal information	Outlines when an APP entity can collect personal information that is solicited. It applies higher standards to the collection of "'sensitive"' information.
Principle Four	Dealing with unsolicited personal information	Outlines how APP entities must deal with unsolicited personal information.
Principle Five	Notification of the collection of personal information	Outlines when and in what circumstances an APP entity that collects personal information must notify an individual of certain matters.
Principle Six	Use or disclosure of personal information	Outlines the circumstances in which an APP entity may use or disclose personal information that it holds. Use or disclosure of personal information
Principle Seven	Direct marketing	An organization may only use or disclose personal information for direct marketing purposes if certain conditions are met.
Principle Eight	Cross-border disclosure of personal information	Outlines the steps an APP entity must take to protect personal information before it is disclosed overseas.
Principle Nine	Adoption, use, or disclosure of government related identifiers	Outlines the limited circumstances when an organization may adopt a government related identifier of an individual as its own identifier, or use or disclose a government related identifier of an individual
Principle Ten	Quality of personal information	An APP entity must take reasonable steps to ensure the personal information it collects is accurate, up to date, and complete. An entity must also take reasonable steps to ensure the personal information it uses or discloses is accurate, up to date, complete and relevant, having regard to the purpose of the use or disclosure.
Principle Eleven	Security of personal information	An APP entity must take reasonable steps to protect personal information it holds from misuse, interference, and loss, and from unauthorized access, modification, or disclosure. An entity has obligations to destroy or de-identify personal information in certain circumstances.

(continued)

Table 4.1 (continued)

APP number	Name of principle	Purposive description
Principle Twelve	Access to personal information	Outlines an APP entity's obligations when an individual requests to be given access to personal information held about them by the entity. This includes a requirement to provide access unless a specific exception applies.
Principle Thirteen	Correction of personal information	Outlines an APP entity's obligations in relation to correcting the personal information it holds about individuals.

serious criminal offences against the Commonwealth. Historically, it was the most extensive legislative instrument addressing federal criminal offences but is now being superseded with the passing of the *Criminal Code Act 1995 (Cth)*, which is a compilation of all the federal offences in Australia [11].

4.2.2.2 Criminal Code Act 1995 (Cth)

Apart from the criminalization of specific activities, Australian law also presents a means to legally address wrongdoing in civil law, which relates to non-criminal law including civil wrongs, contract law, property law, and other areas that concern the rights and duties of individuals amongst themselves [12].

4.2.2.3 Common Law and Civil Tort Law

As in Canadian civil tort law and, unless barred by an existing statute, individuals are entitled to sue other people, or the state, for the purpose of obtaining a civil legal remedy for a legally recognized "tort" or wrongdoing. However, to sue someone in tort law, requires the pre-existence or creation of an applicable tort, through the common law, case law, or challenge in a court. At the time of writing, there is currently no federal or state legislation articulating a specific cause of action for breach of privacy in Australian law.

Although privacy protections exist in the *Privacy Act 1988 (Cth)*, those provisions do not apply to individuals who are not operating a business, businesses with an annual turnover of less than $3 million, media organizations, members of a parliament, contractors for political representatives, and individual volunteers for registered political parties. In 2014, the Australian Law Reform Commission formally recommended the creation of a tort for "serious invasions of privacy" to the federal government in their final report on Serious Invasions of Privacy in the Digital Era.

Although there is no established common law tort to pursue civil causes of action in Australia, the *Criminal Code Act 1995 (Cth)*, in conjunction with the provisions given in the *Spam Act 2003*, the *Australian Government Agencies Privacy Code 2017*, *Privacy Act 1988*, including the *Privacy Amendment 2012*, and the *Privacy Regulation 2013*, make up the majority of Australia's currently existing data privacy and cybersecurity-related federal legislation.

4.3 Review of United Kingdom Cybersecurity Laws

In the United Kingdom, as we have seen in other countries, there is no overarching comprehensive national cybersecurity law, although the *European Union's General Data Protection Regulation* (GDPR), in which the United Kingdom was a member party, came pretty close. For government, businesses, and other private-sector organizations, the UK's *General Data Protection Regulation* (UK-GDPR), the *Data Protection Act 2018*, and the *NIS Regulations* make up the bulk of the law relating to cybersecurity law and risk mitigation in the United Kingdom. For individuals and malicious parties, the UK's *Computer Misuse Act*, which was implemented back in 1990, continues to be a primary law at the forefront of interpersonal digital privacy, even 30 years later.

4.3.1 Regulating Government, Businesses, and Organizations

Government, businesses, and organizations in the United Kingdom are subject to the *General Data Protection Regulation* (GDPR), the *Data Protection Act 2018*, and the *NIS Regulations*. When the Brexit transition period concludes on December 31, 2020, the United Kingdom will have its own *UK General Data Protection Regulation* (UK-GDPR) which will work in conjunction with the current *Data Protection Act 2018*.

4.3.1.1 General Data Protection Regulations and Data Protection Act 2018

The collection, processing, use, and possession of personal data in the European Economic Area is governed by the *General Data Protection Regulation* (GDPR). The *Data Protection Act 2018* is essentially the UK's implementation of the European Economic Area's *General Data Protection Regulation*. Both the GDPR and the *Data Protection Act* require that government, public entities, private-sector businesses, corporations, and organizations reduce the risk of personal data loss and privacy breaches by implementing strict security measures in an effort to safeguard all personal data collected, processed, used, or held by that entity.

These laws require that personal data must be securely kept and access to personal data is only permitted to third parties subject to sufficient guarantees regarding the security of the processing services. They also require the implementation of technical (e.g., firewalls, anti-virus programs, specific software, perimeter scanning tools) and organizational (e.g., policies and procedures regarding cybersecurity) protective measures to safeguard personal data and protect against unauthorized or unlawful access, use, loss, destruction and damage of any personal data. It is interesting to note that, according to these laws, enforcement action to address inadequate safeguards can be taken even in the absence of a reported cyber-attack or personal data breach.

Businesses that are subject to the GDPR and the *Data Protection Act* are required to implement appropriate and proportionate measures to manage their risks. Failing to do so can result in enforcement action, including the imposition of significant fines of up to a maximum of the greater of £17.5 million or 4% of annual global turnover [13].

4.3.1.2 Network and Information Security Regulations 2018

The *Security of Network & Information Systems Regulations (NIS Regulations)* provide legal measures to boost the level of cybersecurity and physical resilience of network and information systems in the provision of essential, and digital, services. Whereas the GDPR is concerned with the security of personal data, the *NIS Regulations* are similarly concerned with the security of information systems.

The *NIS Regulations* establish a range of network and information security requirements and impose cybersecurity-related obligations which apply to operators of essential services and to digital service providers that offer services to individuals within the United Kingdom.

As with the obligations in the GDPR and *Data Protection Act 2018*, businesses subject to the obligations in the *NIS Regulations* have the freedom to determine which measures are appropriate and proportionate to adequately manage the risks posed to network and information systems and to prevent or minimize the impact of incidents which could affect the security of the network and information systems [14].

The penalty for a business failing to meet the requirements of the *NIS Regulations* can result in enforcement action, including the imposition of significant fines. The NIS Directive allows member states to set their thresholds. In the United Kingdom, the maximum penalty is £17 million.

4.3.2 Regulating Interpersonal Relationships and Criminal Activities

Criminal law provisions which mediate relationships between individuals, in the United Kingdom, are governed by federal law. The *Computer Misuse Act 1990* is the primary law dealing with nefarious online activities in the United Kingdom.

4.3.2.1 Computer Misuse Act 1990

The UK's *Computer Misuse Act 1990* criminalizes individuals who attempt to access or modify data on a computer without authorization. This extends to include cyber-attacks, such as malware or ransomware attacks, which seek to disrupt services, obtain information illegally and/or extort individuals or businesses. The *Computer Misuse Act 1990* was designed over 30 years ago with the intention of protecting telephone exchanges; when less than 0.5% of the UK population used the internet and long before our current normalization of network reliance, digital communication, smartphones, and unlimited data plans.

The first offence in the *Computer Misuse Act* is achieving or attempting to achieve access to a computer or the data it stores, by inducing a computer to perform any function with intent to secure access. The second and third offences are aggravated offences, requiring a specific intent to commit another offence and are intended to deter the more serious criminals from using a computer to assist in the commission of a criminal offence or from impairing or hindering access to data stored in a computer.

The implications of this Act are that hackers who program their computers to search through password permutations could be liable under the first section, even if all of their attempts are rejected by the target computer. As well, using another person's login credentials without proper authority to access data or a program, or to alter, delete, copy or move a program or data, or to output a program or data to a screen or printer, or to impersonate that other person using email, online chat programs, web or other services, constitute the offence.

Although it has been amended two since its implementation, some groups in the UK have expressed concern that the *Computer Misuse Act* has been long superseded by technological progress and that it unintentionally inhibits the work of cyber-threat analysts, cybersecurity researchers, network security companies, and penetration testers, all of whom may be inadvertently caught by this Act. As the precondition to liability is that the hacker should be aware that the access attempted is unauthorized, then even if the initial access to a computer or data is authorized, a subsequent exploration (if there is a hierarchy of privileges in the system) may inadvertently lead to entry to parts of the system for which the required authorizations are lacking. Although unintentional, this would make out the commission of the offence [15].

Together, the United Kingdom's *Computer Misuse Act 1990*, the *NIS Regulations*, the *Data Protection Act 2018*, and the *General Data Protection Regulation* (GDPR), make up the bulk of the United Kingdom's cybersecurity and data privacy protection legislative scheme.

4.4 Review of United States Cybersecurity Laws

As we have seen in Canada, in the United Kingdom, and in Australia, there is no singular federal law or federal cybersecurity regulation that governs data privacy in the United States. Rather, there are few sector-specific federal cybersecurity regulations that focus on specific industries, including healthcare, financial institutions, and commercial marketing.

The *Privacy Act of 1974* continues to be the foundational legislation governing federal government use of personal information; however, this does not apply to businesses or organizations outside of government. The three main sector-specific cybersecurity regulations are: the *Health Insurance Portability and Accountability Act of 1996* (HIPAA), the *Gramm–Leach–Bliley Act of 1999*, and the *Homeland Security Act of 2002* which included the *Federal Information Security Management Act* (FISMA).

In essence, these regulations mandate the need for healthcare organizations, financial institutions, and federal agencies to enact and enforce policies to protect their systems, ensure data privacy, and comply with all relevant privacy legislation with regard to the access to and collection, processing, use, and disclosure of personal or private information.

4.4.1 Regulating the Federal Government and Governmental Agencies

In the United States, federal government and governmental agencies are bound by the Privacy Act of 1974 and the Federal Information Security Management Act (FISMA).

4.4.1.1 Privacy Act of 1974

The purpose of the *Privacy Act* is to balance the federal government's need to maintain information about individuals with the rights of those individuals to be protected against unwarranted invasions of their privacy arising from the collection, maintenance, use, and disclosure of personal information by a federal agency.

Only United States citizens and aliens admitted for permanent legal residence are permitted to obtain records under this statute. The *Privacy Act* does not apply to state or local governments unless such entities are involved in a computer matching program with the federal government, or to private companies or organizations unless these entities are under contract with the agency to maintain an agency-approved *Privacy Act* system of records [16].

4.4.1.2 Federal Information Security Management Act (FISMA)

The *Federal Information Security Management Act* (FISMA) applies to all agencies within the United States federal government. This has served to bring greater attention and awareness to cybersecurity issues within the federal government while explicitly emphasizing a "risk-based policy for cost-effective security." Since the law was originally enacted in 2002, the federal government expanded the *Federal Information Security Management Act* to include state agencies that administer federal programs, including Medicare/Medicaid, unemployment insurance, and student loans.

The FISMA requires each federal agency to create, distribute, and enact an agency-wide program to provide information security for the information and information systems that work to support the operations and assets of the agency, including those provided or managed by another agency, contractor, or other sources [17].

4.4.2 Regulating Sector-Specific Industries: Healthcare

Ensuring patient and maintaining doctor-patient confidentiality can promote more effective communication between physician and patient in an effort to enhance the quality of individualized health care and treatment, to improve patient autonomy, and with the goal of preventing economic harm or embarrassment to the patient.

4.4.2.1 Health Insurance Portability and Accountability Act of 1996

The *Health Insurance Portability and Accountability Act of 1996* (HIPAA) is a US federal law that required the creation of national standards to protect sensitive patient health information from being disclosed without the patient's consent or knowledge. The US Department of Health and Human Services issued the Privacy Rule and the Security Rule to implement the requirements of the HIPAA.

The Privacy Rule standards address the use and disclosure of individuals' health information (known as "protected health information") by entities subject to the Privacy Rule. These individuals and organizations are called "covered entities." The Privacy Rule also contains standards for individuals' rights to understand and control how their health information is used. A major goal of the Privacy Rule is to ensure that individuals' health information is properly protected while allowing the flow of health information needed to provide and promote high-quality health care and to protect the public's health and well-being. The Privacy Rule strikes a balance that permits important uses of information while protecting the privacy of people who seek care and healing.

The Security Rule protects a subset of information covered by the Privacy Rule. Specifically, this rule establishes national standards to protect individuals' electronic personal health information that is created, received, used, or maintained by a covered entity. The Security Rule requires appropriate administrative, physical and technical safeguards to ensure the confidentiality, integrity, and security of electronically protected health information. It requires physicians to protect patients' electronically stored, protected health information (known as "ePHI") by using appropriate administrative, physical and technical safeguards to ensure the confidentiality, integrity, and security of this information [18].

4.4.3 Regulating Sector-Specific Industries: Banks/Financial Institutions

Financial institutions are among the most heavily regulated entities, at both the federal and state levels, and similarly are required to protect customer personal information against reasonably foreseeable threats to security.

4.4.3.1 GLBA/Financial Services Modernization Act of 1999

The *Gramm–Leach–Bliley Act* (GLBA), also known as the *Financial Services Modernization Act of 1999*, requires a wide range of financial institutions to adequately explain their information-sharing practices to their customers and to safeguard sensitive personal data. Compliance with the GLBA is mandatory; there must be an adequate policy in place to protect the information from foreseeable threats in cybersecurity and integrity of data protection measures regardless of whether or not a financial institution discloses personal or private information.

The three major components overlaying the collection, disclosure, and protection of consumers' personal information in the *Gramm–Leach–Bliley Act* include: the Financial Privacy Rule, the Safeguards Rule, and Protection from Pretexting.

The Financial Privacy Rule requires financial institutions to provide each consumer with a privacy notice at the time the consumer relationship is initially established and annually thereafter. The privacy notice must explain the information collected about the consumer, where that information is shared, how it is used, and how it is protected. The notice must identify the consumer's right to opt out of the information being shared with unaffiliated parties pursuant to the provisions set out in the *Fair Credit Reporting Act.*

The Safeguards Rule requires financial institutions to develop a written information security plan that describes how the company is prepared for and plans to continue to protect clients' nonpublic personal information. The aim of the Safeguards Rule is to force financial institutions to reexamine their relationship with personal private data and to perform a thorough risk analysis on their current safeguard processes.

Protection from Pretexting is to protect against personal data breaches which occur through impersonation. This is, when someone tries to gain access to personal information without the proper authority to do so. This is related to identity theft and identity fraud. Pretexting includes requesting private information while impersonating the account holder either, by phone, by postal mail, by email, or by phishing. The *Gramm–Leach–Bliley Act* encourages organizations to implement adequate safeguards against pretexting, such as the implementation of multi-factor authentication [19].

4.4.4 Regulating Interpersonal Relationships and Criminal Activities

In the United States, interpersonal relationships and cyber-related activities are governed by the *Computer Fraud and Abuse Act of 1986*, as well as by the common law legal precedents and the established civil tort law. Criminal law within individual states may be governed separately from federal criminal statutes.

4.4.4.1 Computer Fraud and Abuse Act (1986)

The *Computer Fraud and Abuse Act* is both a criminal law and a civil statute that creates a private (tort) right of action, allowing compensation and injunctive or other equitable relief to anyone harmed by a violation of this law. The *National Information Infrastructure Protection Act of 1996* later amended the *Computer Fraud and Abuse Act*, modifying several sections and increasing the penalties for specific crimes [20].

4.4.4.2 Common Law and Civil Tort Law

The United States has a few torts which developed out of the "invasion of privacy" cause of action in tort law. These include:

1. *Public Disclosure of Private Facts*
   The dissemination of truthful private information which a reasonable person would find objectionable.

2. *False Light*
   The publication of facts which places a person in a false light, even though the facts themselves may not be defamatory.
3. *Appropriation*
   The unauthorized use of a person's name or likeness to obtain some benefits.
4. *Intrusion of Solitude/Intrusion Upon Seclusion*
   The intentional intrusion, physically, electronically, or otherwise, upon the private space, solitude, or seclusion of a person, or the private affairs or concerns of a person.

The civil law in the United States recognizes invasion of privacy torts as civil wrongs and allows injured parties to recover for their losses by bringing a cause of action (suing) the other party to recover damages, such as financial compensation or an injunction to legally compel the other party to immediately cease an activity.

Together, the United States' *Computer Fraud and Abuse Act of 1986*, the *Gramm–Leach–Bliley A*ct (GLBA)—aka the *Financial Services Modernization Act of 1999*—the *Health Insurance Portability and Accountability Act of 1996*, the *Federal Information Security Management Act*, and the *Privacy Act of 1974* make up the bulk of the United States' cybersecurity and data privacy protection legislative scheme.

4.5 Common Law Countries, in Brief

In considering the cybersecurity laws of four countries: Canada, the United Kingdom, Australia, and the United States, it is evident that they have each taken different approaches to legislate, and regulate, data privacy and cybersecurity-related concerns within their respective borders. While all four are considered to be "common law" countries, their unique national needs, historical interests, and constitutional values have contributed to the individualized evolution of their statutory law.

Statutory laws often evolve in parallel with (or in response to) social and/or technological change. With the rapid technological advancements that have inundated our nations over the past few decades—indeed since the age of industrialization—the national statutory laws have had to adjust and accommodate to remain applicable to the changing society in which we live. This exceptional period of technological growth, and our increased reliance on digital communications, has culminated in the need for each of these nations to re-evaluate their current national data privacy and cybersecurity-related statutory schemes to adequately protect the interests of the nation and the people who live and work within it.

At the time of writing, all four of these nations have, individually and collectively, been engaged in consultation processes to address their statutory provisions relating to cybersecurity, data privacy, and cybercriminal activities. Indeed, these four international allies (and New Zealand) have been collaborating, through their respective cybersecurity research centers, to create new and improved global cybersecurity standards and report on possible strategies for approaching potentially malicious cybersecurity threats. As we enter into 2021, we can anticipate (with great certainty) that the applicable data privacy, cybersecurity, and cybercriminal provisions in these countries will continue to develop, evolve, and expand over the next decade.

The applicable national laws related to various cybersecurity relationships and/or offences for each of the above nations are summarized in Tables 4.1 and 4.2.

4.6 National Considerations

There are many considerations that factor into governmental decision-making, particularly within those countries which operate using democratic systems of governance. In this section, we will discuss the concepts of national identity, diversity, identity politics, constitutional values, and international considerations which are relevant sources of influence in policy and political decision-making.

4.6.1 Identity and Diversity

National identity refers to the unique cultures, characteristics, and condition of belonging to, and identifying with, a specific nation. This includes the many symbols and expressions that set a particular nation apart from other peoples and cultures of the world. National identities can be built around liberal and democratic political values, and around the shared experiences that provide the connective tissue allowing diverse communities to thrive. National identity has been seen to be a pivotal feature influencing the fortunes of modern states.

4.6.1.1 National Identity

National identity begins with a shared belief in the legitimacy of the country's political system, whether or not that system is democratic. Identity can be embodied in formal laws and institutions that dictate, for example, which language or languages will be considered official ones, or what schools will teach children about their country's past. But national identity also extends into the realm of culture and values. It consists of the stories that people tell about themselves: where they came from, what they celebrate, their shared historical memories, and their expectations about what it takes to become a genuine member of the community [21].

As an example, China, Japan, and Korea all had highly developed national identities well before they began to modernize—indeed, prior to the confrontation with the Western powers that all three countries experienced in the nineteenth century. One reason the economies of China, Japan, and South Korea were able to grow in such spectacular fashion in the twentieth and early twenty-first centuries is that these countries did not have to settle internal questions of identity as they opened up to international trade and investment. They too suffered from civil war, occupation, and division. But they could build on traditions of statehood and a sense of common national purpose once these conflicts were stabilized.

Table 4.2 Applicable national laws related to cybersecurity

Cybercrime	Canada	United Kingdom	Australia	United States
Applicable National Cybersecurity and Data Privacy Laws	*Canadian Charter of Rights and Freedoms* (1982) *Criminal Code of Canada* (1985) *Privacy Act* (1985) *Copyright Act* (1985) *Personal Information Protection and Electronic Documents Act* (2000) *Canada's Anti-Spam Legislation* (2014) *Protecting Canadians from Online Crime Act* (2014)	*Criminal Law Act* (1967) *Theft Act* (1968) *Copyright, Designs and Patents Act* (1988) *Computer Misuse Act* (1990) *Communications Act* (2003) *Privacy and Electronic Communications Regulations* (2003) *Fraud Act* (2006) *General Data Protection Regulation* (2018) *Data Protection Act* (2018) *NIS Regulations* (2018)	*Crimes Act* (1914) *Copyright Act* (1968) *Privacy Act* (1988) *Criminal Code Act* (1995) *Telecommunications Act* (1997) *Spam Act* (2003) *Cybercrime Legislation Amendment Act* (2012) *Privacy Amendment (Enhancing Privacy Protection) Act* (2012) *Australian Government Agencies Privacy Code* (2017) *Security of Critical Infrastructure Act* (2018)	*Privacy Act of* 1974 *Copyright Act of* 1976 *Electronic Communications Privacy Act of* 1986 *Computer Fraud and Abuse Act of* 1986 *Identity Theft and Assumption Deterrence Act of* 1998 *Financial Services Modernization Act of* 1999 *(GLBA) Federal Information Security Management Act of* 2002 *Controlling the Assault of Non-Solicited Pornography And Marketing Act* (2003)
Hacking and/or Unauthorized Access	*Criminal Code of Canada* (1985) s. 184 s. 342.1 s. 380(1) s. 430	*Computer Misuse Act* (1990) *Terrorism Act* (2000)	*Criminal Code Act* (1995) s. 478.1	*Computer Fraud and Abuse Act of* 1986 ss. 1030 *Electronic Communications Privacy Act* of 1986 *Stored Communications Act of* 1986 s. 2702
DOS and DDOS Attacks	*Criminal Code of Canada* (1985) s. 430(1.1)	*Computer Misuse Act* (1990)	*Criminal Code Act* (1995) s. 477.3	*Computer Fraud and Abuse Act of* 1986 (CFAA) s. 1030(a)(5)(A)

Phishing	*Criminal Code of Canada* (1985) s. 380(1)	*Computer Misuse Act* (1990) *Fraud Act* (2006)	*Criminal Code Act* (1995) s. 134.2(1) s. 135.1(1) s. 135.1(3) s. 135.1(5)	*Computer Fraud and Abuse Act of* 1986 s.1030(a)(5)(A) s. 2702
Modification or Impairment of Data	*Criminal Code of Canada* (1985) s. 380(1)	*Computer Misuse Act* (1990)	*Criminal Code Act* (1995) s. 478.1 s. 478.2	*Computer Fraud and Abuse Act of* 1986 s.1030(a)(5)(A)
Interception of Data and/or Electronic Theft	*Criminal Code of Canada* (1985) s. 342.1	*Theft Act* (1968) *Computer Misuse Act* (1990) *Terrorism Act* (2000) *Fraud Act* (2006)	*Criminal Code Act* (1995) s. 478.1	*Computer Fraud and Abuse Act of* 1986 s.1030(a)(2) *Electronic Communications Privacy Act of* 1986 (ECPA) *Stored Communications Act of* 1986 s. 2702
Identity Theft or Fraud	*Criminal Code of Canada* (1985) s. 402.2 s. 403	*Computer Misuse Act* (1990) *Fraud Act* (2006)	*Criminal Code Act* (1995) s. 372.1(a)	*Identity Theft and Assumption Deterrence Act of* 1998
Copyright Infringement	*Copyright Act* (1985) s. 41.1(1)	*Copyright, Designs and Patents Act* (1988)	*Copyright Act* (1968)	*Copyright Act of* 1976
Spam	*Canada's Anti-Spam Legislation* (2014)	*Privacy and Electronic Communications Regulations* (2003)	*Spam Act* (2003)	*Controlling the Assault of Non-Solicited Pornography And Marketing Act* (2003)

4.6.1.2 Diversity

Diversity, in the context of national politics, is the practice or quality of including or involving people from a range of different social and ethnic backgrounds and of different genders, sexual orientations, etc. within the legal and political decision-making process, from meaningful consultation to representative heads of government. There are many benefits to encouraging diversity in a society. For example, exposure to different ways of thinking and acting can often stimulate innovation, creativity, and entrepreneurship. Diversity provides interest and excitement, as well as being critical to resilience.

Even in the natural world, environmental biologists have pointed out that many crop monocultures are often highly vulnerable to disease because they lack genetic diversity. Indeed, genetic diversity is the catalyst of evolution itself, which relies on genetic variation and adaptation. Ecologists have long worried about the loss of diversity in many species around the world, in part because the reduction of genetic diversity poses a real and substantial threat to long-term biological resilience.

Yet diversity is not the solution for everything. For example, Syria and Afghanistan are very diverse places, but their unique diversity has yielded violence and conflict rather than creativity and resilience. In Kenya, where there are sharp divisions between ethnic groups, diversity feeds an inward-looking political corruption based on ethnic ties. Ethnic diversity led to the breakdown of the liberal Austro-Hungarian Empire in the decades prior to the First World War, when the Empire's component nationalities began to rebel against living together in a common political structure. Finally, the imperial capital of Vienna was, at one time, a melting pot that produced such luminaries as psychologist Sigmund Freud, novelist and poet Hugo von Hofmannsthal, and composer Gustav Mahler. But when the narrower national identities of peoples within the Empire—Serbs, Bulgarians, Czechs, and Austro-Germans—asserted themselves as distinct identity groups, the region descended into violence and intolerance.

4.6.2 Identity in Politics

Identity is rooted in thymos, a term coined by Plato for the aspect of the human soul that is emotionally experienced through feelings of pride, shame, and anger and that craves recognition of dignity. An individual's thymos has the potential to undermine rational debate and deliberation by promoting blind attachment to one's own community. Yet democracies will not survive if citizens are not in some measure irrationally attached to the ideas of constitutional government and human equality through feelings of pride and patriotism, as can be facilitated through a national identity and the use of that schema in identity politics.

National identities can be built around liberal and democratic political values, and around the shared experiences that provide the connective tissue allowing diverse communities to thrive. Canada, France, India, and the United States are each examples of countries that have tried to cultivate national identities along these lines. Such an inclusive sense of national identity remains critical to maintaining a successful modern political order for a number of reasons.

4.6.2.1 Physical Security

Weak national identity creates other serious security issues. It may threaten the integrity of states, a security risk given that large political units are more powerful than smaller ones and can better protect themselves. Larger states can also more easily shape the international environment to suit their own interests. The benefit of physical security from a strong national identity can be seen, for example, in Britain, which could not have played the geopolitical role that it did over past centuries if Scotland had remained an independent country.

4.6.2.2 Quality of Government

Good government entails effective public services and low levels of corruption, which is heavily dependent on governing officials placing public interest above their own more personal interests. In systemically corrupt societies, politicians and bureaucrats may divert public resources away from that which is in the best interest of the public and, instead, to their own political party, ethnic group, region, tribe, family, or into their individual pockets because they do not feel obligated to serve the interests of the wider community.

4.6.2.3 Economic Development

The third function of national identity is facilitating economic development. In order for the people of a country to work on its behalf, the people must take pride in their country, including the national identity. This is evidenced in the strong national identities in Japan, South Korea, and China which created an elite government intensely focused on the economic development of their country rather than on their own personal enrichment. This is particularly important during the early decades of rapid economic growth seen within these countries. This kind of public focused directness was key to the success of the developmental state in these and other rapidly modernizing economies. Conversely, this was much less commonly seen in regions such as sub-Saharan Africa, the Middle East, and Latin America.

While we can see the benefit to economic development from a strong national identity within the country as a whole, many identity groups based on ethnicity or religion prefer to trade among themselves. While this may be of help to a community of immigrants when they first arrive in a country, their future prosperity will depend on their ability to assimilate with larger economic markets. Economies thrive when citizens have access to the widest possible markets and those in which transactions can be completed without regard to the identities of the buyers and sellers. Provided that national identity does not become the basis for protectionism against other nations, a sense of common national identity helps to bring about this pattern of economic development.

4.6.2.4 Trust

Trust is essential for facilitating healthy economic exchange as well as meaningful political participation. The ability to cooperate with other people based on informal norms and shared values—also called "social capital" is the basis of trust within the scope of a national identity. While smaller community identity groups promote trust among their members, their social capital is often seen to stay limited to the trusted members within that community—that is, the "in-group" members. In this way, strong community identities rather than national identities often serve to decrease the trust between the in-group members and those who are outside of the more narrow social community. Societies thrive on trust, but in order to truly flourish, they need the widest possible radius of trust, which is enabled by an overarching sense of shared national identity.

4.6.2.5 Social Safety Nets

The existence of a strong national identity encourages countries to maintain equally strong social safety nets that serve to mitigate economic inequalities with the population. If those within a society feel that they are members of an extended family and have high levels of trust in one another, they are much more likely to support social programs that aid their weaker fellows. The strong welfare states of Scandinavia are underpinned by equally strong senses of national identity. By contrast, in societies divided into self-regarding social groups whose respective members feel they have little in common, citizens are more likely to regard one another as competitors in a zero-sum contest for resources.

4.6.2.6 Liberal Democracies

A liberal democracy is an implicit contract between citizens and their government, and among the citizens themselves, under which they give up certain rights so as to enable the government to protect other rights that are more basic and important. National identity is built around the legitimacy of this contract; if citizens do not believe they are part of the same polity, the system will not function.

But the quality of democracy depends on more than mere acceptance of the system's basic rules. Democracies need their own culture in order to function. They do not produce automatic agreement; indeed, they are necessarily pluralistic collections of diverse interests, opinions, and values that must be reconciled peacefully. Democracies require deliberation and debate, which can take place only if people accept certain norms of behavior governing what can be said and done. Citizens often have to accept outcomes they do not like or prefer in the interest of a common good. Fostering a culture of tolerance and mutual sympathy is often necessary to overcome personal and/or partisan passions.

When we discuss the creation and application of cybersecurity, data privacy, and cybercriminal laws, it is necessary to consider the national identity of each national individually, as that sense of identity, if strong enough, may be rooted in the psyche of those who make up the nation, influencing the reception and adherence to the law by members of that society. With the threat of weakening a national identity, it is imperative for nations to consider their identity politics in legislating such topics.

One of the places to look for features of identity in politics is to consider the values expressed in constitutions, codes, or other statutory material, as well as the international treaties to which a nation is a signatory.

4.6.3 Constitutional Values

Constitutional values can be found either in express constitutional terms or in terms of established legal doctrine. A constitutional value is an abstract concept, which serves to indicate a standard or a measure of good. In this way, constitutional values can set requirements for the appropriate or desired interpretation and application of the constitution, as well as everything dependent upon it.

If something were not to conform to the standards of a particular value, it would mean that the standards of a lower, different, conflicting, or extra-constitutional measure are being applied, leading to unconstitutional results. Constitutional values may therefore be said to be distinguishable but related to principles in the sense that the principles of the constitution would be founded in and give expression to the values. For example, the principle that the law must be applied fairly and equitably is founded in and gives expression to the values of justice and equality.

There is some level of overlap between the meanings and distinctions of the terms "principles", "values," and "guidelines" in relation to constitutional themes. While this is widely debated in academic circles, it is, however, outside of the scope of this book. For this reason, we will refer to both the generalized overarching themes as well as the specified foundational values as being "constitutional values" in this section, as they are indeed values—of some nature—held and conveyed in some manner through the constitution of a nation [22].

4.6.3.1 Example in Law: Core Constitutional Values of the US

As an example of constitutional values expressed by a nation, we can look to the United States and the core values entrenched within the legal system that operates there. Table 4.3 gives the core values and descriptions for the constitutional values, or principles, which underlay their national legal system.

In order to glean a greater understanding of the individuality of constitutional values and how they differ between nations. We can look at Table 4.4, which describes the constitutional values of the United States, and Table 4.5, which compares a selection of national values from Australia, Canada, Germany, India, Morocco, South Africa, and the United Kingdom.

4.7 International Considerations

International considerations include legal documents and formalized contractual agreements between nations, known as treaties, as well as other international sources of influence on domestic policy-making. In this section, we will discuss the relevant treaties and international agreements related to cybersecurity and cyber law, the creation of the *Tallinn Manual* as a response to expressed international concern over

Table 4.3 Which law applies where and to whom?

Which law applies where and to whom?	Canada	United Kingdom	Australia	United States
Federal/National Government	*Canadian Charter of Rights and Freedoms* (1982) *Privacy Act* (1985)	*General Data Protection Regulation* (2018) *Data Protection Act* (2018) *NIS Regulations* (2018)	*Privacy Act* (1988) *Privacy Amendment (Enhancing Privacy Protection) Act* (2012) *Australian Government Agencies Privacy Code* (2017)	*Privacy Act of* 1974 *Federal Information Security Management Act* (2002)
Private-Sector: All Corporations, Businesses, and Non-Governmental Organizations	*Canadian Charter of Rights and Freedoms* (1982) *Personal Information Protection and Electronic Documents Act* (2000)	*General Data Protection Regulation* (2018) *Data Protection Act* (2018) *NIS Regulations* (2018)	*Privacy Act* (1988) *Privacy Amendment (Enhancing Privacy Protection) Act* (2012) *Australian Government Agencies Privacy Code* (2017)	Based on state-specific legislation, rather than the federal legislation.
Private-Sector: Health Care Specific	*Canadian Charter of Rights and Freedoms* (1982) *Personal Information Protection and Electronic Documents Act* (2000)[a]	*General Data Protection Regulation* (2018) *Data Protection Act* (2018)	*Privacy Act* (1988) *Privacy Amendment (Enhancing Privacy Protection) Act* (2012)	*Health Insurance Portability and Accountability Act of* 1996
Private-Sector: Banking and Financial Services Specific	*Canadian Charter of Rights and Freedoms* (1982) *Personal Information Protection and Electronic Documents Act* (2000)	*General Data Protection Regulation* (2018) *Data Protection Act* (2018)	*Privacy Act* (1988) *Privacy Amendment (Enhancing Privacy Protection) Act* (2012)	*Gramm–Leach Bliley Act (GLBA) aka Financial Services Modernization Act of* 1999

(continued)

Table 4.3 (continued)

Which law applies where and to whom?	Canada	United Kingdom	Australia	United States
Commercial Electronic Messages (CEMs)	*Canada's Anti-Spam Legislation* (2014)	*Privacy and Electronic Communications Regulations* (2003) *General Data Protection Regulation* (2018) *Data Protection Act* (2018)	*Spam Act* (2003)	*Controlling the Assault of Non-Solicited Pornography And Marketing Act* (2003)
Individuals	*Criminal Code of Canada* (1985) *Copyright Act* (1985) *Protecting Canadians from Online Crime Act* (2014)	*Criminal Law Act* (1967) *Copyright, Designs and Patents Act* (1988) *Computer Misuse Act* (1990) *Theft Act* (1990) *Terrorism Act* (2000) *Fraud Act* (2006)	*Copyright Act* (1968) *Criminal Code Act* (1995)	*Copyright Act of* 1976 *Computer Fraud and Abuse Act of* 1986 *Electronic Communications Privacy Act of* 1986 *Identity Theft and Assumption Deterrence Act of* 1998 *Title 18 of the United States Code*[b]

[a]Canadian health care privacy legislation comprises 14 government jurisdictions, each with its own legislative framework for protecting the privacy of personal health information
[b]Note: Individual states have their own Penal, Criminal or Crimes Code legislation dependent on jurisdiction

cyber warfare, and the international legal principles as seen in international humanitarian law and private international law which influence national decision-making.

4.7.1 Treaties and International Agreements

The *United Nations* (UN) is an intergovernmental organization aiming to maintain international peace and security, develop friendly relations among nations, achieve international cooperation, and be a center for harmonizing the actions of nations. One of the legal forms of cooperation used by the United Nations is the signing and implementation of treaties between individual nations.

Table 4.4 United States' constitutional values and descriptions

Core value	Description
Individual Rights	Fundamental to American constitutional democracy is the belief that individuals have certain basic rights that are not created by the government but which the government should protect. These are the right to life, liberty, economic freedom, and the "pursuit of happiness." It is the purpose of the government to protect these rights, and it may not place unfair or unreasonable restraints on their exercise. Many of these rights are enumerated in the Bill of Rights.
Right to Life	The individual's right to life should be considered inviolable except in certain highly restricted and extreme circumstances, such as the use of deadly force to protect one's own or others' lives.
Right to Liberty	The right to liberty is considered an unalterable aspect of the human condition. Central to this idea of liberty is the understanding that the political or personal obligations of parents or ancestors cannot be legitimately forced on people.
The Pursuit of Happiness	It is the right of citizens in the American constitutional democracy to attempt to attain (or pursue) happiness in their own way, so long as they do not infringe upon the rights of others.
Personal Freedom	The private realm in which the individual is free to act, to think and to believe, and which the government cannot legitimately invade.
Political Freedom	The right to participate freely in the political process, choose and remove public officials, to be governed under a rule of law; and the right to a free flow of information and ideas, open debate, and right of assembly.
Economic Freedom	The right to acquire, use, transfer and dispose of private property without unreasonable governmental interference; the right to seek employment wherever one pleases; to change employment at will; and to engage in any lawful economic activity.
Freedom of Religion	There shall be full freedom of conscience for people of all faiths or none. Religious liberty is considered to be a natural inalienable right that must always be beyond the power of the state to confer or remove. Religious liberty includes the right to freely practice any religion or no religion without governmental coercion or control.
Popular Sovereignty	The citizenry is collectively the sovereign of the state and holds ultimate authority over public officials and their policies.
Common Good	The public or common good requires that individual citizens have the commitment and motivation—that they accept their obligation—to promote the welfare of the community and to work together with other members for the greater benefit of all.
Justice	People should be treated fairly in the distribution of the benefits and burdens of society, the correction of wrongs and injuries, and in the gathering of information and making of decisions.
Rule of Law	Both government and the governed should be subject to the law.
Truth	Citizens can legitimately demand that truth-telling as refraining from lying and full disclosure by government be the rule, since trust in the veracity of government constitutes an essential element of the bond between governors and governed.
Diversity	Variety in culture and ethnic background, race, lifestyle, and belief is not only permissible but desirable and beneficial in a pluralist society.

(continued)

Table 4.4 (continued)

Core value	Description
Federalism	Power is shared between two sets of governmental institutions, those of the states and those of the central or federal authorities, as stipulated by the Constitution.
Separation of Powers	Legislative, executive, and judicial powers should be exercised by different institutions in order to maintain the limitations placed upon them.
Representative Government	The republican form of government established under the Constitution is one in which citizens elect others to represent their interests.
Checks and Balances	The powers given to the different branches of government should be balanced, that is roughly equal, so that no branch can completely dominate the others. Branches of government are also given powers to check the power of other branches.
Civilian Control of the Military	Civilian authority should control the military in order to preserve constitutional government

The *Council of Europe* is one of several regional organizations established in the aftermath of World War II. It is separate and distinct from the European Union and has a much larger membership than the EU. The Council's core mission is the protection of human rights, but it also works to promote democracy, the rule of law, and uniform standards. Much of the Council's work is accomplished through the drafting of treaties (Table 4.6).

4.7.2 The *Tallinn Manual* and Cyber Warfare

The *Tallinn Manual on the International Law Applicable to Cyber Warfare* (more simply known as the *Tallinn Manual*) was published by Cambridge University Press in April 2013. The *Manual* was the first comprehensive and authoritative attempt to analyze the application of international law to cyber warfare [23].

In late 2009, the Cooperative Cyber Defence Centre of Excellence convened an international group of legal scholars and practitioners to draft a manual addressing the issue of how to interpret international law in the context of cyber operations and cyber warfare and to bring some degree of clarity to the associated complex legal issues. As an academic and non-binding study, the *Tallinn Manual* followed similar efforts, such as the *San Remo Manual on International Law Applicable to Armed Conflicts at Sea* by the International Institute of Humanitarian Law and the *Manual on International Law Applicable to Air and Missile Warfare*, as written by the Harvard Program on Humanitarian Policy and Conflict Research.

The *Tallinn Manual* was produced between 2009 and 2012 by an international team of legal scholars at the request of the NATO Cooperative Cyber Defence Center of Excellence, which is located in Tallinn, Estonia. While it was produced upon invitation from a NATO organization, the *Tallinn Manual* is not a NATO document, rather it is an independent academic research product representing only the views of its authors in their personal capacity. The manual does not represent the

Table 4.5 Comparison of constitutional values of assorted nations

Country	Citation	Features	Constitutional Values
Australia ("Commonwealth of Australia")	*Commonwealth of Australia Constitution Act, 1900 (UK) s. 9.*	Federal Parliamentary Representative Democracy and Constitutional Monarchy	• Freedom of Speech and Expression • Freedom of Religious Belief • Rule of Law • Mutual Respect and Tolerance • Equality of Opportunity for All • Protection of Individual Freedom • Respect for Individual Dignity
Canada	*The Constitution Act, 1867*	Federal Parliamentary Representative Democracy and Constitutional Monarchy	• Equality and Fairness • Diversity and Inclusion • Consultation and Dialogue • Economic Security • Public Safety • Sustainability • Accommodation and Tolerance
Germany ("Federal Republic of Germany")	*Grundgesetz für die Bundesrepublik Deutschland, 1949*	Democratic Federal Parliamentary Republic	• Respect for Human Dignity • Human Rights • Federalism • Social Responsibility • Self-Determination • Separation of Powers • Unity and Freedom
India	*Constitution of India, 1950*	Federal Parliamentary Constitutional Republic	• Protection of Life • Protection of Personal Liberty and Freedom • Constitutional Supremacy • Separation of Powers • Equality Before the Law • Independent Judiciary • Fundamental Rights and Duties
Morocco ("Kingdom of Morocco")	*Moroccan Constitution of 1996*	Social Democratic Parliamentary Constitutional Monarchy	• Promotion and Realization of African Unity • Promotion of Islamic Unity • Promotion of World Peace and Security • Human Rights • Social Democracy • Popular Sovereignty • Openness, Moderation, and Tolerance

(continued)

Table 4.5 (continued)

Country	Citation	Features	Constitutional Values
South Africa ("Republic of South Africa")	*Constitution of the Republic of South Africa 1996*	Democratic Parliamentary Republic	• Achievement of Equality • Advancement of Human Rights and Freedom • Human Dignity • Non-Racism, and Non-Sexism • Right to Life, Freedom and Security of the Person • Supremacy of the Constitution • Universal Adult Suffrage
United Kingdom ("United Kingdom of Great Britain and Northern Ireland")	"Constitution of the United Kingdom" (uncodified constitution)	Unitary Parliamentary Democracy and Constitutional Monarchy	• Parliamentary Sovereignty • Protection of Democracy • Protection of Freedom • Rule of Law • Human Rights • Internationalism • Separation of Church and State

views of NATO nor any other organization or state, including those represented by the observers [23].

The manual is divided into sections of rules and their accompanying commentary. The rules themselves are, in essence, restatements of international law in the cyber context, as understood and agreed to, by all of the authors. Being the first authoritative restatement of the application and interpretation of international law in the cyber context, however, it may be anticipated that the manual will have an effect on how states and organizations will formulate their approaches and positions in those matters.

In February 2017, a follow-up report, *The Tallinn Manual 2.0 on International Law Applicable to Cyber Operations*, was released. The *Tallinn Manual 2.0* broadens the scope to assess how international legal principles can be applied to malevolent cyber operations that do not rise to the level of an armed attack. The focus of the original *Tallinn Manual* is on the most disruptive and destructive cyber operations—those that qualify as 'armed attacks' and therefore allowing states to respond in self-defence—and those taking place during armed conflict. Since the threat of cyber operations with such consequences is especially alarming to states, most academic research has focused on these issues. *Tallinn 2.0* refers to "cyber operations" as opposed to "cyber conflicts" as in the original *Tallinn Manual [24]*.

It is important to keep in mind that the intent of the project was never to make law or to produce a manual that would have the force of law. As the introduction to the *Tallinn Manual 2.0* makes clear:

Table 4.6 International treaties relating to cybersecurity, data privacy, and cybercrime

Name of treaty	Citation	Authority	Description
Universal Declaration of Human Rights (UDHR)	The United Nations. (1948). Universal Declaration of Human Rights.	United Nations	The Declaration was proclaimed by the U.N. General Assembly in 1948. The right to privacy is enshrined in Article 12. Although the Declaration is not legally binding, many of its principles have been incorporated in international treaties, regional human rights instruments, and national constitutions.
International Covenant on Civil and Political Rights (1966)	999 UNTS 171	United Nations	More than 160 countries are state parties to this multilateral treaty. Article 17 recognizes the right to privacy.
Convention on the Rights of the Child (1989)	1577 UNTS. 3	United Nations	Article 34 of the Convention obligates state parties to protect children from all forms of sexual exploitation and abuse, including prostitution and pornography.
United Nations Convention Against Transnational Organized Crime (2000) also known as the "Palermo Convention"	2225 UNTS 209	United Nations	This treaty, also known as the Palermo Convention, obligates state parties to enact domestic criminal offenses that target organized criminal groups and to adopt new frameworks for extradition, mutual legal assistance, and law enforcement cooperation. Although the treaty does not explicitly address cybercrime, its provisions are highly relevant.
Optional Protocol to the Convention on the Rights of the Child (2001)	2171 U.N.T.S. 227	United Nations	This protocol to the 1981 Convention addresses the sale of children, child prostitution, and child pornography. Article 3(1)(c) prohibits the production, distribution, dissemination, sale, and possession of child pornography. The Preamble mentions the Internet as a means of distribution. The definition of child pornography, set forth in Article 2(3), is broad enough to encompass virtual images of children.

(continued)

Table 4.6 (continued)

Name of treaty	Citation	Authority	Description
United Nations Convention on the Use of Electronic Communications in International Contracts (New York, 2005)	New York, 2005	United Nations Commission on International Trade Law	The Electronic Communications Convention aims at facilitating the use of electronic communications in international trade by assuring that contracts concluded and other communications exchanged electronically are as valid and enforceable as their traditional paper-based equivalents. This went into force in 2013.
Convention for the Protection of Human Rights and Fundamental Freedoms (1950)	E.T.S. 5	Council of Europe	Also known as the European Convention on Human Rights. Article 8 of the Convention recognizes the right to privacy. The European Court of Human Rights (see below) is responsible for monitoring compliance with the Convention.
Convention for Protection of Individuals with Regard to Automatic Processing of Personal Data (1981)	E.T.S. 108	Council of Europe	The Convention, which entered into force in 1985, is the first legal binding international instrument on data protection. It is open to signature by countries that are not members of the Council of Europe.
Additional Protocol to the Convention for the Protection of Individuals with Regard to Automatic Processing of Personal Data, Regarding Supervisory Authorities and Transborder Data Flows (2001)	E.T.S. 181	Council of Europe	The additional protocol provides for the establishment of national data protection authorities to monitor compliance with laws adopted pursuant to the original Convention and regulates the transmission of data across national boundaries.
Budapest Convention on Cybercrime (2001) also known as the "Budapest Convention"	E.T.S. 185	Council of Europe	Also known as the Budapest Convention, this is the first international agreement aimed at reducing computer-related crime by harmonizing national laws, improving investigative techniques, and increasing international cooperation.

(continued)

Table 4.6 (continued)

Name of treaty	Citation	Authority	Description
Additional Protocol to the Convention on Cybercrime Concerning the Criminalisation of Acts of a Racist or Xenophobic Nature Committed Through Computer Systems (2003)	E.T.S. 189	Council of Europe	State parties which have ratified this protocol to the Budapest Convention are obligated to enact laws to criminalize racist or xenophobic acts that are expressed or otherwise communicated online.
Convention on the Protection of Children against Sexual Exploitation and Sexual Abuse (2007)	C.E.T.S. 201	Council of Europe	This treaty expressly prohibits the use of "information and computer technology (ICT)" to access child pornography (Article 21(1)(f)), to distribute child pornography (Article 30(5)), or to solicit children for sexual purposes (Article 23).
Protocol Amending the Convention for Protection of Individuals with Regard to Automatic Processing of Personal Data (2018)	E.T.S. 223	Council of Europe	This protocol is intended to modernize and improve the original 1981 convention by taking into account the challenges posed by the new forms of information and communications technology that have emerged during the ensuing decades.

Ultimately, Tallinn Manual 2.0 must be understood only as an expression of the opinions of the two International Groups of Experts as to the state of the law .... This Manual is meant to be a reflection of the law as it existed at the point of the Manual's adoption by the two International Groups of Experts in June 2016. It is not a 'best practices' guide, does not represent 'progressive development of the law', and is policy and politics-neutral. In other words, Tallinn Manual 2.0 is intended as an objective restatement of the lex lata [25].

4.7.2.1 Excerpt from Tallinn Manual

The *Tallinn Manual* is divided into two parts: Part A and Part B, listing a total of 95 Rules with accompanying interpretation and application clauses [26]. Part A outlines the "International Cyber Security Law" and contains two Chapters and the first 19 Rules, while Part B discusses the "Law of Cyber Armed Conflict" and contains five Chapters and the remaining 76 Rules. Limiting our sample scope to Part A, the first 19 Rules of the Tallinn Manual are provided below, distinguished by Chapter and Section.

Chapter One of the *Tallinn Manual* discusses "States and Cyberspace" and divides the first 9 Rules into two Sections: (1) Sovereignty, Jurisdiction, and Control; and (2) State Responsibility.

Section One of Chapter One contains the Rules applicable to "Sovereignty, Jurisdiction, and Control":

RULE 1—Sovereignty
A State may exercise control over cyberinfrastructure and activities within its sovereign territory.
RULE 2—Jurisdiction
Without prejudice to applicable international obligations, a State may exercise its jurisdiction:
(a) Over persons engaged in cyber activities on its territory;
(b) Over cyber infrastructure located on its territory; and
(c) Extraterritorially, in accordance with international law.
RULE 3—Jurisdiction of Flag States and States of Registration
Cyberinfrastructure located on aircraft, ships, or other platforms in international airspace, on the high seas, or in outer space is subject to the jurisdiction of the flag State or State of registration.
RULE 4—Sovereign Immunity and Inviolability
Any inference by a State with cyberinfrastructure aboard a platform, wherever located, that enjoys sovereign immunity constitutes a violation of sovereignty.
RULE 5—Control of Cyber Infrastructure
A State shall not knowingly allow the cyberinfrastructure located in its territory or under its exclusive governmental control to be used for acts that adversely and unlawfully affect other States.

Section Two of Chapter One contains the Rules applicable to "State Responsibility":

RULE 6—Legal Responsibility of States
A State bears international legal responsibility for a cyber operation attributable to it and which constitutes a breach of an international obligation.
RULE 7—Cyber Operations Launched from Governmental Cyber Infrastructure
The mere fact that a cyber operation has been launched or otherwise originates from governmental cyberinfrastructure is not sufficient evidence for attributing the operation to that State, but it is an indication that the State in question is associated with the operation.
RULE 8—Cyber Operations Routed Through a State
The fact that a cyber operation has been routed via the cyberinfrastructure located in a State is not sufficient evidence for attributing the operation to that State.
RULE 9—Countermeasures
A State injured by an internationally wrongful act may resort to proportionate countermeasures, including cyber countermeasures, against the responsible State.

Chapter Two discusses "The Use of Force" and divides the next 10 Rules into three Sections: (1) Prohibition of the Use of Force; (2) Self-Defence; and (3) Actions of International Governmental Organizations.

Section One of Chapter Two contains the Rules applicable to "Prohibition of the Use of Force":

RULE 10—Prohibition of Threat or Use of Force
A cyber operation that constitutes a threat or use of force against the territorial integrity or political independence of any State, or that is in any other manner inconsistent with the purposes of the United Nations, is unlawful.
RULE 11—Definition of Use of Force
A cyber operation constitutes a use of force when its scale and effects are comparable to non-cyber operations rising to the level of a use of force.

(continued)

RULE 12—Definition of Threat of Force
A cyber operation, or threatened cyber operation, constitutes an unlawful threat of force when the threatened action, if carried out, would be an unlawful use of force.

Section Two of Chapter Two contains the Rules applicable to "Self-Defence":

RULE 13—Self-Defence Against Armed Attack
A State that is the target of a cyber operation that rises to the level of an armed attack may exercise its inherent right of self-defence. Whether a cyber operation constitutes an armed attack depends on its scale and effects.
RULE 14—Necessity and Proportionality
A use of force involving cyber operations undertaken by a State in the exercise of its right of self-defence must be necessary and proportionate.
RULE 15—Imminence and Immediacy
The right to use force gun self-defence arises if a cyber armed attack occurs or is imminent. It is further subject to a requirement of immediacy.
RULE 16—Collective Self-Defence
The right of self-defence may be exercised collectively. Collective self-defence against a cyber operation amounting to an armed attack may only be exercised at the request of the victim-State and within the scope of the request.
RULE 17—Reporting Measures of Self-Defence
Measures involving cyber operations undertaken by States in the exercise of the right to self-defence pursuant to Article 51 of the United Nations Charter shall be immediately reported to the United Nations Security Council.

Section Three of Chapter Two contains the Rules applicable to "Actions of International Governmental Organizations":

RULE 18—United Nations Security Council
Should the United Nations Security Council determine that an act constitutes a threat to the peace, breach of the peace, or act of aggression, it may authorize non-forceful measures, including cyber operations. If the Security Council considers such measures to be inadequate, it may decide upon forceful measures, including cyber measures.
RULE 19—Regional Organizations
International organizations, arrangement, or agencies of a regional character may conduct enforcement actions, involving or in response to cyber operations, pursuant to a mandate from, or authorization by, the United Nations Security Council.

4.7.2.2 Tallinn Manual 2.0

In February 2017, a follow-up report, *The Tallinn Manual 2.0 on International Law Applicable to Cyber Operations*, was released. The *Tallinn Manual 2.0* broadens the scope to assess how international legal principles can be applied to malevolent cyber operations that do not rise to the level of an armed attack. The focus of the original *Tallinn Manual* is on the most disruptive and destructive cyber operations—those that qualify as "'armed attacks"' and therefore allowing states to respond in self-defence—and those taking place during armed conflict. Since the threat of cyber operations with such consequences is especially alarming to states, most academic research has focused on these issues. *Tallinn 2.0* refers to "cyber operations" as opposed to "cyber conflicts" as in the original *Tallinn Manual [24].*

It is important to keep in mind that the intent of the project was never to make law or to produce a manual that would have the force of law. As the introduction to the *Tallinn Manual 2.0* makes clear:

> *Ultimately, Tallinn Manual 2.0 must be understood only as an expression of the opinions of the two International Groups of Experts as to the state of the law . . . . This Manual is meant to be a reflection of the law as it existed at the point of the Manual's adoption by the two International Groups of Experts in June 2016. It is not a 'best practices' guide, does not represent 'progressive development of the law', and is policy and politics-neutral. In other words, Tallinn Manual 2.0 is intended as an objective restatement of the lex lata [25].*

4.7.3 International Legal Principles in Cyberspace

The law of war is the subset of public international law that governs armed conflicts. It includes criteria for determining whether the use of force is justifiable (in legal terms "*jus ad bellum*"), as well as rules governing the conduct of warfare (or "*jus in bello*"), also known as international humanitarian law. Legal scholars continue to debate whether existing international law principles, including those that govern international warfare, are sufficient to address cyber-attacks or whether a new legal framework is needed to manage conflicts that occur in cyberspace. Although various proposals for drafting a cyberspace treaty have been floated, none have evolved as of yet and it is unlikely that a new treaty will emerge any time soon.

Some of the sources of influence on international legal policy and strategies—that is, the factors which are considered prior to making a legal decision or domestic legal policy with implications to international law—are provided in Fig. 4.1. While there are many sources given in this figure, this list is not exhaustive.

4.7.4 International Dispute Resolution

We have previously discussed the sources of law in Part One of this book and now we have added the sources of influence on law. From contrasting these, we can understand that the sources of international law can include everything that an international tribunal might rely on to decide international disputes. *International disputes* include arguments or conflicts between nations, between individuals or companies from different nations, and between individuals or companies and a foreign nation-state.

4.7.4.1 International Court of Justice

The International Court of Justice (ICJ)—also known as the World Court—is the principal judicial organ of the United Nations, having been established in June 1945 by the Charter of the United Nations. Article 38(1) of the *Statute of the International*

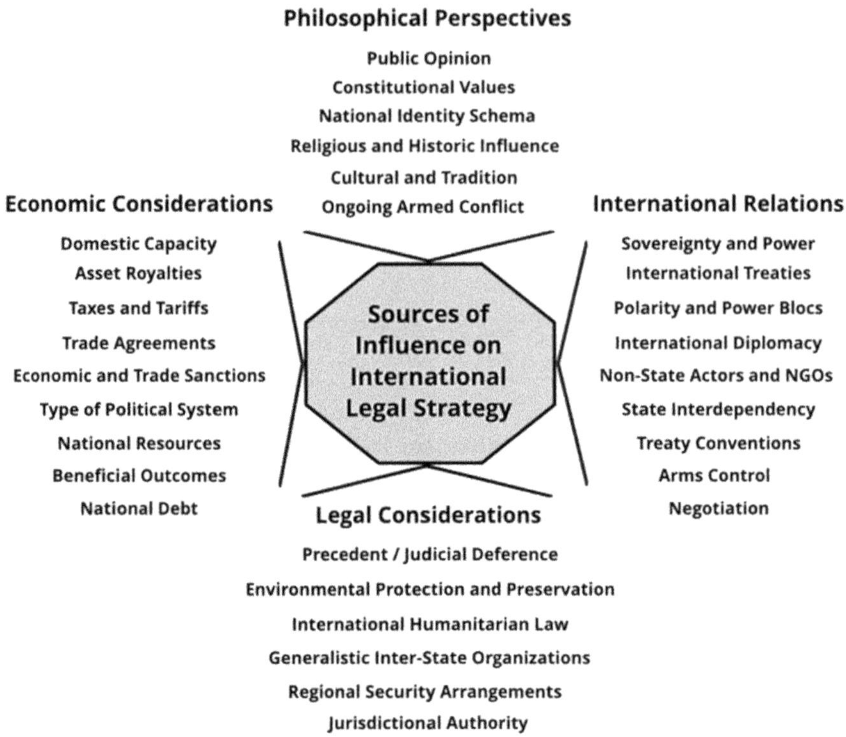

Fig. 4.1 Sources of influence on international legal strategy

Court of Justice lists four sources of international law: treaties and conventions, custom, general principles of law, and judicial decisions and teachings.

The Court is composed of 15 judges, who are elected for terms of office of nine years by the United Nations General Assembly and the Security Council. The election of the first Members of the International Court of Justice took place at the First Session of the United Nations General Assembly and Security Council on February 6, 1946, with work in the court beginning in April 1946. The ICJ only hears lawsuits between nation-states and its jurisdiction is not compulsory, meaning that both nations in a dispute must agree to have the ICJ hear the dispute.

The seat of the Court is at the Peace Palace in The Hague.[1] Of the six principal organs of the United Nations, it is the only one that is not located in New York, in the United States. The role of the International Court of Justice is to settle, in accordance with international law, legal disputes submitted to it by nation-states and to give advisory opinions on legal questions referred to it by authorized United Nations organs and specialized agencies.

[1] In the Netherlands.

4.8 Summary

In this chapter, we have discussed and compared the cybersecurity, cybercriminal, and data privacy laws of four common law countries: Canada, Australia, the United Kingdom, and the United States. We examined the national considerations and influences which shape the laws created by individual nations and the treaties which flow from that posturing as well. We looked at the concept of national identity, diversity, and identity politics which work with the expressed, codified, or implied constitutional values to influence both domestic and international legal development. Finally, we discussed the international considerations, such as treaties and existing legal principles, which may apply to international cyber law as well as traditional law. The answers to the following questions are provided within this chapter:

1. In what ways are the laws of Canada, Australia, the United Kingdom, and the United States, as discussed in this chapter, similar? In what ways are they different?
2. What is national identity?
3. Why might the constitutional values of a nation be relevant to their creation of cybersecurity and data privacy legislation?
4. How is a treaty similar to a contract? How is it different?
5. What is the Tallinn Manual, how did it come to exist, and what is the origin of its name?
6. What is the World Court, which organization is it affiliated with, and why does it matter?

References

1. Privacy Act (RSC 1985, c P-21)
2. Access to Information Act (RSC 1985, c A-1)
3. Personal Information Protection and Electronic Documents Act (SC 2000, c 5).
4. Canada's Anti-Spam Legislation (SC 2010, c 23)
5. Criminal Code (RSC (1985), c C-46)
6. Protecting Canadians from Online Crime Act (SC 2014, c 31)
7. Jones v Tsige (2012 ONCA 32)
8. Privacy Act 1988 (Cth)
9. Privacy Amendment (Enhancing Privacy Protection) Act 2012
10. Spam Bill 2003 (Cth)
11. Crimes Act 1914 (Cth)
12. Criminal Code Act 1995 (Cth)
13. Data Protection Act 2018
14. Network and Information Security Regulations 2018
15. Computer Misuse Act 1990
16. Privacy Act of 1974
17. Federal Information Security Management Act
18. Health Insurance Portability and Accountability Act of 1996
19. Financial Services Modernization Act of 1999

20. Computer Fraud and Abuse Act (1986)
21. Möllers, N. (2021). Making digital territory: Cybersecurity, techno-nationalism, and the moral boundaries of the state. *Science, Technology, & Human Values, 46*(1), 112–138.
22. Venter, F. (2001). Utilizing constitutional values in constitutional comparison. *Potchefstroom Electronic Law Journal/Potchefstroomse Elektroniese Regsblad, 4*(1), 19.
23. Schmitt, M. N. (Gen. ed.) (2013). *Tallinn manual on the international law applicable to cyber warfare*. Cambridge University Press. http://csef.ru/media/articles/3990/3990.pdf
24. Leetaru, K. Forbes. What Tallinn Manual 2.0 teaches us about the new cyber order.
25. Schmitt, M. N. (2017). *Tallinn manual 2.0 on the international law applicable to cyber operations* (2nd ed., pp. 2–3). Cambridge University Press.
26. Schmitt, M. (2013). *Tallinn manual on the international law applicable to cyber warfare*. Cambridge University Press. https://doi.org/10.1017/CBO9781139169288

Emerging Issues 5

In this, our final chapter, we will discuss slime of the emergent, upcoming, and future issues in cybersecurity law, which include: globalization and determination of jurisdictional authority; digital marketplaces and consumer rights; anonymized DarkNet markets and the influx of cryptocurrencies; existing and anticipated challenges to law enforcement; and the issue of digital sovereignty in relation to data governance, private ownership, and privacy protection.

5.1 Globalization and Jurisdictionally

The most popular illegal Dark Web marketplace, called the "Silk Road," was designed to use TOR for user anonymity and Bitcoin as a similarly anonymous transactional currency. Silk Road was created and operated by Ross William Ulbricht from 2011 until his arrest in 2013. As Ulbricht is an American citizen and the arrest took place in the United States, he was indicted under the American criminal justice system for a total of seven offences including: conspiracy to launder money, conspiracy to commit computer hacking, conspiracy to traffic narcotics by the means of the internet, and continuing a criminal enterprise. In May 2015, Ross Ulbricht was sentenced to a double life sentence plus forty years without the possibility of parole and was ordered to pay over $180-million (USD) in fines. Pretty much as soon as the government shut down Ulbricht's Silk Road, another individual quickly launched a Silk Road 2.0 and was promptly charged with the same crimes as Ross Ulbricht for his original Silk Road enterprise [1].

While these Silk Road cases were simplified because the United States had the legal jurisdiction, the often international and cross-jurisdictional nature of the Dark Web makes it essential for criminal investigators to be able to collaborate across law enforcement agencies and without the limitation of borders if our goal is to regulate or enforce law on the Dark Web/Dark Net.

M. Lukings, A. Habibi Lashkari, *Understanding Cybersecurity Law and Digital Privacy*, Future of Business and Finance, https://doi.org/10.1007/978-3-030-88704-9_5

5.1.1 Determining Jurisdiction

In law, *jurisdiction* refers to the practical authority to make, enforce, and administer laws and justice, which is granted to a legal body based on the type and locational circumstances of the case. In more casual terms, jurisdiction can also refer to a specific regional, physical, territorial, or geographic area. When we consider online activities, however, there is not necessarily a defined geographic area to distinguish which governing authority of which nation or state has the legal jurisdiction over that medium. While jurisdiction is often linked to sovereignty over a territorial location, jurisdiction can also exist without a connection to territory. The type of jurisdictional authority held by a governing body indicates whether that nation or state can undertake enforcement action to uphold its law [2]. There are three types of jurisdiction: (1) prescriptive jurisdiction; (2) adjudicative jurisdiction; and (3) enforcement jurisdiction.

Prescriptive jurisdiction—or legislative jurisdiction—refers to the authority of the governing body of a nation or state to establish laws and legal norms that are applicable to individuals, groups, corporations, property, and events, both within and outside of its territory. Under the prescriptive jurisdiction, the laws of a nation or state are still binding on citizens of that jurisdiction while abroad. The same principle of legal scope may also be applicable to certain events or activities conducted abroad that could negatively impact the nation or state which is hoping to assert a prescriptive jurisdiction. For example, a nation may choose to create legislation applicable to crimes that occur abroad which the home nation considers to be a threat to its security or economic interests [3].

Enforcement jurisdiction refers to the power of a nation or state to ensure compliance with prescriptive legal commands which regulate people and situations in the jurisdiction of that nation or state. Enforcement jurisdiction is closely tied to the adjudicative jurisdiction and both can be contrasted with the prescriptive jurisdiction [4].

Adjudicative jurisdiction refers to the power of the governing body of a nation or state to hear and settle legal disputes, as well as the authority to decide and determine the outcomes of competing legal claims.

Both the adjudicative jurisdiction and enforcement jurisdiction are territorially limited. The intention for this is to limit the power of a nation or state to enforce its prescriptive or adjudicative jurisdiction within another nation or state. In this way, the legal enforcement and court systems are restricted to operating within the territorial boundaries of their corresponding nation or state. In the absence of permission, a nation or state cannot exercise its prescriptive jurisdiction—either through enforcement or adjudication—outside of its territory [5].

In common law legal systems, jurisdictional divisions are considered locally, provincially, and federally. Jurisdictional divisions can also refer to the division of legal powers, within the executive and legislative branches of government, to analyze and allocate resources with the aim of promoting and serving the best interests of the people who are governed by the laws within that jurisdiction.

5.1.2 Online Jurisdiction

To better understand how legal jurisdiction applies to encrypted online criminal activities, it is necessary to consider the context and nature of the Deep Web and the Dark Web/DarkNet. Unlike the more visible "traditional" criminal activities, the anonymous nature of the Dark Web/DarkNet can make it challenging for law enforcement to determine whether an offence has occurred, how the offence occurred, from where it was initiated, or at what point the threshold for the commission of the offence was surpassed. When law enforcement has been notified of illegal transactions, the use of a decentralized network for confirmation and verification of Dark Net transactions, limits the ability of law enforcement to localize an offence to a specific jurisdiction, even when there is very clearly a law being broken somewhere by someone. Compounding this issue is the inherent cross-jurisdictional and international nature of the Dark Web/DarkNet, which can be hindered by testy international relations, unsigned treaties, and conflicting interests between jurisdictional parties and law enforcement organizations [6].

When considering cross-jurisdictional criminal activities we must consider whether there are any pre-existing relations between the two (or more) jurisdictions involved, and if so, what the responsibilities of each nation party has within that treaty agreement.

5.1.3 Case Hypothetical: Jurisdiction

As a fun example, if we consider the illustration below, we can see how establishing legal jurisdiction over a specific criminal instance may additionally be complicated by the cross-jurisdictional nature of cybercrime in the following scenarios below. For each hypothetical case, refer to the Jurisdictional Hypothetical figure in Fig. 5.1.

Example One

Blue Government of Blue Nation detects criminal activity coming from Blue Person within Blue Nation and being received by Pink Person in Pink Nation. Blue Government and Pink Government have a treaty agreement which states that each Nation must inform the other when cross-jurisdictional criminal activity is detected online.

Consider:

- Is there an obligation to inform?
- Who has jurisdictional authority?

Blue Nation informs Pink Nation.

Blue Nation and Pink Nation work together.

This is the simplest example.

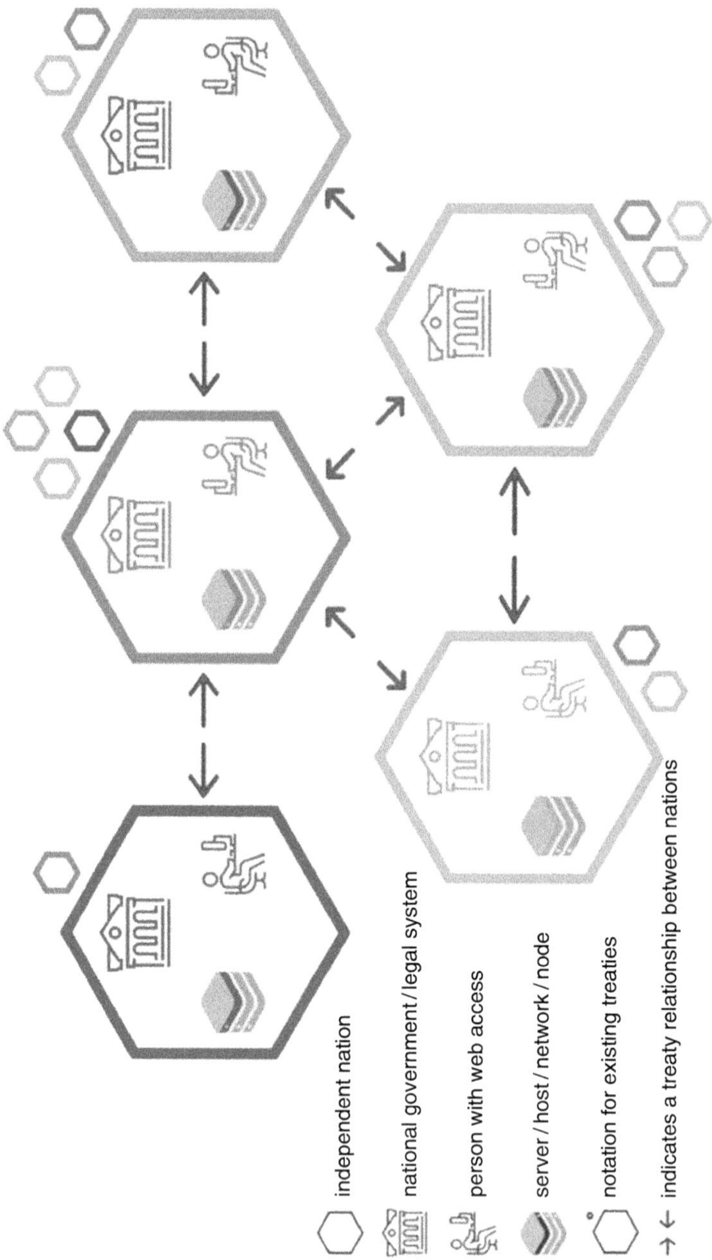

Fig. 5.1 Jurisdiction case hypothetical

Example Two
Blue Government detects criminal activity coming from Blue Person in Blue Nation and being received by Purple Person in Purple Nation. The Blue Government and Purple Government do not have a treaty agreement.

Consider:

- Does Blue Nation have an obligation to inform Purple Nation?
- Does Blue Government have the jurisdictional authority to intervene in Purple Nation for a crime that originated in Blue Nation?

Example Three
Blue Government detects criminal activity coming from Purple Person in Purple Nation and being received by Purple Person in Purple Nation. Blue Nation does not have any tie to the criminal activity other than having detected it. Blue Nation and Purple Nation do not have a treaty agreement.

Consider:

- Does Blue Nation have an obligation to inform Purple Nation?

Example Four
Blue Government detects criminal activity coming from Blue Person in Pink Nation and being received by Purple Person in Purple Nation. Pink Government has individual treaty agreements with both Blue Government and Purple Government which state that each Nation must inform the other when cross-jurisdictional criminal activity is detected online. The Blue Government and Purple Government do not have a treaty agreement.

Consider:

- We know that Blue Nation must inform Pink Nation. Does Blue Nation also have an obligation to inform Purple Nation?
- We know that the Pink Government has a treaty with both Blue Government and Purple Government and is aware that there is no existing treaty relationship between Blue Government and Purple Government. Does Pink Nation have an obligation to inform Purple Nation about criminal activity detected between Pink Nation and Purple Nation if that activity was detected and shared to Pink Nation by Blue Nation?
- Does Blue Nation have the jurisdictional authority to intervene in Purple Nation for a crime that originated with Blue Person in Pink Nation?

Example Five
Blue Nation and Green Nation have vastly different laws. What is criminalized in Green Nation is not always criminalized in Blue Nation. Purple Government detects criminal activity coming from Green Person in Pink Nation and being received by Purple Person with Blue Server in Blue Nation. The nature of this particular activity is not illegal in Blue Nation. Purple Government, who detected the activity, has treaties with Pink Government and Green Government which state that each Nation

must inform the other when cross-jurisdictional criminal activity is detected online. Green Government has similar treaties with Purple Government, Pink Government, and Orange Government, but not with Blue Government. Pink Government has treaties with Blue Government, Green Government, Purple Government, and Orange Government. The Blue Government only has a treaty with the Pink Government.

Consider:

- Who has jurisdictional authority?
- Which Nation has the obligation to inform which other Nation(s)?
- Does it matter if the activity is not illegal in Blue Nation?

Cross-jurisdictional considerations add a level of complexity to the issue of detecting, informing, and enforcing laws on encrypted global networks. Where a localized crime may be easy to assign within a legal jurisdiction, where an online crime may pass through multiple jurisdictions can be substantially more complicated. The area of law which specifically deals with cross-jurisdictional or inter-jurisdictional legal conflicts is called international law. Recall that international law can be either public or private, as discussed in Part One.

5.2 Digital Marketplaces and the Consumer

In this section, we will discuss the current issues relating to digital marketplaces with respect to consumer data and transactions done over the course of conducting business. We will start by looking at consumer rights, as they are applied in the global marketplace, including data protection agreements, and issues of privacy in online communication services. We will then explore the issues surrounding the regulation of commercial electronic messages (CEMs), also known as SPAM. Finally, we will examine the commercial application of data privacy, personal information protection, and cybersecurity laws on the international stage.

5.2.1 Rights of the Consumer in the Global Marketplace

Consumer rights refer to the protections provided under consumer protection legislation, which is implemented and enforced by the government and governmental bodies [7]. The specific rights of the consumer which are protected vary between jurisdictions. Some of the consumer rights which have been included in consumer protection legislation are the:

1. Right to Basic Needs
2. Right to Consumer Education
3. Right to Redress
4. Right to Healthy Environment
5. Right to Be Informed

6. Right to Be Heard
7. Right to Choose
8. Right to Safety

In this section, we will discuss the use of Consumer Data Privacy Agreements which exist to protect consumer data and personal information and the issue of privacy in online communications, particularly in organizations that collect, use, share, or otherwise interact with the personal data of consumers [8].

5.2.1.1 Data Protection Agreements

Data protection agreements are used to protect personal information (PI) about customers when organizations are sharing information. These agreements are usually entered into when one organization outsources or subcontracts part of their work to a third-party organization. In doing so, the contracting organization must often give the subcontractor personal information about its customers, in the course of regular business interactions, to allow the subcontractor to complete the work.

Personal information, in relation to data protection agreements, can include information about individual customers, employees, or other individuals. The protection of the personal information being shared always remains the responsibility of the organization responsible for collecting the information. That organization is responsible for ensuring that personal information is protected and handled in compliance with applicable laws [9].

As a result, it is of the utmost importance for organizations to take proper measures to protect any personal information collected, held, or otherwise used before transferring that information to a third-party service provider or subcontractor. Some of the measures that can be undertaken by organizations include:

- Scheduling regular reviews of their written privacy policies
- Consulting with experts about the past practices of the organization with regard to handling personal and other sensitive information
- Compiling information about prior privacy complaints and data breaches
- Entering into data protection agreements, or including privacy provisions as part of any service agreements

Data protection agreements should be specific to the parties involved, the exact data to be shared, the services to be provided, and the steps being undertaken to keep the data protected [10].

Most data protection agreements will include the following information:

- The ownership of the personal information
- The type and nature of the information that is being transferred
- The purpose for which the information can be collected, used, and disclosed
- Any confidentiality requirements
- Any restrictions on access to the information
- Any required safeguards put in place to protect personal information
- The procedure for updating, correcting, and deleting the information

- The right to inspect how the information is being protected
- Any restrictions on further transfer or access to the personal information
- An agreement to comply with privacy laws
- Any requirements to disclose government access requests or other disclosure orders—where permitted by law
- Any requirement to notify the organization and/or customer in the case of a breach
- The procedure for destroying and/or returning the information at the termination of the contract
- The consequences of breaching the data protection agreement obligations
- The consequences of breaching privacy laws

5.2.1.2 Privacy in Online Communications

Generally, individuals have the right to have their private communications remain private. In most circumstances, it is an invasion of privacy for someone to monitor or disclose the contents of private communications. However, different rules may apply for email communications that are sent or received over an employment-based email system or on an employer's computer. For this reason, it is important for employers to have policies in place that describe what kind of computer activities are permitted, which are prohibited, and the consequences for engaging in prohibited activities. The best way to avoid problems with Internet and email usage at the workplace is for employers to develop a written policy. The policy should include guidelines about topics such as: visiting inappropriate websites, spreading computer viruses, confidentiality, personal use, and copyright infringement. Most employers will also want to include an explicit right to monitor the electronic communications of their employees [11].

A note for employees:

Even if your employer does not have a policy about Internet and email use, you should assume that your employer can track all the websites you visit and read all the messages you send or receive, even after you have deleted them. If you use the computer system at your workplace to send or receive inappropriate messages, it could be considered "just cause" for your employer to fire you.

5.2.2 Commercial Electronic Messages

Our increased reliance on electronic messages, particularly in the context of doing business, exposes individuals and organizations to the increased risk of receiving unsolicited *commercial electronic messages*, which we call "spam."

Spam with respect to computer privacy refers to unwanted or unsolicited "commercial electronic messages" (CEMs) received over the internet. A *commercial electronic message* is any electronic message that encourages participation in a commercial activity, such as an email that contains a coupon or tells customers about a promotion or sale. That said, a message that includes hyperlinks to a website or contains business-related information does not make it a commercial electronic message.

Spam messages can be found on Internet forums, in text messages, blog comments, and social media. As an activity, "spamming" involves the use of computer messaging systems to send unwanted messages, often unsolicited advertising, to a large number of individual recipients for a prohibited purpose. Spamming is a serious security concern as it may be used as a means to deliver Trojan horses, viruses, worms, spyware, etc [12].

We can see spamming in the use of advertisement emails for stores, services, and other profitable enterprises, which, until recently, were not required to be sent with the consent of the recipient. The widespread implementation of anti-spam legislative provisions in many countries added a level of regulation to this type of advertising scheme, with violations of these some provisions being punishable by substantial fines.

While regular spam is simply any unsolicited email, messaging which contains infected attachments, phishing messages, or malicious URLs is more specifically known as "*malspam.*"

One of the most well-known malspamming threats faced by cybersecurity experts involves the use of a weaponized Rich Text Format (RTF) document—a file format used by Microsoft products, including MS Word and MS Office—to exploit a remote code execution vulnerability within MS Office. This is then used to download and execute a Warzone remote access Trojan.

A "*remote code execution*" (RCE) refers to the ability of a cyberattacker to access and make changes to a computer owned by another, without authority, and regardless of where the computer is geographically located. A "*remote access Trojan*" (RAT) is a type of malware program that provides a back door for remote access and administrative control over the target computer. RATs are often downloaded invisibly through a user-requested program—like a game—or sent as an email attachment.

Imperva, a cybersecurity software and services company based in California, has provided data indicating that at the height of the cryptocurrency boom in December 2017, almost 90% of all remote code execution attacks were driven by cryptocurrency mining. They also reported that 88% of all remote code execution attacks in December 2017 involved having a request sent to an external source to try to download a cryptocurrency mining malware.

> *These attacks try to exploit vulnerabilities in the web application source code, mainly remote code execution vulnerabilities, in order to download and run different crypto-mining malware on the infected server... [which] usually uses all CPU computing power, preventing the CPU from doing other tasks and effectively denies service to the application's users.*
>
> — Imperva

Spammers aim to reroute their outbound spam through an external computer, making it less detectable by Spamhaus, the world leader in supplying real-time highly accurate threat intelligence to the Internet's major networks. One of the most common techniques to achieve this is by using an inventory of compromised systems, called a "botnet," which can be remotely controlled by an external "*botmaster.*" When the botmaster issues a command to the botnet to begin sending out malspam in a widespread attack, it is called "spamming botnet attack" [13].

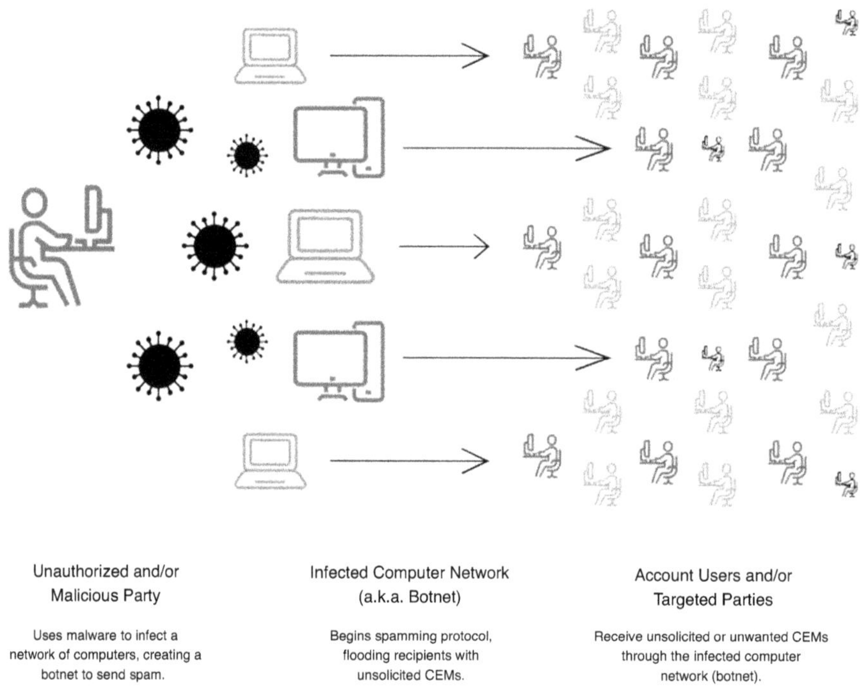

Fig. 5.2 Spamming botnet attack

5.2.2.1 Case Hypothetical: Using SPAM as a Cyber Attack

As an example of a *spamming botnet attack*, we can consider Fig. 5.2, which illustrates the hypothetical case of Person A, an unauthorized or malicious party, who wishes to send out mass communications for the purpose of phishing. In this example, Person A uses malware to infect a network of computers, which creates a botnet. The botnet begins spamming account users or targeted parties, flooding them with unsolicited commercial electronic messages. In this case, the recipients of these unsolicited messages will then be the target of phishing by Person A and potentially exploited for illegal financial gain.

5.2.3 International Commercial Application

International commercial law is a body of legal rules, conventions, treaties, domestic legislation, and commercial customs or usages, that govern international commercial or business transactions [14]. International commercial contracts are sale transaction agreements made between parties from different countries. The methods of entering the foreign market, with choice made balancing costs, control, and risk, include [15]:

1. Export directly
2. Use of a foreign agent to sell and distribute
3. Use of a foreign distributor to on-sell to local customers
4. Manufacture products in the foreign country by either setting up business or by acquiring a foreign subsidiary
5. License to a local producer for manufacturing
6. Enter into a joint commercial venture with a foreign entity
7. Appoint a franchisee in a foreign country

In international commercial law, a transaction is considered to be *international* when elements or entities of more than one country are involved [16].

5.2.3.1 Sources of International Commercial Law

The primary sources of international commercial law are:

1. Treaties and conventions
2. Decisions of the courts in various countries—including nation or state-specific domestic decisions
3. Decisions of regional courts—such as the European Court of Justice
4. Decisions by regional trade organizations—such as the North American Free Trade Agreement (NAFTA)
5. Resolutions of the United Nations (UN)
6. Agreements, resolutions, and decisions facilitated and regulated through the World Trade Organization (WTO)

We have previously touched on most of these sources earlier in this book but we have not yet discussed the World Trade Organization, which facilitates trade in goods, services, and intellectual property among participating countries. We will discuss that in more detail next.

5.2.3.2 The World Trade Organization (WTO)

As the global trade volume increases, contrasting national differences in trading rules bring about recurrent issues of protectionism, trade barriers, subsidies, and violation of intellectual property, and others. When these types of issues arise, the World Trade Organization serves as the mediator between the nation parties. The World Trade Organization (WTO) commenced operations in January 1995, replacing the previous General Agreement on Tariffs and Trade (GATT) which had been established and operational since 1948 [17].

The World Trade Organization is an intergovernmental organization that regulates and facilitates international trade between nations by providing a framework for negotiating trade agreements, which usually aim to reduce or eliminate tariffs, quotas, and other restrictions [18]. The WTO also administers independent dispute resolution for enforcing participants' adherence to trade agreements and resolving trade-related disputes.[1] Member governments look to the WTO to establish, revise, and enforce the agreed-upon rules that govern international trade. When created, these agreements are signed by representatives of national member governments and then ratified by the legislature within each individual nation-state [19].

The functions of the World Trade Organization can be summarized as [20]:

1. Overseeing the implementation, administration, and operation of the Agreements
2. Providing a forum for negotiations and for settling disputes
3. Reviewing and promoting the national trade policies
4. Ensuring the coherence and transparency of trade policies of the Agreements
5. Assisting the developing, least-developed, and low-income countries in transition to adjust to WTO rules and disciplines
6. Facilitating the implementation, administration, and operation—and furthering the objectives—of this Agreement and of the Multilateral Trade Agreements
7. Providing the framework for the implementation, administration, and operation of the Multilateral Trade Agreements
8. Providing the forum for negotiations among its members concerning their multilateral trade relations in matters which are listed in the Annexes of the Agreement
9. Administering the Understanding on Rules and Procedures Governing the Settlement of Disputes as well as the Trade Policy Review Mechanism [21]
10. Cooperate, as appropriate, with the International Monetary Fund (IMF) and with the International Bank for Reconstruction and Development (IBRD) and its affiliated agencies

The WTO establishes a framework for trade policies, but it does not define or specify outcomes as it is specifically concerned with setting the rules of "trade policy." As an organization, the WTO prohibits discrimination between trading partners but provides exceptions for environmental protection, national security, and other important goals. The five primary principles underpinning the WTO are: (1) non-discrimination; (2) reciprocity; (3) binding and enforceable commitments; (4) transparency; and (5) safety values. These are summarized in Table 5.1.

5.3 Anonymized DarkNet Markets and Cryptocurrencies

The rapid growth of encryption technology has revolutionized the online marketplace and helped to enable the creation of anonymous online networks, like the DarkNet—a hidden forum for which has attracted individuals who wish to engage in criminal activities while remaining anonymous and untraceable. Cybercriminal activity, unlike typical localized or neighborhood crimes, is not confined by national or provincial

[1] "U.S. Trade Policy: Going it Alone vs. Abiding by the WTO | Econofact". *Econofact*. 15 June 2018.

Table 5.1 Principles of the World Trade Organization (WTO)

Principle	Description
Non-Discrimination	Members of the WTO must apply the same favorable trade conditions—which are applied to another WTO member—equally to all trade with other WTO members. AND Imported goods should be treated no less favorably than domestically produced goods. BUT Exceptions can be made to allow preferential treatment for developing countries, regional free trade areas, and customs unions.
Reciprocity	Concessions between WTO members should be balanced or reciprocated. That is, trade policy alterations that change the volume of imports for each country should be of equal value to any changes in the volume of its exports.
Binding and Enforceable Commitments	Tariff commitments made by WTO members in multilateral trade negotiations and accessions are enumerated in a schedule of concessions, which also establish "ceiling bindings." This means that a country may only change its bindings after negotiating with its trading partners. If satisfaction is not achieved, the dissatisfied country can invoke the WTO dispute settlement procedures.
Transparency	Members of the WTO are required to publish their trade regulations, to maintain institutions allowing for the review of administrative decisions affecting trade, to respond to requests for information by other members, and to notify changes in trade policies to the WTO. These internal transparency requirements are supplemented and facilitated by periodic trade policy reviews through the Trade Policy Review Mechanism.
Safety Values	Members of the WTO are able to restrict trade or take other measures in specific circumstances to protect not only the environment but also public health, animal health, and plant health

borders or limited by physical geography. The fairly recent creation and development of cryptocurrencies, through the DarkNet, has created the possibility of full transactional anonymity for those involved in criminal activities both on- and offline.

For the most part, crime hidden on the Dark Web (accessed via the DarkNet) or committing using the DarkNet is not a novel crime; it is an established crime the commission of which is being facilitated through the use of anonymous encrypted networks. Rather than being a unique section of Canadian criminal law, the Dark Web merely acts as a different forum for activities that were already criminalized outside of the context of the Dark Web. The difficulty in creating laws to regulate Dark Web/DarkNet activity arises from the dual issues of detection/tracing and legal jurisdiction within an essentially unlimited and fully anonymous global encrypted network.

In this section, we will discuss the legal issues relating to encrypted online criminal activities, specifically those involving or facilitated by the use of Dark Web browsers and cryptocurrencies (such as TOR and Bitcoin, respectively) which provide anonymity to both parties in an illegal transaction. Cybercriminal activity is not confined by national borders or limited by geography so the main legal issues which stem from hidden online criminal activities are the inherent difficulties of detection/tracing on encrypted networks and the legal puzzle of navigating jurisdictional authority and balancing foreign and domestic relations, treaties between nations, and potentially conflicting interests on the international stage.

5.3.1 Illegal Content and Dark Web Marketplaces

Illegal content, such as child sexual abuse material (as we have discussed in Sect. 3.1.1) and DarkWet marketplaces go hand in hand, as individuals who are looking to acquire illegal content in exchange for consideration typically want their identity and the record of the transaction to be as discreet as possible. As DarkNets provide the most encryption, through anonymization, it makes sense that purveyors of illegal content would migrate to Dark Web marketplace forums accessed anonymously through the DarkNet [22].

5.3.1.1 DarkNet

The *DarkNet* is an online file-sharing network that provides users with anonymity through encryption and other cybersecurity technologies. This enables criminals to broker illegal goods and services on the Internet and avoid detection through anonymous online networks. The DarkNet attracts criminal activity by concealing online transactions, such as the online buying and selling of illegal drugs, pirated media, counterfeit goods, and other illicit products.

Through the use of the DarkNet and other anonymous online forums, criminals can easily purchase cybercrime tools, services, and supporting infrastructure. This service-based online market enables more criminals to take part in technologically advanced cybercrime activities, such as DDoS attacks or malware distribution through botnets. The online availability of such tools and services means that more criminals can outsource their cybercrime operations in part or in whole.

5.3.1.2 DarkMarkets and Virtual Currencies

DarkWeb Marketplaces (or DarkMarkets) act as a forum to facilitate illegal, or fringe, commercialized online transactions; a place in which illegal content, illicit and/or stigmatized goods, and unregulated services can be bought and sold without a record of the buyer, seller, or the transaction at all. Many times, these DarkMarket transactions are not only encrypted and anonymized, but are also completed with neither the buyer nor the seller having any knowledge of the name, location, or any identifying information of the other. The most anonymized transactions also involve the exchange of one or more cryptocurrencies.

Virtual currency schemes, such as Bitcoin, can also be used by criminals to launder their proceeds online. These types of currency schemes provide organized criminal networks with new ways to hide their earnings. The criminal use of virtual currencies is quite often associated with darknets, in which virtual currencies and anonymous online networks are used to obtain payments for illegal goods and services and launder revenue associated with criminal transactions.

Beyond simply providing an anonymized exchange of goods and services, the Dark Web has also been connected with the international humanitarian issue of human trafficking, formally known as trafficking in persons.

5.3.1.3 Illegal Trafficking in Persons or Goods

Trafficking in persons (or *human trafficking*) is the illegal, exploitative, and non-consensual transportation of persons for personal gain and is considered a criminal offence regardless of whether it occurs entirely within one jurisdiction—domestic trafficking—or involves the transportation of trafficked persons across national borders—international trafficking. However, the increasing use of digital technology—specifically the seeping growth in criminal awareness of, and familiarity with, untraceable access to the DarkNet and Dark Web content—has made it necessary for national legislators around the world to consider their respective understanding, law enforcement capacity, and individual national interests in working together to combat illegal online human trafficking on a global level.

The *Protocol to Prevent, Suppress and Punish Trafficking in Persons, Especially Women and Children* (the Palermo Protocol) is one of three protocols adopted by the United Nations to supplement the *United Nations Convention against Transnational Organized Crime* (the Palermo Convention); a multilateral treaty against organized crime which was drafted in 2000, ratified by many in 2002, and fully came into force in September 2003 [23]. The convention and its three protocols all fall under the jurisdiction of the United Nations Office on Drugs and Crime (UNODC) [24].

The Palermo Protocol and the Palermo Convention—collectively the *Protocol to Prevent, Suppress and Punish Trafficking in Persons, Especially Women and Children,* supplementing the *United Nations Convention against Transnational Organized Crime*—is the primary international instrument that deals with human trafficking. It aims to: prevent trafficking in persons; protect and assist victims of trafficking; bring traffickers to justice; and promote cooperation among the signatory countries. Within this Protocol, "human trafficking" is defined as:

> *...the recruitment, transportation, transfer, harbouring or receipt of persons, by means of the threat or use of force or other forms of coercion, of abduction, of fraud, of deception, of the abuse of power or of a position of vulnerability or of the giving or receiving of payments or benefits to achieve the consent of a person having control over another person, for the purpose of exploitation. Exploitation shall include, at a minimum, the exploitation of the prostitution of others or other forms of sexual exploitation, forced labour or services, slavery or practices similar to slavery, servitude or the removal of organs [25].*

This currently seems to be the most internationally accepted definition of human trafficking, at the time of writing [26].

As of November 2020, the *United Nations Convention against Transnational Organized Crime*—commonly known as the Palermo Convention—and the *Protocol to Prevent, Suppress and Punish Trafficking in Persons, Especially Women and Children*—also known as the Palermo Protocol—have a total of 190 parties, including 185 United Nation member states and 147 signatory parties.

While trafficking in persons is indeed a form of coercive and exploitative control—a defining feature of slavery—the transportation and possession of another person(s), often for the purpose of some variety of exploitation, it is by no means a "modern" trend [27]. As a comparison, historical experts have calculated that approximately 13 million people were captured and sold as slaves between the 15th and 19th centuries [28]. In 2014, a report from the International Labour Organization (ILO) estimated that over 21 million people globally were victims of human trafficking at that time [29].

Just three years later, a 2017 investigative report in the United Kingdom estimated that "slavery affects more than 40 million people worldwide, which is more than at any other time" in recorded history. To consider this in financial terms, research published in 2017 showed that individuals trafficking in persons make a return on their initial investment which is 25–30 times higher than that of the slave traders in the 18th and 19th centuries [30]. Also in 2017, the United Nations' Office on Drugs and Crime (UNODC) publicly recognized that many ongoing and escalating global conflicts were exposing more and more vulnerable populations to human trafficking and domestic forms of slavery, bringing the crime of human trafficking on par with firearms dealing and drug trafficking as a global criminal industry, in both scope and scale.[2]

In his 2017 book *Modern Slavery: A Global Perspective*, Siddharth Kara estimates that sex trafficking specifically accounts for around 50% of the total illegal profits generated by human trafficking. These calculations were based on data drawn from 51 countries over a 15 years period and from detailed interviews with more than 5000 individuals who have experienced victimization through human trafficking. This is made additionally shocking when the statistics he cites indicate that victims of sex trafficking only account for 5% of the total victims of trafficking [31].

It is important to note and be aware of the distinction between the subset of human sex trafficking (5%)—which is estimated to make up over 50% of the total illegal profits from all human trafficking—and consensual sexual activities which are done outside of the realm of human trafficking, violence, or sexual exploitation. This distinction exists even when the consensual sexual activities are done in exchange for some kind of benefit in consideration or as part of a mutually beneficial arrangement which features both consensual sexual activities and the provision of consideration.

Additionally, we can distinguish between the offences of human trafficking and human smuggling, which are distinct in terms of express consent, overlap with exploitation, and transnational nature. The smuggling of humans—although often undertaken in dangerous or degrading conditions—involves the intentional movement of migrant people who have given their consent to, or even provided consideration for, their being smuggled. In contrast, victims of human trafficking have either never consented to being trafficked or, if consent had initially been willingly given, their consent has since been rendered meaningless. As well, whereas human smuggling eventually ends with the migrant arriving at their destination, human trafficking tends to involve the ongoing exploitation of the trafficked victim. Finally,

[2] Updated statistics from the UN Office on Drugs and Crime (UNODC) are available for convenient and casual public perusal online at: unodc.org.

smuggling is always transnational, whereas human trafficking may not be transnational, as in domestic trafficking. This is because, in contrast to human smuggling, human trafficking can occur regardless of whether victims are transported across or between jurisdictions, nations, states, regions, or municipalities.

5.3.2 Differentiating the Dark from the Deep

We have previously discussed the distinction between cyber-dependent, cyber-enabled, and computer-supported crimes. To refresh: *cyber-enabled crimes* are those which can be committed without the use of technology, but are increased in their scale or reach by the use of a computer, network, or other technology; *cyber-dependent crimes* are crimes that can only be committed using a computer, a computer network, or other technology; and finally, *computer/cyber-supported crimes* are those in which the use of the computer or network is only incidental to the actual commission of the crime. The Dark Web is the medium in which these three classifications of cybercrime all converge. But first: definitions.

Net is a truncated form of the word network and refers to a network that includes several computers, servers, and connectors (e.g., a switch, hub, router, etc.). The network of computers can be either Intra-net or Inter-net.

Intranet (or intra-net)[3] is a private network such as your home network, a company or university network, or any other private network. An Intranet is naturally private until the user makes it public. At that point, the now-public Intra-net connects to other Intra-nets within the larger Inter-net.

The *Internet* (or inter-net)[4] is the larger network made up of all of these Intra-nets when they are made publicly available and accessible.

A *web page* (or web-page) is a page of content in a publicly available server, called a *web-server* which contains data and information. Combining several web-pages together creates a *website* (or web-site). Thus, a *web* is a collection of websites that could be legal or illegal. When you pay for your internet connection through your Internet Service Provider (or "ISP"), the ISP gives you the ability to connect to the public Inter-net through their Intra-net.

Depending on the level or lack of accessibility, the type of web being accessed falls within one of the layered categories of the internet: Surface Web, Deep Web, and Dark Web. To browse the Surface Web-sites in the Internet-Web (WWW) you need to use a browser like Firefox, Chrome, Safari, or Internet Explorer. To access the Dark Web, you need to use an anonymous encrypted browser like The Onion Router (called "TOR").

The *Surface Web* (or *Clear Web*) refers to your standard internet browsing experience. The Surface Web includes indexed websites which are accessible through traditional search engines and internet browsers. Anything that you can

[3]We will be using the terms intranet and intra-net interchangeably.

[4]For consistent inconsistency, we will also be using the terms internet and inter-net interchangeably.

find through a simple keyword search is considered to be Surface Web content and can be accessed through a typical internet connection. Examples of Surface Web sites include Google, Facebook, Yahoo, Wikipedia, and many news sites.

DeepWeb and *DeepNet* refer to the content and internet websites that exist and can be accessed on an encrypted network through the use of a password or other login credentials. It includes all unindexed sites; those which are not publicly accessible through a standard internet search on a typical internet browser. In most cases, these unindexed sites are not accessible because they are password-protected, encrypted, or require a login to gain access. Network administrators can connect to the Deep Web using the DeepNet when they have the username and password and use the assigned IPs.

The creation of the Deep Web in the 1970s was originally intended to protect and isolate networks from the Advanced Research Projects Agency Network and to hide the locations and IP addresses of US military operations for security purposes. Much of the content on the Deep Web comprises academic resources, patent information, and large-scale databases which are maintained by universities, governmental organizations, and other institutions. Examples of Deep Web content include online banking, personal email accounts, libraries, user databases, members-only sites, and other similar content which requires a password, login, or specific credential in order to gain access.

The *Dark Web* (or DarkWeb)[5] is the part of the greater unindexed Deep Web, which is both encrypted and anonymized, thus making it an attractive medium of communicating and transacting for the purpose of engaging in illegal activities. Reported illegal Dark Web activities include illegal file-sharing; intellectual property theft; drug and weapons dealing; trading in other illegal goods or criminalized services; human trafficking; accessing, creating, and distributing child pornography; and, allegedly, a myriad of just about anything else you could imagine.

In recent years, illegal Dark Web marketplaces have acted as a catalyst for the development of cryptocurrencies because online exchanges which are completed using cryptocurrency protect the identity of both the buyer and the seller in the transactions, which can be highly desirable for both parties. The anonymity of cryptocurrency also helps in preventing the build-up of a "paper trail" of traceable evidence from being created while engaged in illegal activities. Without clear, definitive, traceable evidence to tie an individual or group to a crime, the anonymized Dark Web enables people who are engaging in online criminal activities to better evade detection and identification by law enforcement.

The *DarkNet* (or Dark Net)[6] refers to the unused address space of the internet which is not speculated to interact with other computers in the world. It is "Dark" because of its inherently anonymous nature, virtual marketplace, and use of cryptocurrency. The Dark Web could be accessible through the DarkNet, beyond the reach of the World Wide Web search engines.

---

[5] As is likely suspected, we will be using the forms Dark Web and DarkWeb interchangeably.

[6] Once again, we will be using the forms Dark Net and DarkNet interchangeably. This should no longer be a surprise.

The DarkNet is a network of IPs that attackers can use as a medium for illegal activities, such as connecting to the Dark Web to access illegal content without detection and identification or to execute large-scale cyber-attack scenarios with 100% anonymity. As an example, a potential cyber-attacker could use thousands of unassigned IPs in the DarkNet to prepare a DDoS attack on a large organization knowing that no one will be able to trace the attack back to them. Together, the Dark Web and DarkNet provide anonymous and encrypted access to hidden and potentially illegal web content within the larger Deep Web.

These three layers of the overall internet are illustrated in Fig. 5.3, using the popular iceberg metaphor [32].

5.3.2.1 Encryption and Anonymization

"TOR" or *"The Onion Router"* is a commonly used encrypted browser that can be used to connect the user to the DarkNet and allow access to the Dark Web. The TOR model uses encryption from the user point of contact to the Entry Node, through an unknown Relay Node, to an Exit Node, where it is then decrypted at the receiving end. The onion is used as a metaphor as it compares peeling back each layer of encryption to peeling off the layers of protective outer skin on an onion. The type of encryption used in the TOR model is provided in Fig. 5.4 [32].

5.3.2.2 Deep Dark Legal Questions, Simplified

While some tech-savvy internet users prefer the encrypted browsing option to guarantee their privacy and anonymity and/or to prevent tracking or monitoring software from collecting data about their online activities and behaviors, many other internet users are unfamiliar with browsers like TOR and so are unsure of the legal implications of using such a browser. We have created a list of commonly asked questions about the law and the Dark Web to try to answer the easiest questions in the most straightforward way.

Is the Dark Web Illegal?

No.

—The Dark Web itself is not illegal. While there are many websites within the Dark Web that specialize in illegal products, marketplaces, activities, or services, for the most part the content on the Dark Web is not illegal. That said, using the Dark Web or DarkNet to engage in criminal activities would absolutely be illegal; however, it would be the activity itself that is criminalized, not the Dark Web as a medium.

Is It Illegal to Access the Dark Web?

No, but. . .

—The act of simply accessing the Deep or Dark Web is not a criminal offence in most common law countries. However, an offence of illegally accessing private data in a Deep Web network for which you are not authorized to have access (e.g., hacking, intrusion upon seclusion, privacy breach) could be considered an offence under laws that we have previously discussed.

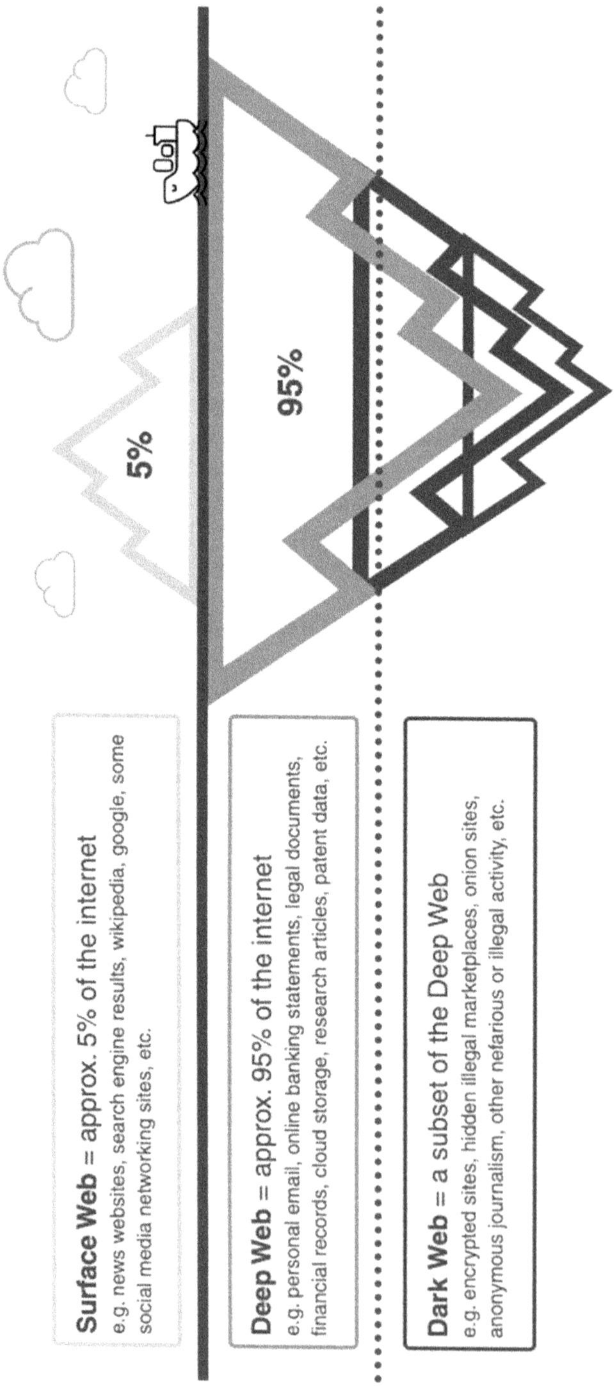

Fig. 5.3 Dark web iceberg model [32]

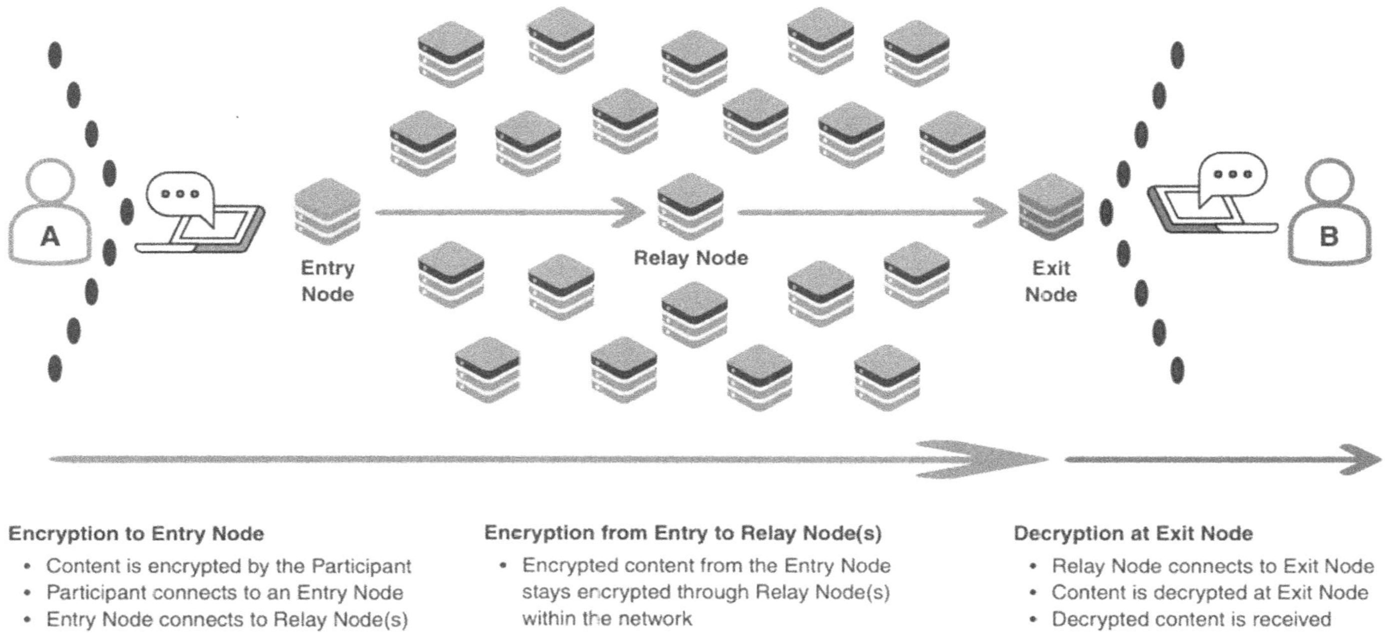

Fig. 5.4 TOR encryption model [32]

Is It Illegal to use an Encrypted Browser to Explore the Dark Web?
No.

— It is not illegal to use an encrypted browser, like TOR, to explore the Dark Web. It is not uncommon for internet users who are concerned about monitoring and tracing (e.g. journalists, researchers, and patent owners) to use encrypted web browsers to anonymously and confidentially communicate without jeopardizing their personal safety, security, or personal private data. That said, it is illegal to use an encrypted browser to commit a criminal offence. The browser itself is not illegal but using it as a tool for illegal activities could be a crime.

Is the Dark Web/DarkNet Actively Monitored by Law Enforcement?
Yes, sort of…

—Canadian law enforcement does try to monitor Dark Web content and activity; however, there is no currently available law enforcement software—based on our Surface Web search—that can adequately detect and monitor illegal access, communications, activities, and encrypted content transmitted over the Dark Web.

Does Law Enforcement Care About the Dark Web/DarkNet?
Yes.

—Law enforcement would like to be able to detect and trace criminal activities done over the Dark Web. Some of the most commonly highlighted goals of law enforcement with regard to the Dark Web are to prevent child pornography, to shutdown illegal marketplaces which provide a forum for exchanging goods or services for consideration—which sometimes may take the form of payment in one or more cryptocurrencies—and to combat the problem of global and domestic human trafficking as enabled or otherwise facilitated using encrypted networks, or DarkNet.

Can I Get into Legal Trouble by Accessing the Dark Web/DarkNet?
Maybe.

—While simply accessing the Dark Web is not a criminal offence, there is a possibility that you will stumble upon sites that host illegal marketplaces for purchasing drugs, weapons, other illegal goods, as well as child pornography, snuff porn, criminals for hire, and human trafficking. If you were to engage with one of these illegal sites and break a law, then you could be charged with a crime and end up in legal trouble.

Do I Have Any Legal Responsibilities on the Dark Web/DarkNet?
Yes.

—Your responsibilities on the Deep Web and Dark Web are the same as those on the Surface Web, which are similar to the legal responsibilities you have when you are offline, or in real life. As would be the case in other mediums, here are some examples of individual responsibilities with regard to creating and controlling content on the internet, based on the common law legal system:

- If you create or exercise control over content on the internet, then you may be responsible for any damage caused by that content.
- If you have control over content that you learn is infringing upon a law or the individual rights of another person and you choose to do nothing about it then you may be liable for your inaction.
- If you intentionally or knowingly infringe upon the rights of another person, then you may be liable for any damages caused as a result.
- If you use the Deep Web/DeepNet or Dark Web/DarkNet to commit an act elsewhere that is illegal in your country, you may still be held accountable and legally responsible under the law of your country of origin.
- If you develop or create illegal content, even if that content is subsequently made available only from a server located outside of your country, you may still be held criminally responsible.
- If you commit a criminal offence, regardless of whether it takes place on- or offline, then you can be charged for that criminal offence and be held legally responsible.

The Deep/Dark Web is not a separate or distinct legal realm, but merely an alternative medium for communicating and interacting remotely with others. Criminal activities are illegal regardless of whether they take place in person, at a distance, remotely, or through the use of technology. If you commit a crime then you can be charged for that crime.

5.3.3 Cryptocurrencies

Some transactions, on both the Surface Web and the Dark Web, take place using cryptocurrencies. Since its first introduction in 2009, the popularity of cryptocurrencies, also called digital currencies, has grown substantially. Legislators and corporations are finding it necessary to consider the widespread social, legal, and financial implications of a growing online world of decentralized currencies, in the form of cryptocurrencies, which can be used to anonymize online transactions on the Surface Web just as they can on the DarkNet. As an extra bonus, some cryptocurrencies can also be used—albeit infrequently—for purchases in traditional physical in-person stores and marketplaces, known as “brick and mortar businesses.”

Cryptocurrencies, like Bitcoin, are anonymous and cannot be traced because they are decentralized. This allows a buyer in one region to convert their national currency to a common cryptocurrency and complete an online transaction with a seller in another region using that cryptocurrency. The seller, upon receipt of the cryptocurrency at the end of the transaction, could then convert the cryptocurrency from the buyer into the national currency of their region. The currency conversion on both ends would be done anonymously and encrypted over the DarkNet, circumventing the use of banking institutions for currency conversion, and essentially eliminating all banking fees related to currency conversion services. Cutting the cost of the conversion service provided by a bank also allows for individuals to send money to family in other countries or regions without having to use a banking and wire transfer service at a highly inflated cost, allowing the individual to retain more of their own money.

Over the last decade, cryptocurrency schemes have become increasingly accessible, with increased public awareness and understanding as the years have passed. The inherent benefits of the anonymous nature of cryptocurrency transactions were quickly picked up and used by criminals to obtain payments for illegal goods and services and to launder illegal revenue, from criminal activities, from the comfort of their own homes.

A recent special report published by the *Association of Certified Financial Crime Specialists*, explains that cryptocurrency gained traction in the financial world as access to bitcoin became more widespread which started the gradual shift of criminal enterprises from more traditional financial products to cryptocurrency. This massive shift along with the protective features offered by the use of DarkWeb and DarkNet technology made it inevitable that the human trafficking industry would begin to use cryptocurrencies as well [33].

For the purpose of cyber-enabled human trafficking, it should be noted that cryptocurrencies can be used in a wide variety of online and in-person transactions relating to human trafficking, including payment to the trafficker; remittance of funds to an organization leader; and/or dispersion of profits to all involved in trafficking the individual, which would typically appear in the pattern of periodic large cryptocurrency purchases and remittances. Additionally, cryptocurrencies can be used to make untraceable payments to websites that advertise sexual services, paid pornography sites, and other activities related to the nightly business of prostitution, all of which would typically appear in an account as many frequent "low dollar" transactions [34]. The result of all of this appears as a frequent but inconsistent variety of transaction amounts and frequencies, at all times of the day, all of which may be indicative of human trafficking [33].

Along with being associated with nefarious activities for which anonymization would be fairly necessary, cryptocurrencies are also known for being especially volatile as a trading option in the market.

The data in Table 5.2 below, which was sourced from CoinDesk Research, is based on dividing bitcoin volatility into three ranges: high, mid, and low. High is volatility at or above 100%. Mid is volatility at or above 50%, and below 100%. Low is volatility below 50%. Volatility is the 30-day standard deviation of daily log returns, annualized at 365 days of trading.

5.3.4 Corporate Considerations

In our quickly changing world, it has become necessary for corporations to examine their own strategies on how to either implement or avoid the influx of encrypted tech, the expansion of cryptocurrencies, and the looming threat of large-scale data breaches and ransomware attacks which are becoming more and more common.

Table 5.2 Average duration of bitcoin volatility periods

YEAR	HIGH	MID	LOW	ALL
2014	40	38	45	40
2015	28	49	57	48
2016	N/A	62	114	79
2017	13	72	85	61
2018	136	87	58	92
2019	23	70	40	44
2020	36	56	46	50
2021	32	62	N/A	52
ALL	38	60	58	54

Source: CoinDesk Research, April 25 2021.
Volatility = annualized 30d std dev of daily log returns. "High" = 30d avg vol >= 1.0; 1.0 > "Mid" >= 0.5; "Low" < 0.5.

The increasing use of encryption technology and the Dark Web as a platform for intellectual property infringement as well as commercial and other crimes requires governments, businesses, and individuals to be mindful of any current and future potential impact of Dark Web activity in relation to their interests. Often, when private corporate records obtained in data breaches are published and offered for sale, the forum used to leak this stolen data involves the use of the Dark Web/Dark Net.

5.3.4.1 The DarkNet

With the growth and expansion of the online marketplace, even before the COVID-19 pandemic lockdowns had people switching from in-person to online shopping, we are entering a new frontier of commercial enterprise. The rise in popularity of encryption technology and interest in cryptocurrencies presents a novel medium, or forum, for previously criminalized criminal activities. This advancement has allowed illegal online activities to become truly borderless, as browsing and transactions can now be completed not only with encryption but with full anonymity.

It is now possible, and not at all uncommon, for an individual in one jurisdiction to connect to a remote server in another jurisdiction, which can then connect to or host content that is not available or highly illegal in the jurisdiction in which the individual is operating. The Dark Web/Dark Net provides access to a hidden realm in which the lack of detection, monitoring, and tracing ability of law enforcement enables an absence of accountability for the user.

As large-scale malicious data breaches and extortion via data theft is now a reality for companies operating online and using cloud networks, it is worth considering the question of liability for corporations with respect to data protection and the Dark Web. Certainly, at the very least, requiring additional authentication for approved user access to Deep Web material is an obvious initial preventative and protective measure, but it is also important to proactively prepare for what happens when prevention and protection are not enough and irreparable widespread damage is caused from a privacy or data breach of a large magnitude.

This technology is powerful and unprecedented. We are more connected to our devices and the online world than ever before. Now, more than ever, it is necessary for corporations and legislators alike to become more aware and informed of encrypted online networks and the risks of massive, large-scale data hacks and subsequent anonymous Dark Web data dumps. The added complexity of determining legal jurisdictional authority in a naturally cross-jurisdictional and international encrypted and anonymized realm, while ominous and off-putting, is a challenge that must be tackled before international Dark Web/Dark Net cryptocurrency-enabled cross-jurisdictional crimes become more prevalent and we are forced to deal with the influx of class-action lawsuits which may inundate us sooner than we ever thought possible.

5.3.4.2 Cryptocurrencies

For businesses who want to connect with the anonymous online market or accept a wider range of international currencies, this could involve expanding current financial services to accept specific cryptocurrencies as payment for both online and in-person transactions or providing a variable conversion rate for specified cryptocurrencies. This would allow a buyer in one region to convert their national currency to a common cryptocurrency, complete an online transaction with a seller in another region using the agreed-upon cryptocurrency. The seller, upon receipt of the cryptocurrency at the end of the transaction, could then convert the cryptocurrency into the national currency of their region.

For example, in Canada, the law of securities regulation and banking is under the federal division of power. This means that any laws or legislation relating to the regulation and legal exchange of cryptocurrencies (as a security) falls under federal legal jurisdiction. The main issues facing federal legislators in tackling the cryptocurrency markets are a general lack of understanding and awareness of cryptocurrencies, the perceived complexity of blockchain structure, the lack of a centralized data depository for keeping records of transaction history, the difficulty in tracing and identifying the individual parties on either side of a transaction, the inability to determine the contents or context of a transaction, and the general uncertainty and fear of a notoriously volatile online currency which many in government and law still do not fully understand.

5.3.4.3 Corporate Liability

As large-scale malicious data breaches and extortion via data theft is now a reality for companies operating online and using cloud networks, it is worth considering the question of liability for corporations with respect to data protection and the Dark Web. Certainly, at the very least, requiring additional authentication for approved user access to Deep Web material is an obvious initial preventative and protective measure, but it is also important to proactively prepare for what happens when prevention and protection are not enough and irreparable widespread damage is caused from a privacy or data breach of a large magnitude [35].

5.3.4.4 Case Hypothetical: Corporate Data Breach

Company X is an online and app-based dating and social networking service which is marketed primarily to people who are married or already in relationships. Sadly, polyamory is frowned upon and highly socially stigmatizing in this hypothetical world. As a result of social norms and stigma, Company X markets its websites to potential customers based primarily on the security and discretion which their services offer to subscribers, describing the sites as being "safe, secure, and worry-free."

In an effort to appeal to a wide range of subscribers, Company X launched three sites: one paid premium site, one free site, and one pay-what-you-can site. All three sites generated a high level of site traffic, allowing Company X to generate additional profits by selling website advertising space to other companies, also with a wide range of customers and consumers. After building up an impressive subscriber base, Company X launched an initial public offering, issuing a new publicly traded stock for interested investors. Over the following years, profits continued to soar.

During this time, the paid subscription site quickly became the primary source of profit generation for Company X, growing in popularity as well as notoriety. Unfortunately, while on its journey to success, Company X had garnered the unwanted attention of a cluster of malicious parties, becoming the frequent target of cyberattacks. The majority of these attacks were aimed at accessing the personal and financial information of Company X's subscribers.

Eventually, one of the malicious parties, Group A, was able to successfully hack into the user database for all three of the sites. Once the data breach had reached news media organizations and catalyzed a suitable amount of panic amongst site users, Group A enthusiastically announced and took ownership of their vigilante activism, while remaining anonymous behind the facade of the Group. Group A demanded two things: a ransom of $1,000,000 to be converted to an untraceable cryptocurrency and transferred over the DarkNet to a digital wallet held by Group A; and for all three sites to immediately be shut down.

To encourage compliance with their demands, Group A threatened to release the full names, home addresses, search histories, chat logs, and personal member credit card numbers of all current and former subscribers of all sites operated by Company X if those sites were not removed—and the full ransom paid—within three days. To further complicate the issue, Group A offered to extend the deadline by 24 hours for each time Company X made a lump sum payment of $100,000 to the Group. As specified with the main random, these "extension payments" were also to be converted into an untraceable cryptocurrency and transferred over the DarkNet, but to a different digital wallet. Initially, the executives of Company X doubted the validity of the claims made by Group A and chose to ignore the looming threat.

By the following day, word of the massive cyberattack and data breach had funneled through the news channels on all varieties of medium. The public was soon informed of the threats that had been made by Group A and the subsequent demands for the large ransom payment and website removal. The public also became aware of the offer made to Company X to make "extension payments" to delay the data release by 24 hours for each payment. Chaos ensued but Company X publicly refused to give in to the demands made by Group A.

The time slowly crept by, and the third day came along. Public outcry seemed to grow by the hour and public opinion became markedly more divisive with factions breaking out between: those who felt the data should be released regardless of a ransom; those who felt the data should be protected at all costs; those who felt it was the responsibility of Company X to take care of any necessary ransom payments in order to protect the data; and those who did not care. After receiving substantial feedback from fearful subscribers and gathering plentiful input from a variety of investors and stakeholders, Company X declined to submit to Group A's demand and waited in anticipation of what they hoped was a bluff.

On the fourth day, as was threatened, the first mass data release occurred. Over 60GB of subscriber personal information was made available via the DarkNet and quickly spread to mainstream surface internet forums. The breach was promptly validated by cybersecurity experts who found the personal information to be highly accurate and the chat logs to be extensive and disturbingly detailed. Company X continued to refuse to submit to Group A's demands and held strong.

The second successful breach took place on the fifth day, with the release of a further 80GB of user data. By this time, after only 36 hours of the personal information being available online, some of Company X's subscribers reported receiving extortion mails requesting payment in cryptocurrency to prevent the public release of their personal information. Other subscribers, specific to the paid site, were threatened with the release of all of their in-app chat logs and account information to their significant other.

The sixth day followed with an additional 20GB of data. Police services indicated reports of suicide and many extortion attempts associated with the leak of individual user profiles. Company X responded by offering a reward of and offered a reward of $500,000—notably higher than the total amount of "extension payments" which would have been made for a 3-day delay on the data releases—for any information which would lead to the arrest of the hackers.

On the seventh day, Group E returned with the results of their investigation into the cyberattack, the data breach, and the subsequent data release. The reports suggested that Company X was using an outdated cybersecurity system which was a couple of years behind the standard cybersecurity system used in other websites with high traffic and user-generated content. As well, Group E had uncovered a few years' worth of emails in the Junk mailbox folder of the CEO of Company X, which specifically warned that the cybersecurity system was about to expire, and then expired, out-of-date, and in need of an upgrade. While these emails did come from the previous cybersecurity system provider, they were mislabelled as SPAM and ended up in the Junk folder, unbeknownst to the CEO.

Following this massive data breach, a $500 million class-action lawsuit was filed against Company X by subscribers who had been negatively impacted by the data breach and who alleged that Company X was negligent and should be held responsible for damage incurred because of the data breach. No one associated with Group A has been identified by law enforcement and there are no leads at this time.

Consider:

1. Whose data, is it?
2. Who has ownership?
3. Who has possession?
4. Who has interest?
5. Where is the data located?
6. Who is responsible for the data?
7. Who should be held liable for the breach?
8. What could have been done to protect the data?
9. What could have been done to mitigate the damage?
10. At what point, if any, should Company X be obligated to respond, and in what way?
11. What do you think the outcome should be?

5.4 Challenges to Law Enforcement

Law enforcement faces many challenges in their work to enforce and apply the laws within their respective jurisdictions. Some of the challenges in applying the law include the issues of: decentralization; detection, tracing, and localization; determination of jurisdiction and type of jurisdiction necessary to enforce and apply the law; and the issue of law enforcement capacity and resource allocation. Regarding enforcing existing laws against online crime and illegal activity, there are four main goals of law enforcement:

1. *Detection*—initial front-line red flags, access, transmission source, type of action, content, context
2. *Tracing*—access point, transmission source, location of action, content source, content context, transmission destination
3. *Evidence Collection*—admissible, relevant, material, collected at all points during transaction from point of access to transmission destination and receipt
4. *Enforcement*—must be within jurisdictional authority or be party to a treaty with that jurisdictional authority

Sites and content on the Dark Web cannot be indexed by a crawling web browser like Google. The IPs on the DarkNet are not assigned to any user, so are anonymous. This makes it definitely difficult for law enforcement to find and access specific Dark Web/DarkNet websites and connection methods, to detect and monitor illegal activities, to trace and localize the source of the illegal activities, and to enforce the applicable laws on the involved parties [36].

The often international and/or cross-jurisdictional nature of the DarkWeb and DarkNet makes it essential for criminal investigators to be able to collaborate across law enforcement agencies and without the limitation of borders to have any chance of effectively regulating or enforcing law on the DarkWeb and DarkNet.

5.4.1 Decentralization

Cryptocurrencies, such as Bitcoin, Litecoin, Etherium, etc., are anonymous and cannot be easily traced because the ledgers for cryptocurrency transactions are decentralized. This allows a buyer in one region to convert their national currency to a common cryptocurrency and complete an online transaction with a seller in another region using that cryptocurrency. The seller, upon receipt of the cryptocurrency at the end of the transaction, could then convert the cryptocurrency balance received from the buyer into their own national or regional currency. The currency conversion on both ends would be done anonymously and encrypted over the DarkNet, circumventing the use of banking institutions for currency conversion, and essentially eliminating all banking fees related to currency conversion services [37].

By cutting the cost of the conversion service provided by a bank also allows for individuals to send money to family in other countries or regions without having to use a banking and wire transfer service at a highly inflated cost, allowing the individual to retain more of their own money.

In Fig. 5.5, the structural and operational differences between centralized network transactions and decentralized network transactions are visually provided for better understanding.

5.4.2 Detection, Tracing and Localization

The Dark Web/DarkNet are "dark" because they are hidden. Sites and content on the Dark Web cannot be indexed by a crawling web browser like Google. The IPs on the DarkNet are not assigned to any user, they are anonymous. This makes it definitively difficult for law enforcement to find and access specific Dark Web/DarkNet websites and connection methods, to detect and monitor illegal activities, to trace and localize the source of the illegal activities, and to enforce the applicable criminal laws on the involved parties.

For example, over two million people per day use TOR to access the Dark Web, but we do not yet have a highly accurate solution to detect the content and behaviors in the users' activities on TOR. In 2014, He Gaofeng and his team from the China Electronic Power Resource proposed an idea that would detect the Browsing, File Transfer, and P2P Connection activities in TOR traffic within 600 seconds. Later in 2016, Dr. Lashkari and his team from the University of New Brunswick (UNB) proposed a highly accurate solution using network traffic analysis to detect and characterize user behaviors on TOR and VPN within ten seconds.

Few currently available solutions have coverage that is sophisticated enough to be truly effective at detecting, monitoring, characterizing, and tracing TOR-based activity. As a result, there is a lot of fear, uncertainty, and doubt concerning the effectiveness of cybersecurity laws in this complex, rapidly evolving arena. As research in this field continues, there are likely to be novel solutions proposed to deal with criminal activity on the Dark Web. Since 2015, Dr. Lashkari and his team working in this area, and recently as 2020, they proposed a new solution using image

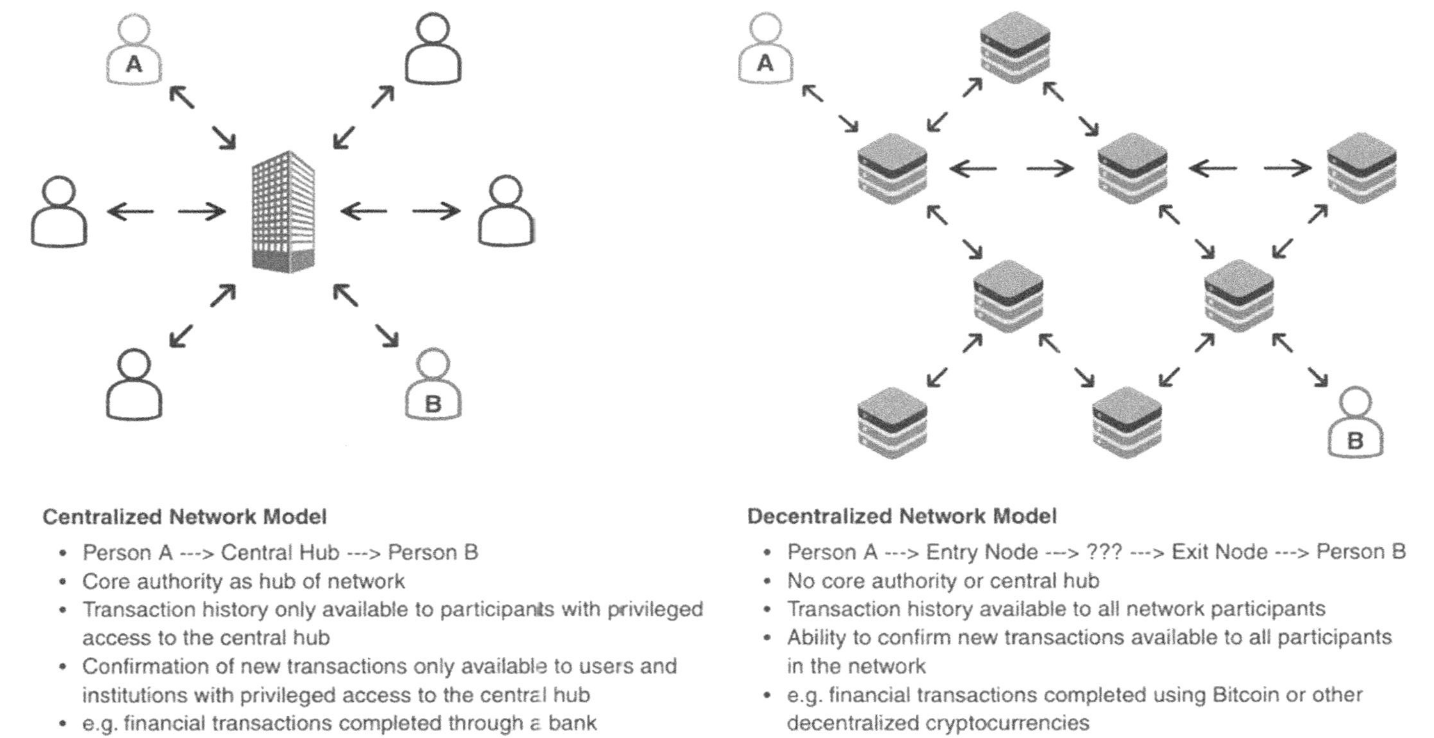

Fig. 5.5 Centralized vs decentralized network transactions

processing and AI, called "Deep Image DarkNet" (or "DIDarknet") to detect and characterize user activities [38]. So far, these activities include detection and characterization for browsing, chat, email communication, file transfers, streaming, VoIP and P2P, and can already be applied to over eighteen representative applications, including Facebook, Skype, Spotify, and Gmail.

5.4.3 Jurisdiction and Enforcement

Unlike visible criminal activity on the street, the anonymous nature of the Dark Web/DarkNet makes it challenging for law enforcement to immediately know when a law is being broken or harm is being done. When law enforcement has been notified of illegal transactions, the use of a decentralized network for confirmation and verification of Dark Net transactions limits the ability of law enforcement to localize an offence to a specific jurisdiction, even when there is very clearly a law being broken somewhere by someone. Compounding this issue is the inherent cross-jurisdictional and international nature of the Dark Web/DarkNet, which can be hindered by testy international relations, unsigned treaties, and conflicting interests between jurisdictional parties and law enforcement organizations.

5.4.4 Digital Evidence Collection

Digital evidence, also known as electronic evidence, refers to evidence that is stored or transmitted in digital form that a party to a court case may use at trial. The use of digital evidence has increased tremendously as courts have allowed the use of emails, ATM transaction logs, mobile phone message histories, databases, the contents of computer hard drives, computer printouts, GPS logs, and digital video and audio files [39].

As with other types of evidence, the courts require proper use and presentation of the electronic evidence under current provincial and federal evidence legislation. In addition, because electronic evidence can be both more accurate and more easily tampered with than other forms of evidence, the courts may require additional information before allowing the evidence to be introduced.

It is estimated that over two million people use TOR to access the DarkWeb every day, but we do not yet have a highly accurate solution to detect the content and behavior context in activities on the DarkWeb. Few currently available solutions have data coverage that is sophisticated enough to be effective at detecting, monitoring, characterizing, and tracing TOR-based activity. This flows into the next challenge: how to gather evidence when the activities cannot be accurately detected and traced. For this topic, we must turn to the Law of Evidence.

Evidentiary law is the body of regulations governing the proof of the existence of a fact before a court. It is the machinery by which substantive laws are set and kept in motion. So it can be said that the law of evidence deals with rights, as well as, procedures. The general meaning of the term "evidence" is "the available body of facts or information indicating whether a belief or proposition is true or valid."

The law of evidence is also concerned with the quantum (amount), quality, and type of proof needed to prevail in litigation. The rules vary depending upon whether the venue is a criminal court, civil court, or family court, and they vary by jurisdiction. The quantum of evidence is the amount of evidence needed; the quality of proof is how reliable such evidence should be considered. Important rules that govern admissibility, concern hearsay, authentication, relevance, privilege, witnesses, opinions, expert testimony, identification, and the rules of physical evidence. There are various standards of evidence, standards showing how strong the evidence must be to meet the legal burden of proof required in a given situation, ranging from reasonable suspicion to preponderance of the evidence, to clear and convincing evidence, or to beyond a reasonable doubt. The rules vary depending upon whether the venue is a criminal court, civil court, or family court, and they vary by jurisdiction. As an example, we can look at the Law of Evidence in Canada [40].

5.4.5 Example in Law: Canada's Evidence Act

Section 31.1 of the *Canada Evidence Act* allows electronic evidence to be admitted into evidence as long as the person seeking to admit such evidence proves its authenticity.[7]

31.1 Any person seeking to admit an electronic document as evidence has the burden of proving its authenticity by evidence capable of supporting a finding that the electronic document is that which it is purported to be.

31.2 (1) The best evidence rule in respect of an electronic document is satisfied

(a) *on proof of the integrity of the electronic documents system by or in which the electronic document was recorded or stored; or*

(b) *if an evidentiary presumption established under section 31.4 applies.*

(2) Despite subsection (1), in the absence of evidence to the contrary, an electronic document in the form of a printout satisfies the best evidence rule if the printout has been manifestly or consistently acted on, relied on or used as a record of the information recorded or stored in the printout.

31.3 For the purposes of subsection 31.2, in the absence of evidence to the contrary, the integrity of an electronic documents system by or in which an electronic document is recorded or stored is proven

(a) *by evidence capable of supporting a finding that at all material times the computer system or other similar device used by the electronic documents system was operating properly or, if it was not, the fact of its not operating properly did not affect the integrity of the electronic document and there are no*

[7] *Canada Evidence Act* (RSC, 1985, c C-5), s 31.1.

other reasonable grounds to doubt the integrity of the electronic documents system

(b) *if it is established that the electronic document was recorded or stored by a party who is adverse in interest to the party seeking to introduce it; or*

(c) *if it is established that the electronic document was recorded or stored in the usual and ordinary course of business by a person who is not a party and who did not record or store it under the control of the party seeking to introduce it.*

Without relevant, material, and admissible evidence, it would be nearly impossible to convict someone of a crime if all communications and transactions were to take place over the DarkNet.

5.4.6 Case Hypothetical: Challenges to Law Enforcement

Country X taxes all personal income generated by its citizens and requires all individuals, businesses, and organizations to report any earnings or losses made throughout the fiscal year.

Country Z—a neighboring country of Country X—has far less taxation on income than Country X. Also, conversely to Country X, Country Z is known for having an extremely strict criminal justice system in which the laws are heavily enforced.

Person A is a citizen of Country X, but has been living in Country Z for the last six months. During that time, Person A has generated a large sum of cash that was gained through transactions related to activities that are illegal in Country Z but not in Country X. The cash is in the form of a currency used by Country X, not Country Z. Person A would like to launder the cash through the DarkNet to avoid any taxation costs or other penalties assigned by Country X, as that is where Person A is expected to pay taxes on income.

To this end, Person A converts the cash—through a third party based in Country Y—to a popular digital currency. Person A then transfers the decentralized currency through multiple holding parties, each of which are anonymized and spread over many different jurisdictions. Finally, Person A converts the digital currency into the local currency used by Country Z. Person A reports no income on taxes from this series of transactions.

Officer K is a law enforcement officer in Country X who has received information from a private citizen—Person B—that leads them to believe that Person A has been wilfully evading taxes. Officer K is put in charge of the investigation into the tax evasion activities of Person A. In Country Z, Officer Q is assigned to be the liaison for inter-jurisdictional matters between Country Z and Country X.

A few of the issues:

- Who has jurisdiction for taxation?
- Who has jurisdiction for criminal law?
- Is there a treaty or other agreement between Country X and Country Z?

- Does tax evasion relate to Country X matter to Officer Q of Country Z?
- Does illegal activity in Country Z matter to Officer K of Country X?
- Where does Country Y fit into this?
- Can the currency conversions and transactions be traced by Officer K?
- What obstacles to digital evidence collection will be encountered by Officer K?

5.5 Digital Sovereignty and Data Governance

Over the last decade, digital sovereignty has become a central element in policy discourses on digital issues. Although it has become popular in both authoritarian and democratic countries alike, the concept remains highly contested.

In July 2020, in its officially published program for its presidency of the European Council, the German government announced its intention "to establish digital sovereignty as a leitmotiv of European digital policy."[8] This is one of many recent examples in which the term "digital sovereignty" has been used within government to convey the suggestion that states should have the power to assert their authority over the internet, and the ability to protect their citizens, businesses, and organizations from changes to online self-determination.

Digital sovereignty refers to the ability to control the use of the data, hardware, and software that you rely on and create and to direct international actors through the use of digital technologies such as the Internet, social media, and other digital media. The movement towards the pursuit of digital sovereignty—in which a fundamental principle is to regulate and access, entry, content, connectivity, networks, and infrastructure—has been escalating the complications and uncertainties of international cyberspace legislation [41].

5.5.1 Challenges to Digital Sovereignty in International Cyber Law

One of the biggest challenges is that existing binding and well-directed international law does not yet effectively apply to governing states that are granted access to challenges taking place outside the realm of public international law in terms of jurisdiction, arbitration, legal instruments, and jurisprudence. Put simply, international law in cyberspace is currently beyond the scope of what it imposes on state actors and none of this can be overcome without a clear understanding of how international law can be effectively applied to all governing states and how it will address various issues at cyberspace, from cybercrime to procedural formalities.

---

[8] *The German Presidency of the EU Council*, 2020, p. 8.

5.5.2 Online Content Regulation

Online content—also known as digital media—comes in many forms, from text, audio, and videos files to graphics, animations, programs, and images. Digital content can be online—that is, available on the internet—or offline, such as content stored on a USB flash drive. When a governmental body seeks to apply a set of laws, rules, guidelines, provisions, or policies with regard to what can and cannot be uploaded, downloaded, accessed, published, or even created for public consumption, this becomes an issue of online content regulation—a form of online censorship.

Online digital content can come from a wide range of sources, from large media companies to small businesses to content entrepreneurs to social media account users. Generally, "digital content" refers to information that is made available for download or distribution on electronic media, such as an ebook, mobile game, video, or audio file. However, many creative content and online media producers have argued that "digital content" extends to anything that can be published. For the purposes of this book, we will consider the terms "online content," "digital content," and "digital media" as equivalent, synonymous, umbrella terms for all shared electronic, digital, and/or online content or media [42].

Flowing from the premise that online digital content and electronic media includes all publishable digital information shared between internet users, it follows, then, that every tweet, every hashtag, every status update, every video upload, every blog update, and every social media share, etc. all fall under the umbrella of "digital content" as it applies in our context. Some of the different types of online content are summarized in Table 5.3.

5.5.3 Digital Content Creation and the Gig Economy

In a gig economy, temporary, flexible jobs are commonplace, and companies tend to hire independent contractors and freelancers instead of full-time employees. A gig economy undermines the traditional economy of full-time workers who often focus on their career development. The result of a gig economy is cheaper, more efficient services, such as Uber or Airbnb, for those willing to use them. People who do not use technological services such as the Internet may be left behind by the benefits of the gig economy. Cities tend to have the most highly developed services and are the most entrenched in the gig economy.

What this looks like is large numbers of people working in part-time or temporary positions or as independent contractors. The concept of a gig covers a wide range of jobs from writing code or freelance articles to gaining a contract as an adjunct and part-time professor.[9] Colleges and universities can cut costs and match professors to their academic needs by hiring more adjunct and part-time professors. Gig workers

[9] Adjunct and part-time professors are contracted employees as opposed to tenure-track or tenured professors.

Table 5.3 Types of online/digital content

Type of digital content	Description of content
Ad/Advertisement	Online advertising, also known as Internet advertising, digital advertising or web advertising, is a form of marketing and advertising which uses the Internet as a medium to contain website traffic and deliver promotional marketing messages to targeted consumers. Online ads can take the form of display and video ads, social media ads, commercial electronic messages, push notifications, mobile advertising, and other forms.
App/Application	An app, which is short for "application," is a type of software that can be installed and run on a computer, tablet, smartphone, or other electronic devices. An app most frequently refers to a mobile application or a piece of software that is installed and used on a computer.
Article	A piece of writing, usually nonfiction and on a specific topic, forming an independent part of a book, newspaper, magazine, journal, or other publication.
Blog/Weblog	A blog, which is short for "weblog," is a discussion, reflection, or informational website published on the internet and consisting of discrete, often informal journal or diary-style textual entries, called posts.
Comic/Cartoon	These are mediums used to express ideas with images, often combined with text or other visual information contained in speech bubbles, captions, or conveyed through other textual devices. Comics typically take the form of a sequence of panels of images whose size and arrangement contribute to narrative pacing.
Data Archive	Data archiving is the process of collecting older data that is no longer actively used and moving it to a separate secure storage location or device for long-term retention. A data archive is the storage place for data that is important but does not need to be accessed or modified regularly—or at all—so that it can be retrieved if needed.
Digital Audio Files	A method of preserving sound in digital form—that is, the form in which audio signals are digitized and transformed into a series of pulses that correspond to patterns of binary digits and are recorded as such on the surface of a magnetic tape or optical disc.
E-Book	An e-book, also known as an ebook or eBook, is a downloadable book publication made available in digital form, consisting of text, images, or both, which is readable on the flat-panel display of computers or other electronic handheld devices. They can consist of just the electronic text or may contain extra features, such as audio, video, or hyperlinks.
GIF/Graphical Interchange Format	A GIF, which stands for Graphical Interchange Format, is a bitmap image format consisting of a series of images or soundless video that will loop continuously without the user clicking anything.
Infographic	An infographic, a portmanteau derived from "information" and "graphic," that is, a means of conveying information through a visually appealing collection of imagery, charts, and minimal text. Infographics provide a quick way to synthesize data, distilled in a way that is accessible and easy to digest, and presented in a clear and uncomplicated, and manner.

(continued)

Table 5.3 (continued)

Type of digital content	Description of content
Livestream	A livestream refers to online streaming media simultaneously recorded and broadcast in real-time—live and uncensored. It is often referred to simply as streaming, but this abbreviated term is ambiguous because "streaming" may refer to any media delivered and played back simultaneously without requiring a completely downloaded file.
Meme	A meme is a virally transmitted image embellished with text, usually sharing pointed commentary on cultural symbols, social ideas, systems of behavior, or current events. A meme is typically a photo or video, although sometimes it can be a block of text.
Podcast	A podcast is an episodic series of spoken word digital audio files. These files are made available for download by followers and subscribers of the podcast's channel.
Social Media Post	Content shared on social media through a user's profile. It can be as simple as a blurb of text, but can also include images, videos, and links to other content. Other users of the social network can like, comment, and share the post.
User-Generated Content	Any form of content; written, videoed, posted, blogged, created, and uploaded to a forum by individual people rather than commercial brands, organizations, or companies. It can include images, videos, text, and/or audio that has been posted by the user on online platforms.
Webinar	A webinar is an online seminar that turns a presentation into a real-time conversation from anywhere in the world. A webinar allows a speaker from the hosting organization or company to share PowerPoint presentations, videos, web pages, or other multimedia content with audiences that can be located anywhere.

can be independent contractors, online platform workers, contract firm workers, on-call workers, and temporary workers who enter into formal agreements with on-demand companies to provide services to the company's clients.

Content creation involves creating content either as a hobby, a marketing tool, freelance gig, or side hustle. In this way, the Creator Economy is similar to the Passion Economy—When a content creator uses this skill as the foundation of a sustainable business, they become a content entrepreneur.

In addition to creators and entrepreneurs, there are also content marketers. Content marketing is the business of marketing content created by content entrepreneurs. In this way, a new(er) form of art is monetized: the ability to manage many short-term freelance opportunities in which creativity is a necessary component. Commercialized content creation is a large issue with many implications to our society at large, as it intersects with constitutional issues as well as freedom of expression rights which are protected in some jurisdictions. We will discuss these topics in much greater depth in a future publication.

5.6 Future Directions

While we cannot always accurately predict the issues which lay before us, what is certain is that issues in data privacy, cybersecurity, cybercrime, digital sovereignty, and many others will absolutely have an impact on the evolution of our laws. As our dual worlds—the "real world" and the online world—become more entwined, it is only natural to expect that the laws of the real world would have to somehow shift to be applied equally to issues arising digitally.

As fun as it might be to discuss all potential upcoming, emergent, and mildly foreseeable issues in cybersecurity and law, it would surely not be feasible to do so in only one chapter of a book. Undoubtedly the future will include discussions on a wide range of topics that intersect with the legal and the digital worlds. In addition to what we have already covered in the preceding pages of this chapter, we can foresee upcoming cybersecurity/data privacy legal issues touching on areas in:

1. Taxation law in relation to cryptocurrencies and jurisdiction
2. Family law regarding whether—and to what extent—having regular, virtual online access to a child fulfills the custody, access, and/or contact requirements of child custody agreements
3. Intellectual property law in relation to joint, layered, viral, and/or memed digital content creation and creators

Those are just three examples. The future is infinite and so are the possibilities. Our universe is expanding and so is the scope of our collective legal repertoire.

5.7 Summary

In this chapter, we have discussed some of the upcoming relevant issues in cybersecurity law including globalization and the implications on determining jurisdiction; consumer protection regulations for the digital marketplace; emerging anonymized DarkNet marketplaces; the challenges for law enforcement; digital sovereignty, and data governance; and online content regulation. We concluded by emphasizing the limitless potential of future legal directions as our connection to networks and technology deepens. The answers to the following questions are provided within this chapter:

1. What are the three types of jurisdiction?
2. Why might data protection agreements be important for corporations and organizations?
3. What are the benefits and/or arguments in favor of cryptocurrencies?
4. What are some of the challenges which stem from digital evidence collection?
5. What are five examples of online content?
6. Why might the creation of regulations for user-generated content and the implementation of online censorship laws be controversial?

7. What alternative avenues might be available for individuals to share and exchange digital content if the public internet is censored?

References

1. Lacson, W., & Jones, B. (2016). The 21st century DarkNet market: Lessons from the fall of silk road. *International Journal of Cyber Criminology, 10*(1).
2. Ryngaert, C. (2015). Jurisdiction in international law. OUP Oxford.
3. Timofeeva, Y. A. (2004). Worldwide prescriptive jurisdiction in Internet content controversies: a comparative analysis. *Conn J Int'l L, 20*, 199.
4. Ghappour, A. (2017). Searching places unknown: Law enforcement jurisdiction on the dark web. *Stan L Rev, 69*, 1075.
5. Brilmayer, L., Haverkamp, J., Logan, B., & Lynch, L. (1987). General look at general jurisdiction. *Tex L Rev, 66*, 721.
6. Kohl, U. (2007). *Jurisdiction and the Internet: Regulatory competence over online activity*. Cambridge University Press.
7. Cassel, D. (2001). Human rights and business responsibilities in the global marketplace. *Business Ethics Quarterly*, 261–274.
8. Alboukrek, K. (2003). Adapting to a new world of e-commerce: The need for uniform consumer protection in the international electronic marketplace. *Geo Wash Int'l L Rev, 35*, 425.
9. Irion, K., Yakovleva, S., & Bartl, M. (2016). Trade and Privacy: Complicated Bedfellows? How to achieve data protection-proof free trade agreements. How to achieve data protection-proof free trade agreements (July 13, 2016).
10. Lindqvist, J. (2018). New challenges to personal data processing agreements: is the GDPR fit to deal with contract, accountability and liability in a world of the Internet of Things? *International Journal of Law and Information Technology, 26*(1), 45–63.
11. Robison, W. J. (2009). Free at what cost: Cloud computing privacy under the stored communications act. *Geo LJ, 98*, 1195.
12. Moustakas, E., Ranganathan, C., & Duquenoy, P. (2006). E-mail marketing at the crossroads: A stakeholder analysis of unsolicited commercial e-mail (spam). *Internet Research*.
13. Matwyshyn, A. M. (2005). Material vulnerabilities: Data privacy, corporate information security, and securities regulation. *Berkeley Bus LJ, 3*, 129.
14. Mo, J. S. International Commercial Law (2003) 1.
15. Gilligan, Colin and Hird, Marin; *International marketing: Strategy and management* (1986) 99.
16. Pryles, Jeff Waincymer, and Davis, Martin; *International trade law* (2004) 74.
17. WTO Agreement. (1994). *Marrakesh agreement establishing the world trade organization*, Apr. 15, 1994, 1867 U.N.T.S. 154, 33 I.L.M. 1144.
18. Oatley, T. (2019). *International political economy* (6th ed., pp. 51–52). Routledge.
19. Malanczuk, P. (1999). International Organisations and space law: World trade organization. *Encyclopædia Britannica, 442*, 305.
20. Main Functions. Archived 30 December 2006 at the Wayback machine, WTO official site.
21. DSU. (1994). *Dispute settlement rules: Understanding on rules and procedures governing the settlement of disputes, marrakesh agreement establishing the World Trade Organization*, Annex 2, 1869 U.N.T.S. 401, 33 I.L.M. 1226.
22. Rudesill, D. S., Caverlee, J., & Sui, D. (2015). *The deep web and the darknet: A look inside the internet's massive black box* (p. 3). Woodrow Wilson International Center for Scholars, STIP.
23. Pianta, L. *Researchers simulate mafia and terrorism recruitment*, Phys.org, 25 July 2019.
24. United Nations. Protocol to prevent, suppress and punish trafficking in persons, especially women and children, supplementing the United Nations convention against transnational organized crime (was signed in New York in November 2000 and came into force in December 2003).

25. United Nations. protocol to prevent, suppress and punish trafficking in persons, especially women and children, supplementing the united nations convention against transnational organized crime, article 3(a).
26. Housefather, A. (2018). Moving forward in the fight against human trafficking in canada, 24th report of the standing committee on justice and human rights. 1st Session. In *42nd parliament*, Ottawa. www.ourcommons.ca/DocumentViewer/en/42-1/JUST/report-24
27. Tetlow, E. M. (2004). Sumer. In *Women, crime and punishment in ancient law and society: Volume 1: The ancient near east*. A&C Black. isbn: 9780826416285.
28. Kelly, A. (2017, July 31). 'Human life is more expendable': Why slavery has never made more money. In *Modern-day slavery in focus, UK*. The Guardian. https://www.theguardian.com/global-development/2017/jul/31/human-life-is-more-expendable-why-slavery-has-never-made-more-money
29. "Ratifying countries are now obliged to implement the treaty and report on measures taken." Committee on Forced Labour, ILC 2014.
30. Kelly, A. (2017, July 31). 'Human life is more expendable': Why slavery has never made more money. In *Modern-day slavery in focus, UK*. The Guardian. https://www.theguardian.com/global-development/2017/jul/31/human-life-is-more-expendable-why-slavery-has-never-made-more-money
31. Siddharth, K. (2017). *Modern slavery: A global perspective*. Columbia University Press.
32. Lashkari, A., & Lukings, M. "Deep, dark, and (un)detectable – Canadian jurisdictional considerations in global encrypted networks (article 7)" understanding Canadian cybersecurity Laws. (Online: ITWorldCanada.com, 2020).
33. Sattler, S. (2020, December 12). Special ATII report: Crypto transactions and human trafficking – A non-traditional investigation perspective for traditional financial institutions. US: Association of Certified Financial Crime Specialists. https://www.acfcs.org/special-atii-report-crypto-transactions-and-human-trafficking-a-non-traditional-investigation-perspective-for-traditional-financial-institutions/
34. FinCEN. Guidance on recognizing activity that may be associated with human smuggling and human trafficking – financial red flags. FIN-2014-A008. September 11, 2014. (Available online at: https://www.fincen.gov/sites/default/files/advisory/FIN-2014-A008.pdf).
35. Wright, C. S. (2000). Actual versus legal control: Reading vicarious liabilty for copyright infringement into the Digital Millennium Copyright Act of 1998. *Wash L Rev, 75*, 1005.
36. Fidalgo, E., Alegre, E., Fernández-Robles, L., & González-Castro, V. (2019). Classifying suspicious content in tor darknet through semantic attention keypoint filtering. *Digital Investi gation, 30*, 12–22.
37. Wright, A., & De Filippi, P. (2015). Decentralized blockchain technology and the rise of lex cryptographia. Available at SSRN 2580664.
38. "DIDarknet: A contemporary approach to detect and characterize the darknet traffic using deep image learning", Arash Habibi Lashkari, Gurdip Kaur, Abir Rahal, The 10th International Conference on Communication and Network Security (ICCNS2020), Tokyo, Japan, September 2020.
39. Taylor, M., Haggerty, J., Gresty, D., & Hegarty, R. (2010). Digital evidence in cloud computing systems. *Computer Law & Security Review, 26*(3), 304–308.
40. Sopinka, J., Fuerst, M. K., Lederman, S. N., & Bryant, A. W. (1991). *The law of evidence in Canada*. LexisNexis.
41. Floridi, L. (2020). The fight for digital sovereignty: What it is, and why it matters, especially for the EU. *Philosophy & Technology, 33*(3), 369–378.
42. Gorwa, R. (2019). The platform governance triangle: Conceptualising the informal regulation of online content. *Internet Policy Review, 8*(2), 1–22.

Conclusion

We have reached the end of our journey—for now. While more books in this series are surely to follow, we have reached the end of our preliminary dive into the intersection of law and cybersecurity, and a greater understanding of cybersecurity law. To wrap up, let us briefly summarize the general topics that we have covered so far in this book.

In the first chapter, on legal foundations, we discussed the purpose and principles of law and legal jurisprudence. From there, we extended into the sources of law and legal influence, the various systems and categories of law, and some of the forms of legal governance. Finally, we rounded off chapter one with a look at the concept of constitutionalism and the division of jurisdictional power and authority.

In chapter two, we looked at property and privacy in context; outlining some of the historical perceptions of property before moving on to distinguish between the interwoven concepts of ownership, possession, and interest. We examined the relationship between property and privacy, as well as the intersection of property, privacy, and cybersecurity in the law and legal system.

Chapter three, on cybersecurity and cybercrime, started off with the categorization of cybercriminal activities into three groups—cyber-enabled offences, cyber-dependent offences, and cyber-supported offences—along with a description of the nature of these different types of offences. We went on to discuss the growing prevalence of cybercrime, digital privacy infringement, data theft, and other online offences. Finally, we rounded off by neatly sorting the specific subsets of criminal offences respectively within each of the three branches of cybercriminal activity categorization.

The fourth chapter looked at the global relevance of cybersecurity law, using four common law nations as comparators. We started off by reviewing the Canadian cybersecurity laws, followed by those of Australia, then the United Kingdom, and finally the United States. Using tables, we compared and contrasted the methods of regulating cyber offences between these four example nations. After establishing an understanding of some of the different strategies employed by individual nations to apply existing law to the online world, we outlined some of the national and international considerations which influence individual national and/or state policies pertaining to cybersecurity, data privacy, and online crime.

M. Lukings, A. Habibi Lashkari, *Understanding Cybersecurity Law and Digital Privacy*, Future of Business and Finance, https://doi.org/10.1007/978-3-030-88704-9

In our fifth and final chapter, we discussed some of the emerging issues in cybersecurity and data privacy law. We outlined the dual-headed issue of globalization and jurisdictionality on an international stage and examined the relationship between digital marketplaces and the online consumer. We then ventured onto the DarkNet, giving an overview of anonymized darkness marketplaces and the rise of transactions and online exchangers made using cryptocurrencies. Stemming from these unique issues, we branched into a discussion on some of the existing challenges to law enforcement, as well as the complexity of digital sovereignty and data governance in law. We finished off this chapter by discussing some of the potential future directions for further research and exploration into the field of cybersecurity law.

When we initially set out to write this book, our goal was to bridge the knowledge gap between the dually insular worlds of cybersecurity research and development and that of the legal profession. While this book may be part of the solution to bridge this gap, further engagement from both of these "ivory towers" is necessary to fully integrate an understanding of the law within cybersecurity education, research, and industry. Respectively, further engagement is also necessary in order to integrate an understanding of some of the challenges of cybersecurity, and the complexities of the online world, with those who teach, learn, or research in the field of law and legal education, as well as those who choose to practice law.

While we may have only just begun to scratch the surface of the deeper issues of our increasingly digitally-reliant society, we hope that this book has been a solid stepping stone onto the bridge, and over the knowledge gap. It is our great hope that some of the topics covered in this book have served as a catalyst to encourage readers to further engage with the material.

If our future is limitless, then our law must be limitlessly adaptable as well. In our rapidly changing world of technological advancements and increased digital connectedness, having an integrated knowledge of cybersecurity and the law is absolutely fundamental and necessary as a step forward to securing our successes in the future.

GPSR Compliance
The European Union's (EU) General Product Safety Regulation (GPSR) is a set of rules that requires consumer products to be safe and our obligations to ensure this.

If you have any concerns about our products, you can contact us on

ProductSafety@springernature.com

In case Publisher is established outside the EU, the EU authorized representative is:

Springer Nature Customer Service Center GmbH
Europaplatz 3
69115 Heidelberg, Germany

www.ingramcontent.com/pod-product-compliance
Ingram Content Group UK Ltd.
Pitfield, Milton Keynes, MK11 3LW, UK
UKHW020818290926
15470UKWH00003B/1242
9783030887032